IEE PROFESSIONAL APPLICATIONS OF COMPUTING SERIES 1

Series Editors: Professor P. Thomas
Dr. R. Macredie

KNOWLEDGE DISCOVERY AND DATA MINING

IEE PROFESSIONAL APPLICATIONS OF COMPUTING SERIES

For professional engineers, information about the latest developments and their significance means continued professional standing. Nowhere is this so obvious than computing. The pace of change – in hardware, software and new applications – is breathtaking, and the development of global communications is increasing the pace of change on an international scale.

To help the professional engineer understand new developments in computing, this new series of books is aimed at professionals working in computing. The Professional Applications of Computing Series will cover new developments in computing in the context of real applications and industry needs.

The series will develop to contain books on the applications of computing across various core sectors, which may include:

- high-performance computing
- microelectronics
- applications of mobile computing
- distributed information management
- software development tools
- privacy and security issues
- the Internet

However, as developing topics gain prominence and new topics arise with rapidity, the series will also aim to cover emerging topics within areas such as:

- education and training
- e-commerce
- embedded computing
- multimedia
- intelligent systems

KNOWLEDGE DISCOVERY AND DATA MINING

Edited by

M A Bramer

The Institution of Electrical Engineers

Published by: The Institution of Electrical Engineers, London,
United Kingdom

© 1999: The Institution of Electrical Engineers

The Institution of Electrical Engineers,
Michael Faraday House,
Six Hills Way, Stevenage,
Herts. SG1 2AY, United Kingdom

British Library Cataloguing in Publication Data

A CIP catalogue record for this book
is available from the British Library

ISBN 0 85296 767 5

Printed in England by Short Run Press Ltd., Exeter

Contents

Preface   xiii
Contributors   xvii

Part I   KNOWLEDGE DISCOVERY AND DATA MINING IN THEORY   1

1   Estimating concept difficulty with cross entropy.
    K. Nazar and M.A. Bramer   **3**
    1.1   Introduction   3
        1.1.1   Attributes and examples   4
    1.2   The need for bias in machine learning   4
        1.2.1   Bias interference   5
    1.3   Concept dispersion and feature interaction   7
    1.4   Why do we need to estimate concept difficulty?   8
    1.5   Data-based difficulty measures   10
        1.5.1 μ-ness   10
        1.5.2   Variation   11
        1.5.3   Blurring   11
    1.6   Why use the *J* measure as a basis for a blurring measure?   14
    1.7   Effects of various data characteristics on blurring and variation   15
        1.7.1   Irrelevant attributes   17
    1.8   Dataset analysis   19
    1.9   Problems with information-theoretic-based blurring measures   21
    1.10 Estimating attribute relevance with the RELIEF algorithm   22
        1.10.1 Experiments with RELIEFF   23
    1.11 Blurring over disjoint subsets   26
    1.12 Results and discussion   27
    1.13 Summary and future research   28
    1.14 References   30

2   Analysing outliers by searching for plausible hypotheses.
    X. Liu and G. Cheng   **32**
    2.1   Introduction   32
    2.2   Statistical treatment of outliers   33

2.3   An algorithm for outlier analysis   35
2.4   Experimental results   38
      2.4.1   Case I: onchocerciasis   38
      2.4.2   Case II: glaucoma   39
2.5   Evaluation   41
2.6   Concluding remarks   44
2.7   Acknowledgments   44
2.8   References   44

3   **Attribute-value distribution as a technique for increasing the
    efficiency of data mining.**   *D. McSherry*   **46**
3.1   Introduction   46
3.2   Targeting a restricted class of rules   48
3.3   Discovery effort and yield   50
3.4   Attribute-value distribution   53
3.5   Experimental results   55
      3.5.1   The contact-lens data   55
      3.5.2   The project-outcome dataset   60
3.6   Discussion and conclusions   62
3.7   References   63

4   **Using background knowledge with attribute-oriented data mining.**
    M. Shapcott, S. McClean and B. Scotney   **64**
4.1   Introduction   64
4.2   Partial value model   66
      4.2.1   Definition: partial value   66
      4.2.2   Definition: partial-value relation   66
      4.2.3   Example   66
      4.2.4   Aggregation   67
      4.2.5   Definition: simple count operator   67
      4.2.6   Example   68
      4.2.7   Definition: simple aggregate operator   68
      4.2.8   Example   68
      4.2.9   Aggregation of partial values   69
      4.2.10 Definition: partial value aggregate operator   69
      4.2.11 Example   69
      4.2.12 Definition: partial-value count operator   70
      4.2.13 Theoretical framework   70
4.3   Reengineering the database – the role of background
      knowledge   71
      4.3.1   Concept hierarchies   71
      4.3.2   Database-integrity constraints   73
      4.3.3   Definition: simple comparison predicate   73
      4.3.4   Examples of simple comparison predicates   74
      4.3.5   Definition: table-based predicate   74

	4.3.6	Example of a table-based predicate	74
	4.3.7	Expression of rules as table-based predicates	74
	4.3.8	Reengineering the database	74
4.4	Multiattribute count operators		76
	4.4.1	Example	77
	4.4.2	Example	77
	4.4.3	Example	78
	4.4.4	Quasi-independence	79
	4.4.5	Example	81
	4.4.6	Interestingness	81
	4.4.7	Example	82
4.5	Related work		82
4.6	Conclusions		83
4.7	Acknowledgments		84
4.8	References		84

5 A development framework for temporal data mining.
X. Chen and I. Petrounias   **87**

5.1	Introduction		87
5.2	Analysis and representation of temporal features		89
	5.2.1	Time domain	89
	5.2.2	Calendar expression of time	90
	5.2.3	Periodicity of time	92
	5.2.4	Time dimensions in temporal databases	94
5.3	Potential knowledge and temporal data mining problems		95
	5.3.1	Forms of potential temporal knowledge	95
	5.3.2	Associating knowledge with temporal features	97
	5.3.3	Temporal mining problems	98
5.4	A framework for temporal data mining		100
	5.4.1	A temporal mining language	100
	5.4.2	System architecture	102
5.5	An example: discovery of temporal association rules		104
	5.5.1	Mining problem	104
	5.5.2	Description of mining tasks in TQML	106
	5.5.3	Search algorithms	107
5.6	Conclusion and future research direction		110
5.7	References		110

6 An integrated architecture for OLAP and data mining. *Z. Chen*   **114**

6.1	Introduction		115
6.2	Preliminaries		116
	6.2.1	Decision-support queries	116
	6.2.2	Data warehousing	116
	6.2.3	Basics of OLAP	117
	6.2.4	Star schema	118

6.2.5   A materialised view for sales profit   118
6.3 Differences between OLAP and data mining   119
       6.3.1   Basic concepts of data mining   119
       6.3.2   Different types of query can be answered at different
               levels   120
       6.3.3   Aggregation semantics   120
       6.3.4   Sensitivity analysis   122
       6.3.5   Different assumptions or heuristics may be needed at
               different levels   123
6.4 Combining OLAP and data mining: the feedback sandwich
     model   123
       6.4.1   Two different ways of combining OLAP and data
               mining   124
       6.4.2   The feedback sandwich model   125
6.5 Towards integrated architecture for combined OLAP/data
     mining   126
6.6 Three specific issues   128
       6.6.1   On the use and reuse of intensional historical data   128
       6.6.2   How data mining can benefit OLAP   131
       6.6.3   OLAP-enriched data mining   133
6.7 Conclusion   135
6.8 References   135

**Part II   KNOWLEDGE DISCOVERY AND DATA MINING IN
            PRACTICE   137**

**7 Empirical studies of the knowledge discovery approach to
    health-information analysis.**   *M. Lloyd-Williams*   **139**
7.1 Introduction   139
7.2 Knowledge discovery and data mining   140
       7.2.1   The knowledge discovery process   140
       7.2.2   Artificial neural networks   147
7.3 Empirical studies   149
       7.3.1   The 'Health for all' database   149
       7.3.2   The 'Babies at risk of intrapartum asphyxia' database   153
       7.3.3   Infertility databases   155
7.4 Conclusions   157
7.5 References   158

**8 Direct knowledge discovery and interpretation from a multilayer
    perceptron network which performs low-back-pain classification**
    M.L. Vaughn, S.J. Cavill, S.J. Taylor, M.A. Foy and A.J.B. Fogg   **160**
8.1 Introduction   160
8.2 The MLP network   161
8.3 The low-back-pain MLP network   163

8.4	The interpretation and knowledge-discovery method	163
	8.4.1 Discovery of the feature-detector neurons	163
	8.4.2 Discovery of the significant inputs	164
	8.4.3 Discovery of the negated significant inputs	164
	8.4.4 Knowledge learned by the MLP from the training data	166
	8.4.5 MLP network validation and verification	167
8.5	Knowledge discovery from LBP example training cases	168
	8.5.1 Discovery of the feature detectors for example training cases	168
	8.5.2 Discovery of the significant inputs for example training cases	168
	8.5.3 Data relationships and explanations for example training cases	168
	8.5.4 Discussion of the training-example data relationships	170
	8.5.5 Induced rules from training-example cases	170
8.6	Knowledge discovery from all LBP MLP training cases	173
	8.6.1 Discussion of the class key input rankings	173
8.7	Validation of the LBP LMP network	176
	8.7.1 Validation of the training cases	176
	8.7.2 Validation of the test cases	176
8.8	Conclusions	177
8.9	Future work	177
8.10	Acknowledgments	178
8.11	References	178

9	**Discovering knowledge from low-quality meteorological databases.**		
	C.M. Howard and V.J. Rayward-Smith		**180**
	9.1	Introduction	180
		9.1.1 The meteorological domain	180
	9.2	The preprocessing stage	182
		9.2.1 Visualisation	182
		9.2.2 Missing values	182
		9.2.3 Unreliable data	185
		9.2.4 Discretisation	186
		9.2.5 Feature selection	187
		9.2.6 Feature construction	188
	9.3	The data-mining stage	188
		9.3.1 Simulated annealing	189
		9.3.2 SA with missing and unreliable data	190
	9.4	A toolkit for knowledge discovery	195
	9.5	Results and analysis	196
		9.5.1 Results from simulated annealing	198
		9.5.2 Results from C5.0	198
		9.5.3 Comparison and evaluation of results	199
	9.6	Summary	199

9.7   Discussion and further work   200
9.8   References   201

10 A meteorological knowledge-discovery environment.
A.G. Büchner, J.C.L. Chan, S.L.Hung and J.G. Hughes   **204**
10.1   Introduction   204
10.2   Some meteorological background   205
       10.2.1   Available data sources   206
       10.2.2   Related work   208
10.3   MADAME's architecture   211
10.4   Building a meteorological data warehouse   212
       10.4.1   The design   212
       10.4.2   Information extraction   213
       10.4.3   Data cleansing   214
       10.4.4   Data processing   215
       10.4.5   Data loading and refreshing   216
10.5   The knowledge-discovery components   217
       10.5.1   Knowledge modelling   217
       10.5.2   Domain knowledge   221
10.6   Prediction trial runs   222
       10.6.1   Nowcasting of heavy rainfall   222
       10.6.2   Landslide nowcasting   223
10.7   Conclusions and further work   224
10.8   Acknowledgments   224
10.9   References   225

**11 Mining the organic compound jungle – a functional programming
approach.**   *K.E. Burn-Thornton and J. Bradshaw*   **227**
11.1   Introduction   227
11.2   Decision-support requirements in the pharmaceutical
       industry   227
       11.2.1   Graphical comparison   228
       11.2.2   Structural keys   228
       11.2.3   Fingerprints   229
       11.2.4   Variable-sized fingerprints   230
11.3   Functional programming language Gofer   230
       11.3.1   Functional programming   231
11.4   Design of prototype tool and main functions   234
       11.4.1   Design of tool   234
       11.4.2   Main functions   235
11.5   Methodology   236
11.6   Results   236
       11.6.1   Sets A, B and C (256, 512 and 1024 bytes)   237
       11.6.2   Set D (2048 bytes)   237
11.7   Conclusions   238

11.8   Future work   239
11.9   References   239

**12 Data mining with neural networks – an applied example in
understanding electricity consumption patterns.**
P. Brierley and B. Batty   **240**
   12.1   Neural networks   241
      12.1.1 What are neural networks?   241
      12.1.2 Why use neural networks?   242
      12.1.3 How do neural networks process information?   242
      12.1.4 Things to be aware of . . .   244
   12.2   Electric load modelling   250
      12.2.1 The data being mined   250
      12.2.2 Why forecast electricity demand?   252
      12.2.3 Previous work   253
      12.2.4 Network used   254
   12.3   Total daily load model   255
      12.3.1 Overfitting and generalisation   264
   12.4   Rule extraction   266
      12.4.1 Day of the week   267
      12.4.2 Time of year   268
      12.4.3 Growth   269
      12.4.4 Weather factors   271
      12.4.5 Holidays   272
   12.5   Model comparisons   274
   12.6   Half-hourly model   276
      12.6.1 Initial input data   276
      12.6.2 Results   277
      12.6.3 Past loads   286
      12.6.4 How the model is working   286
      12.6.5 Extracting the growth   287
      12.6.6 Populations of models   288
   12.7   Summary   288
   12.8   References   289
   12.9   Appendixes   292
      12.9.1 Backpropagation weight update rule   292
      12.9.2 Fortran 90 code for a multilayer perceptron   299

Index   **304**

Preface

Modern computer systems are accumulating data at an almost unimaginable rate and from a very wide variety of sources: from point-of-sale machines in the high street to machines logging every cheque clearance, bank cash withdrawal and credit-card transaction, to Earth observation satellites in space.

Three examples will serve to give an indication of the volumes of data involved:

- the 1990 US census collected over a million million bytes of data;
- the human genome project will store thousands of bytes for each of several billion genetic bases;
- NASA Earth observation satellites generate a terabyte (i.e. 10^9 bytes) of data *every day*.

Alongside advances in storage technology which increasingly make it possible to store such vast amounts of data at relatively low cost, whether in commercial data warehouses, scientific research laboratories or elsewhere, has come a growing realisation that such data contains buried within it knowledge that can be critical to a company's growth or decline, knowledge that could lead to important discoveries in science, knowledge that could enable us accurately to predict the weather and natural disasters, knowledge that could enable us to identify the causes of and possible cures for lethal illnesses, knowledge that could literally mean the difference between life and death. Yet the huge volumes involved mean that most of this data is merely stored—never to be examined in more than the most superficial way, if at all.

Machine-learning technology, some of it very long established, has the potential to solve the problem of the tidal wave of data that is flooding around organisations, governments and individuals.

Knowledge discovery has been defined as the 'nontrivial extraction of implicit, previously unknown and potentially useful information from data'. The underlying technologies of knowledge discovery include induction of decision rules and decision trees, neural networks, genetic algorithms, instance-based learning and statistics. There is a rapidly growing body of successful applications in a wide range of areas as diverse as:

- medical diagnosis;
- weather forecasting;
- product design;
- electric load prediction;
- thermal power-plant optimisation;
- analysis of organic compounds;
- automatic abstracting;
- credit-card fraud detection;
- predicting share of television audiences;
- real-estate valuation;
- toxic-hazard analysis;
- financial forecasting.

This book comprises six chapters on the technical issues of knowledge discovery and data mining followed by six chapters on applications.

Part I of the book, 'Knowledge discovery and data mining in theory', looks at a variety of technical issues, all of considerable practical importance for the future development of the field.

'Estimating concept difficulty with cross-entropy' by Kamal Nazar and Max Bramer presents an approach to anticipating and overcoming some of the problems which can occur in applying a learning algorithm owing to unfavourable characteristics of a particular dataset such as feature interaction.

'Analysing outliers by searching for plausible hypotheses' by Xiaohui Liu and Gongxian Cheng describes a method for determining whether outliers in data are merely noise or potentially valuable information and presents experimental results on visual function data used for diagnosing two blinding diseases: glaucoma and onchocerciasis.

'Attribute-value distribution as a technique for increasing the efficiency of data mining' by David McSherry describes a method for efficient rule discovery, illustrated by generating rules for the domain of contact-lens prescription.

'Using background knowledge with attribute-oriented data mining' by Mary Shapcott, Sally McClean and Bryan Scotney looks at the important question of how background knowledge of a domain can be used to aid the data-mining process.

'A development framework for temporal data mining' by Xiaodong Chen and Ilias Petrounias is concerned with datasets which include information about time. The chapter presents a framework for discovering temporal patterns and a query language for extracting them from a database.

'An integrated architecture for OLAP and data mining' by Zhengxin Chen examines features of data mining specific to the data-warehousing environment where online analysis processing (OLAP) takes place. An integrated architecture for OLAP and data mining is proposed.

Part II of the book, 'Knowledge discovery and data mining in practice', begins with a chapter entitled 'Empirical studies of the knowledge discovery approach to health-information analysis' by Michael Lloyd-Williams which introduces the basic concepts of knowledge discovery, identifying data mining as an information-processing activity within a wider knowledge-discovery process (although the terms knowledge discovery and data mining are often used interchangeably). The chapter presents empirical studies of the use of a neural-network learning technique known as the Kohonen self-organising map in the analysis of health information taken from three sources: the World Health Organisation's 'Health for all' database, the 'Babies at risk of intrapartum asphyxia' database and a series of databases containing infertility information.

The next chapter, 'Direct knowledge discovery and interpretation from a multilayer perceptron network which performs low-back-pain classification' by Marilyn Vaughn *et al.*, discusses the uses of a widely used type of neural network, the multilayer perceptron (MLP), to classify patients suffering from low-back pain, an ailment which it is estimated that between 60 and 80 per cent of the population will experience at least once at some time in their lives. A particular emphasis of this work is on the induction of rules from the training examples.

The two chapters on medical applications are followed by two on meteorology.

'Discovering knowledge from low-quality meteorological databases' by Craig Howard and Vic Rayward-Smith proposes a strategy for dealing with databases containing unreliable or missing data based on experiences derived from experiments with a number of meteorological datasets.

'A meteorological knowledge-discovery environment' by Alex Büchner *et al.* describes a knowledge-discovery environment which allows experimentation with a variety of textual and graphical geophysical data, incorporating a number of different types of data-mining model.

The final two chapters are concerned with the application of knowledge-discovery techniques in two other important areas: organic chemistry and the electricity-supply industry.

'Mining the organic compound jungle—a functional programming approach' by Kathryn Burn-Thornton and John Bradshaw describes experiments aimed at enabling researchers in the pharmaceutical industry to determine common substructures of organic compounds using data-mining techniques rather than by the traditional method involving visual inspection of graphical representations.

'Data mining with neural networks—an applied example in understanding electricity consumption patterns' by Philip Brierley and Bill Batty gives further information about neural networks and shows how they can be used to analyse electricity-consumption data as an aid to comprehension of the factors influencing demand. Fortran 90 source code for a multilayer perceptron is also provided as a way of showing that 'implementing a neural network can be a very simple process that does not require sophisticated simulators or supercomputers'.

This book grew out of a colloquium on 'Knowledge discovery and data mining' which I organised for Professional Group A4 (Artificial Intelligence) of the Institution of Electrical Engineers (IEE) in London on May 7 and 8 1998. This was the third in a series of colloquia on this topic which began in 1995. The colloquium was co-sponsored by BCS–SGES (the British Computer Society Specialist Group on Expert Systems), AISB (the Society for Artificial Intelligence and Simulation of Behaviour) and AIED (the International Society for AI and Education).

The chapters included here have been significantly expanded from papers presented at the colloquium and were selected for inclusion following a rigorous refereeing process. The book should be of particular interest to researchers and active practitioners in this increasingly important field. I should like to thank the referees for their valuable contribution and Jonathan Simpson (formerly of the IEE) for his encouragement to publish the proceedings in book form. I should also like to thank my wife, Dawn, for preparing the index.

Max Bramer
December 1998

Contributors

J Bradshaw
Glaxo Wellcome Research &
Development
Medicines Research Centre
Gunnels Wood Road
Stevenage
Hertfordshire SG1 2NY
UK

A G Büchner
Northern Ireland Knowledge
Engineering Laboratory
University of Ulster
Shore Road
Newtownabbey
Co. Antrim BT37 0QB
UK

M Bramer
University of Portsmouth
School of Computer Science and
Mathematics
Mercantile House
Hampshire Terrace
Portsmouth PO1 2EG
UK

K E Burn-Thornton
Data Mining Group
School of Computing
Plymouth University
9, Kirkby Place
Plymouth PL4 8AA
UK

P Brierley
NeuSolutions Ltd
34 Pontamman Road
Ammanford
Carmarthenshire
SA18 2HX
UK

J C L Chan
Centre for Environmental
Science and Technology
Faculty of Science and
Engineering
City University of Hong Kong
Tat Chee Avenue
Kowloon
Hong Kong

X Chen
Department of Computing and
Mathematics
Manchester Metropolitan
University
John Dalton Building
Chester Street
Manchester M1 5GD
UK

Z Chen
Department of Computer
Science
University of Nebraska at Omaha
Omaha NE 68182-0500
USA

**C M Howard and V J Rayward-
Smith**
School of Information Systems
University of East Anglia
Norwich NR4 7TJ
UK

J G Hughes
Faculty of Informatics
University of Ulster
Newtownabbey
Co. Antrim BT37 0QB
UK

S L Hung
Department of Computer
Science
Faculty of Science and
Engineering
City University of Hong Kong
Tat Chee Avenue
Kowloon
Hong Kong

X Liu and G Cheng
Department of Computer
Science
Birkbeck College
University of London
Malet Street
London WC1E 7HX
UK

M Lloyd-Williams
School of Information Systems
and Computing
University of Wales Institute
Cardiff
Colchester Avenue
Cardiff CF3 7XR
UK

D McSherry
School of Information and
Software Engineering
University of Ulster
Coleraine BT52 1SA
UK

K Nazar
Point Information Systems
Embassy House
Ballsbridge
Dublin 4
Ireland

I Petrounias
Department of Computation
UMIST
PO Box 88
Manchester M60 1QD
UK

**C M Shapcott, S McClean and
B Scotney**
School of Information and
Software Engineering
Faculty of Informatics
University of Ulster
Cromore Road
Coleraine BT52 1SA
UK

**S J Taylor, M A Foy and
A J B Fogg**
Orthopaedic Department
Princess Margaret Hospital
Okus Road
Swindon SN1 4JU
UK

M L Vaughn and S J Cavill
Knowledge Engineering
Research Centre
Department of Informatics and
Simulation
Cranfield University (RMCS)
Shrivenham
Swindon SN6 8LA
UK

Part I
Knowledge discovery and data mining in theory

Chapter 1
Estimating concept difficulty with cross entropy

K. Nazar and M. A. Bramer
University of Portsmouth, UK

1.1 Introduction

In concept learning the features used to describe examples can have a drastic effect on the learning algorithm's ability to acquire the target concept.[1] In many poorly understood domains the representation can be described as being low level. Examples are described in terms of a large number of small measurements. No single measurement is strongly correlated to the target concept; however, all information for classification is believed to be present. Patterns are harder to identify because they are conditional. This is in contrast to problems where a small number of attributes are highly predictive of the concept. Clark and Thornton [1] call these type-2 and type-1 problems, respectively. Many current approaches perform very poorly on type-2 problems because the biases which they employ are poorly tuned to the underlying concept. In this chapter we discuss reasons why attempting to estimate concept difficulty before any learning takes place is desirable. Some current approaches to learning type-2 problems are described together with several measures used to estimate particular sources of difficulty, their advantages and disadvantages and an estimate based on the Δ_j measure [2] which addresses many of the shortcomings of previous approaches.

---

[1] A concept is a classification rule which describes a subset (class) of instances and separates them from instances which do not satisfy the rule. A target concept is the one concept that classifies all the examples in the domain correctly.

1.1.1 Attributes and examples

Representation concerns the attributes used to describe examples which are either instances of the concept to be learned (referred to as positive examples) or not (negative examples). Each example is a list or vector described in terms of a sequence of ordered features (the predicting variables or attributes) and a class attribute (the predicted variable or attribute), with each feature assuming one of a possible number of values from its domain.

Assume that each example is described by n attributes $Y_1, Y_2, \ldots, Y_n$, where Y_i is the set or range of allowable values for discrete attribute i. An n-dimensional instance space is described by $Y_1 \times Y_2 \times, \ldots, \times Y_n$. Not all problems use this convention, but all representations use some descriptive language to communicate particular aspects of articles used to describe the problem. The idea of representation described here is only concerned with the attributes used to describe the examples which form an input to the learning algorithm. This is distinct from internal representation languages used to express hypotheses.

1.2 The need for bias in machine learning

For all but the most trivial data sets, the space of all possible hypotheses is so vast that generating and testing the entire set is not possible. In order to learn a reasonable approximation of the target concept in an acceptable time, learning algorithms must restrict the space of hypotheses which they generate. Bias allows a learner to focus attention on particular areas of the hypothesis space by imposing a preference or ordering on this space, so focusing attention primarily on areas more likely to be useful. Utgoff [3] describes bias in machine learning as any factors which affect hypothesis selection, aside from positive and negative instances of the concept being learned. This type of bias is also referred to as extra-evidential and the language hypotheses which are described in this chapter are included in this definition. This language restriction is one process by which the space of hypotheses can be limited. When primitive features are unsuitable for acquiring the target concept, and the algorithm's hypothesis language restriction means that its internal representation is also poorly adjusted, the algorithm's approximation of the concept is likely to be far removed from the true concept.

Table 1.1   Exclusive-OR over two binary attributes

	y_2	y_1	class
example1	0	0	0
example2	0	1	1
example3	1	0	1
example4	1	1	0

1.2.1 Bias interference

Several methods have been used to alleviate the computational burden associated with exhaustive search. Beam-search techniques track the best alternatives to the top-ranking hypothesis by keeping a size-limited set (the beam). At each stage of hypothesis formation, candidates are specialised and ranked according to some quality function (e.g. entropy). The beam is then trimmed back to a predetermined size (often user defined). Hypotheses falling outside the beam are discarded; only those inside the beam are considered for further specialisation. However, where conditional patterns occur (for example in parity-type problems[2]), promising solutions may be overlooked when employing a beam coupled with a general-to-specific search, because initial candidates (i.e. single-attribute values) may seem unpromising (until specialised or combined with other variables) and so fall outside the beam.

Greedy search techniques are used in many learning algorithms [4–6]. Algorithms employing a greedy bias are essentially using beam search but with the beam width set to one.

Similarity-based learning bias (SBL) —a form of language restriction— is also employed in many algorithms, sometimes referred to as selective induction. Systems that utilise SBL biases assume that neighbouring points in instance space are highly predictive of each other's class membership values (i.e. their class label or predicted variable). Such systems tend to classify unseen examples, like nearby ones which were seen during the training phase.

Given an exclusive-OR-type concept over two attributes ($y_1 \oplus y_2$), the entire space of examples is detailed in Table 1.1. This type of concept has many real-world manifestations, for example in medical diagnosis. Simple combinations of patient symptoms are rarely certain forecasts of disease. Some diagnostic rules have complex logical forms—they

---

[2] Parity-type concepts are simply higher-order variants of exclusive-OR.

may require that a patient presents more than a certain number of symptoms.

Examples 3 and 4 appear to be close (they differ in only one attribute), and examples 1 and 2 exhibit the same closeness. However, both pairs have different class values. Examples 2 and 3 are maximally dissimilar because they differ in both attributes, although these examples share the same classification.

Some neighbouring points appear to be close but violate the SBL assumption because of dependencies between attributes.

SBL/greedy splitting algorithms are attractive computationally. Such systems are only slowed linearly as sample size increases; speed depends on the product of the number of data, number of attributes and the number of disjuncts in the output concept. Because of the different biases employed by various learning systems, learning difficulty can vary considerably from one algorithm to another; different approaches may be biased or tuned towards a certain input representation.

The basic SBL assumption is valid in many problems where the primitive attributes are at a suitable level of abstraction, because the domain is well understood and experts are available to designate appropriate measurements. For example, in a domain concerned with diagnosing eating disorders and with a target concept of anorexia, if while recording patient details the doctor asks whether the patient suffers from anorexia (i.e. the data set has a binary-valued attribute of anorexic), then there will be a very clear correlation between this predicting attribute and the predicted (class) attribute. However, if the doctor does not record this information but does record the patient's age, height and weight,[3] then the information required to discover the concept is present in the data, but is recorded in a number of small, insignificant measurements. Taken together these sets of data are complete enough to identify the underlying concept. This is a common situation in poorly understood domains — examples may be described in terms of many small measurements or attributes because the appropriate level of abstraction is unknown or difficult to communicate (for example in relational-type concepts).

Some real-world learning tasks have been shown to be problematic across a wide assortment of learning approaches which leads to the conclusion that the representations characterising these problems are poor in a more general way.

---

[3] Anorexia is dependent on the ratio of patient height and weight: a ratio greater than a certain threshold (dependent on the patient's sex) is an indicator of the condition.

Class-membership probability

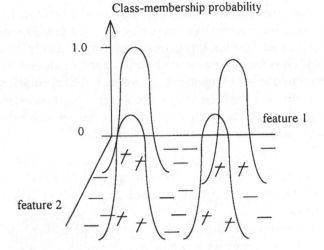

Figure 1.1   Concept dispersion visualised as a probability surface

There are many reasons for poor learning performance including noise, class distribution, number of attributes and number of data in the training sample. However, here we assume that intrinsic accuracy[4] is high (i.e. all relevant information required for class separability has been included), and that difficulty is caused by a poor representation. Rendell and Seshu [7] describe problems of this nature (i.e. those with high intrinsic accuracy which produce poor results over a wide range of algorithms) as being hard. When intrinsic accuracy is high but learning performance is poor, the concept needs to be expressed in terms of more complex expressions involving the primitive attributes. This is because each one is more distantly related to the target concept, which makes classification information difficult to identify because patterns are conditional.

1.3 Concept dispersion and feature interaction

Some of the aspects of problem difficulty can be visualised if the concept is thought of as a two-dimensional probability surface. The horizontal axes in Figure 1.1 represent two relevant features and the vertical axis represents class membership probability (for a given class variable $X = x_j$). If Y_1 and Y_2 are the set of allowable values for feature 1 and feature 2, respectively, then the vertical axis is simply the probability of $X = x_j$ conditional on each member of the set formed by

---

[4] Given a set of attributes, intrinsic accuracy is the largest attainable accuracy for the class membership function using those attributes and perfect class membership information [7].

$Y_1 \times Y_2$ (i.e. the cross product of Y_1 and Y_2). As can be seen from Figure 1.1, the probability surface has many peaks and troughs or areas of high and low class membership probability,[5] respectively. The peaks or areas of high class membership probability are of primary concern.

Problems encountered owing to low-level representations can be described in terms of two indicators: concept dispersion and feature interaction. Concept dispersion is a symptom of underlying inter-actions and is influenced by a number of factors:

(i)   the number of peaks: the smallest number of peaks which describe the underlying concept to a given accuracy;
(ii) peak shape: the average number of disjuncts needed to describe each peak;
(iii) peak arrangement: the smallest number of features which must be considered together to achieve a certain accuracy.

The number of peaks is the principal factor in concept dispersion and is a measure of concept density. Many algorithms encounter difficulty as the number of peaks increases. A larger number of peaks implies greater interactions, and therefore as the number of peaks increases so does the difficulty in finding them. Since each peak represents a disjunct of the target concept, each separate disjunct (which consists of one or more conjoined attribute values) represents a local region of the instance space. Separate disjuncts associate groups of more remotely connected regions, so increasing numbers of peaks reduces concept concentration. For example, if we have a particular learning problem described by n nominal relevant attributes each with v possible values, then there are $n * v$ singleton attribute values. However, if we discover that there are P peaks, where $P > n * v$, this implies that the concept involves some combination of singleton attribute values. The greater the disparity between P and $n * v$ the greater the combinatorial extent.[6]

1.4 Why do we need to estimate concept difficulty?

The justification for estimating concept difficulty (resulting from concept dispersion/feature interaction) is the need to alter learning

[5] For simplicity, the metric used here to estimate class membership probability includes no significance component. A combination of n attribute values (n_c) can have a high conditional probability with respect to the class variable, with n_c occurring very rarely. A more useful metric would also include some measure of the *a priori* probability of this combination.
[6] Calculating the actual number of peaks beforehand is only possible given the form of the target concept. Otherwise all combinations of primitive attributes would have to be generated and tested up to depth n (given n attributes).

strategy when the initial problem description is inappropriate for acquiring the target concept. On the other hand, if the problem description is at an appropriate level of abstraction for the algorithmic biases employed, then any transformation or change of strategy is unnecessary. Detecting the need for this transformation is required because the processes involved (changing representation or employing algorithms which do not employ greedy SBL biases) are computationally more expensive and should only be utilised when warranted by the current problem. We will concentrate on methods used to change the initial representation, as this is a strategy often used when initial representations are poor but intrinsic accuracy is high. These methods attempt to make classification information more apparent to the underlying algorithm by reformulating the original attributes. Other methods improve learning by employing algorithms which use biases that are more suitable for the problem at hand (i.e. biases which are not affected as much by feature interaction).

Three primary strategies are prevalent when deciding to change representation or deal with poorly correlated features:

(i)　always carry out transformation regardless of the initial representation;

(ii)　analyse the initial data set—described with primitive attributes (data-based detection);

(iii)　analyse the base learner's concept description (hypothesis-based detection).

There are some systems that are blind constructive learners, i.e. they always carry out transformations regardless of the initial problem representation. Examples include GALA [8] and AQ17-HCI [9]. Unwarranted feature construction can lead to a degradation in performance because searching for more complex correlations amounts to overfitting; this has been shown to harm learning [10].

Hypothesis-based detection is more common; the results of the learning system (i.e. the resulting classifier–decision tree, rule set, decision list etc.) are analysed for certain pattern types (for example, replications[7] in decision trees or excessive disjunctive components). In other systems, rules or hypothesis fragments of high quality (quality measures include accuracy, conciseness, comprehensibility) are identified and used as new attributes. Often, the detection and selection (selecting appropriate elements for reuse) phases are less distinct

---

[7] A symptom of feature interaction manifested by many decision-tree learners [11].

because components highlighted in the detection phase are selected as new feature components.

Many systems that use hypothesis-based detection construct new attributes based on the results of the analysis and perform an iterative cycle of hypothesis formation, analysis and attribute construction until some stopping criterion is satisfied. The aim is to gradually make classification information more visible to the underlying induction system. However, all hypothesis-driven approaches to difficulty detection attempt to alleviate the problem by this iterative improvement, and are dependent on the quality of the original classifier. When the form of the target concept is very complex and hidden by the primitive attributes, these methods can fail because of the low quality of the initial hypotheses. Problems can occur when the base learner's biases are poorly tuned to acquiring either this concept or any intermediate forms which could be used as new attributes, for example, FRINGE-like algorithms [12], which attempt to learn in domains where feature interaction occurs by identifying global replications. However, as interactions increase, replications become more obscure and unrelated to the target concept. Because of this, hypothesis-based detection ultimately becomes of little use.

Data-based detection methods analyse the training examples directly, whereas hypothesis-based methods examine them indirectly (i.e. by analysing a classifier built using the examples), but are obviously influenced by the base learner's biases. Data-based approaches examine the training examples without attempting to learn; they typically try to estimate the amount of variation or roughness in the instance space. If the underlying concept contains relatively little interaction, then it is safe to assume that selective induction methods will perform well; if not, then greedy methods employing one-dimensional splitting criteria will be less useful and other methods should be employed.

1.5 Data-based difficulty measures

Various data-based difficulty measures have been proposed in the past, some of which are detailed in the next sections.

1.5.1 μ-ness

A μ-DNF concept [13] is one in which each attribute appears no more than once in the concept's description. For example, $x_1 x_2 + x_3 x_4$ is μ-DNF but $x_1 \bar{x}_2 + \bar{x}_1 x_2$ is not. μ-ness is a function of term and literal complexity—the number of terms and literals in the concept's description. Restricting concept complexity to μ-type descriptions limits the amount of feature interaction exhibited. A concept can only be described in terms of μ-ness if its form is known; for synthetic test concepts this presents no problem, but for real-world data the form of the underlying concept is seldom known. Finally, μ-ness is an all-or-nothing measure of concept difficulty: a concept is either μ or non-μ, hence the measure is not particularly fine grained.

1.5.2 Variation

Variation [7] measures the unevenness of the concept by examining the instances which describe it, and requires the gathering of neighbouring examples. Here, neighbouring means that examples differ in the value of a single attribute only. Over the entire instance space for attribute i with v values, a given example will have $(v-1)$ neighbouring points.

The variation of an n-dimensional Boolean concept is:

$$V_n = \frac{1}{n2^n} \sum_{i=1}^{n} \sum_{neigh(x,y,i)} \delta(x, y) \qquad (1.1)$$

if example1 & example2 (neighbouring) belong to the same class
    then δ(example1, example2) = 0
    else δ(example1, example2) = 1

The second summation is taken over all 2^n pairs of neighbouring points that disagree only in their ith attribute. The additional multiplication averages the sum and normalises it to the range $[0, 1]$. Random binary-valued concepts lean towards variation values of 0.5, because the neighbours of a given random example will yield an approximately even split between the classes. So, a variation value of 0.5 is considered high (but not the maximum achievable value for a concept).

1.5.3 Blurring

1.5.3.1 Definitions

We define a rule as a propositional if–then statement (we will also refer to a tentative rule as a hypothesis). If proposition y occurs then x occurs with probability p, and $\bar{x}$ occurs with probability $(1-p)$. $\mathbf{X}$ and $\mathbf{Y}$ are discrete random variables with x and y being letters from their discrete alphabets. Rules are of the form: if $\mathbf{Y} = y_i$ then $\mathbf{X} = x_i$.

1.5.3.2 General definition for relevance assumed by entropy-based blurring measures

Feature value, y_i, is relevant if there exists some y_i and x for which:

$$p(Y_i = y_i) > 0 \qquad (1.2)$$

and

$$p(X = x \mid Y_i = y_i) \neq p(X = x) \qquad (1.3)$$

i.e. the attribute is irrelevant if there is no difference in the class *a priori* and *a posteriori* probabilities (the latter conditional on the attribute). However, this definition does not hold under some circumstances. For some problems, differences between relevant and irrelevant attributes are not apparent, for example in parity-type problems.

1.5.3.3 Blurring (Δ)

Concept difficulty has been described using entropy [14], commonly considered as a goodness-of-split measure. Rendell and Ragavan [15] describe an entropy-based measure called blurring (Δ). A difficulty measure based on entropy amounts to class entropy, conditional on each relevant attribute and averaged over those attributes. This blurring measure estimates feature interaction because each term is a one-dimensional projection onto instance space. If the underlying concept is dispersed then one attribute would provide little information about class membership. As the amount of interaction increases the information content of each attribute would drop, as a single attribute provides less information on its own and patterns become increasingly dependent on other predicting attributes—assuming that the data's intrinsic accuracy is high.

More formally:

$$i(X; Y = y) = H(X) - H(X \mid Y = y) = \sum_x p(x) \log \frac{1}{p(x)}$$

$$- \sum_x p(x \mid y) \log \frac{1}{p(x \mid y)} \qquad (1.4)$$

If we have n relevant attributes for X (the class variable depends on these attributes alone) the blurring of X is

$$\Delta = \sum_{i=1}^{n} \frac{H(X \mid Y = y)}{n}$$

where $H(X | y_i)$, the entropy of X conditional on y_i, is:

$$-\sum_y p(Y=y)\,(\,p(x|Y=y)\,\log_2 p(x|Y=y) + p(\bar{x}|Y=y)\,\log_2 p(\bar{x}|Y=y))$$

$$(1.5)$$

over all values y of Y.

This blurring measure is simply the *a posteriori* entropy of X, conditional on each relevant attribute and averaged over that number.

1.5.3.4 Blurring (Δ_j)

The J measure is the average mutual information between events X and Y with the expectation taken with respect to the *a posteriori* probability of X. Smyth and Goodman [16] describe the J measure as the only nonnegative information theoretic; it is a measure of hypothesis simplicity $p(y)$ and confirmation with the data $j(X; Y=y)$, hence $J(X; Y=y) = p(y).j(X; Y=y)$.

For rules of the form if $Y = y$ then $X = x$:

$$j(X; Y=y) = p\,(x|y)\,.\log_2 \frac{p(x|y)}{p(x)} + (1-p(x|y))\,.\log_2 \frac{(1-p(x|y))}{(1-p(x))} \quad (1.6)$$

$j(X; Y=y)$ is known as the cross entropy [16].

Limits or bounds can be imposed on the information content of a rule's or hypothesis' j measure. These bounds allow unpromising areas of the search space to be pruned, essentially halting further specialisation once a tentative rule's j measure has reached its limiting value:

$$j_s \leqslant \max\left\{ p(x|y)\,.\log_2 \frac{1}{p(x)},\ (1-p(x|y))\,.\log_2 \frac{1}{(1-p(x|y))} \right\} (1.7)$$

Hence, we are able to impose a limit on the maximum utility of an attribute by using the j measure and its limiting property. A blurring measure based on the j measure takes the form:

$$\Delta_j = 1 - \frac{j(X; Y=y)}{j_s} \quad (1.8)$$

A blurring measure based on entropy as in eqn. 1.5 also has limiting properties. The minimum value for a hypothesis or rule is zero (i.e.

minimum entropy=maximum ease) —which occurs when the transition probability $p(x \mid y) = 1.0$.

Given a data set, both blurring measures return a value [0.0, 1.0]. If a data set contains no feature interaction at all and its intrinsic accuracy is high, we would expect Δ_j averaged over all relevant attributes to be closer to zero, because for each relevant attribute value $j(X; Y = y) \approx j_s$. For data sets with a large degree of feature interaction (in the extreme case, when no attributes are relevant according to eqns. 1.2 and 1.3, such as in parity-type problems), we would expect $\Delta_j \approx 1.0$ because $j(X; Y = y) \approx 0.0$, for each relevant attribute value. A further comparison between Δ_j and Δ shows that Δ_j has no component indicating an attribute value's *a priori* probability (i.e. $p(y)$). Obviously, an attribute value can give very high instantaneous information content with respect to a predicted value, but be very unlikely (i.e. have a low *a priori* probability). Calculating each attribute value's *a priori* probability is trivial, and once this has been achieved those falling below a user-defined threshold can be discarded.

1.6 Why use the J measure as a basis for a blurring measure?

A blurring measure based only on the *a posteriori* entropy of X (the class variable) has certain disadvantages. If, for a particular input, the *a posteriori* probabilities of X form a permutation of the class of *a priori* probabilities, problems can occur.

If we have a binary-valued class variable, where a particular value of X ($x = 1$) is very likely *a priori*, the other value of X ($x = 0$) is relatively unlikely *a priori*. Consider the case where we have a domain consisting of examples described by a certain number of binary attributes, one of which is colour. Let us say that we are interested in the goodness of the attribute colour, and we wish to gauge its contribution to the blurring measure.

Case 1:

$p(x = 1) = 0.8$
$p(x = 0) = 0.2$
$p(x = 1 \mid \text{colour} = \text{red}) = 0.2$
$p(x = 0 \mid \text{colour} = \text{red}) = 0.8$

eqn. 1.5 (instantaneous information content only) gives 0.72 bits
eqn. 1.8 gives 1.2 bits

Case 2:

$p(x=1) = 0.8$
$p(x=0) = 0.2$
$p(x=1 \mid \text{colour}=\text{red}) = 0.8$
$p(x=0 \mid \text{colour}=\text{red}) = 0.2$

eqn. 1.5 (instantaneous information content only) gives 0.72 bits
eqn. 1.8 gives zero instantaneous information

A blurring measure based only on the *a posteriori* probability of *x* is the same, and is independent of which probabilities are assigned to which events in the event space of the variable. In case 1, a particular event (*x*=0) has a low *a priori* probability, but the attribute value colour=red predicts this relatively rare event with a high degree of probability. Case 2 shows the situation where the attribute colour gives us no additional information about the class variable at all, as the *a priori* and *a posteriori* probabilities are identical, i.e. the predicted event is no more likely given this value of the predicting variable. A blurring measure based on the *j* measure is able to distinguish between these events, but a measure which ignores any *a priori* belief in *X* is unable to distinguish between these two very different cases.

This information paradox (the fact that information has been received about *X* but there is no change in entropy) can cause problems for heuristics when used as measures of goodness for rules or as a measure of attribute goodness as with blurring.

1.7 Effects of various data characteristics on blurring and variation

Entropy-based measures and variation are based on very different strategies, and so have differing advantages and disadvantages. Variation's advantages over blurring (or entropy-based measures) occur because of its reliance on local estimates of concept character, i.e. appraisal over neighbouring examples. Blurring (Δ_j) is based on averaging mutual information between the class and each attribute. However, when each individual attribute provides no information about the class (owing to higher-order relations), blurring gives no information at all, regardless of the complexity of the concept's form. For example, two possible concepts described by *n* binary attributes are: $y_1 \oplus y_2$ and $y_1 \oplus y_2 \oplus, \ldots, \oplus y_n$. For both concepts, each attribute (relevant or irrelevant) gives zero information gain, entropy, (hence Δ

or Δ_j), even though they have very different structures. Variation is able to differentiate between these two concepts and assign a greater degree of difficulty to the second.

However, blurring measures are more closely related to hypothesis assessment techniques employed in many algorithms. They are more likely to track learning difficulty in algorithms which employ a general-to-specific search strategy because they utilise one-dimensional projections. When they experience maximum difficulty then a different strategy should be adopted (e.g. specific-to-general search) regardless of the concepts underlying the structure. For this reason the ability of blurring measures to identify underlying concept structure when all attributes are irrelevant (with regard to eqns. 1.2 and 1.3) is not seen as a major disadvantage.

The advantage that variation has in being able to identify differences in concept character for problems beyond the range of entropy-based measures (which use one-dimensional projections as a basis for estimation) is due to its assessment over local regions of the instance space. However, the measure's reliance on these local estimates can also cause problems. Variation gives reliable measures of concept difficulty provided that all examples are available for assessment. Measures of concept difficulty using variation are unreliable when using only samples of the data. The problem is the need to fill the gap left by unobserved instances when calculating Hamming distances for a given example. If no neighbouring instances can be found, e.g. when two clusters of positive instances are detected with no observed instances in between, should these unobserved instances be considered as positive, negative or some mixture of both? If a data set contains many of these gaps then variation estimates can be unsafe.

Some studies have been carried out on the use of penalty factors and attribute scalings or orderings. This information can be used to reduce the influence of estimates based on nonneighbouring instances by reducing their contributions based on some notion of the relative importance of various attribute distances (e.g. given two instances, differences in the attribute colour might be more important than differences in the attribute size; instances which differ in the colour attribute should be regarded with greater caution, i.e. their contributions should carry less weight, than neighbours which differ in size). In this way, nonneighbouring instances can be ranked according to the number and type of differences (attributes involved) which they exhibit. However, these attribute scalings are a form of background knowledge and require experts to supply knowledge likely to be of use.

Table 1.2   Exclusive-OR over two binary attributes with y_3 irrelevant

y_3	y_2	y_1	class
0	0	0	0
0	0	1	1
0	1	0	1
0	1	1	0
1	0	0	0
1	0	1	1
1	1	0	1
1	1	1	0

In poorly understood domains, expert intervention cannot be assumed.

This is a major drawback with variation. Given synthetic data all examples are often available but this is not the case with real-world domains. In contrast, blurring can be estimated safely from samples of data and gives stable estimates for very small sample sizes.

1.7.1 Irrelevant attributes

Variation and blurring are affected differently by the presence of irrelevant attributes. Table 1.2 shows the Boolean concept $y_1 \oplus y_2$; y_1 and y_2 are relevant to the concept and y_3 is irrelevant. Additional attributes such as y_3 expand the space of possible examples, the highlighted area, i.e. the instance space given attributes y_1 and y_2 is replicated when y_3, an irrelevant attribute, is also measured. For n additional attributes each with a set of values S_i, the entire space of possible examples is expanded by a factor of:

$$\prod_{i=1}^{n} |S_i|$$

However, information theoretic measures which use *a priori* and *a posteriori* probabilities will not see this expansion as these measurements do not alter dramatically (over the entire space of examples they do not alter at all). In contrast, the variation measure decreases with this expansion because variance is decreasing (over relevant attributes, the number of duplicated patterns is increasing). Heuristics that utilise frequency counts instead of probability measures based on one-dimensional projections are able to detect this expansion, which in

Table 1.3   Contiguous examples for $y_1 \oplus y_2$

	y_2	y_1	class
example 1	0	0	0
example 2	0	1	1
example 3	1	0	1
example 4	1	1	0

Table 1.4   Addition of an irrelevant attribute (y_3) results in nonneighbouring examples becoming contiguous

	y_3	y_2	y_1	class
example 3i	0	1	0	1
example 3ii	1	1	0	1
example 4i	0	1	1	0
example 4ii	1	1	1	0

some cases can actually aid learning in problems exhibiting limited feature interaction [9]. Nevertheless, this expansion does not alleviate problems with variation caused by lack of data. The addition of irrelevant attributes when estimating variation over noncontiguous areas of the instance space can cause underestimates of concept difficulty. Looking at the Boolean concept $y_1 \oplus y_2$ again, Table 1.3 gives the entire instance space for relevant attributes y_1 and y_2; from our previous discussion we can see that the instance space breaches the fundamental SBL assumption because neighbouring points are not predictive of one another's class membership values. If a third, irrelevant attribute, y_3, is added and examples 1 and 2 are removed the resulting instance space can be seen in Table 1.4.

The same structure (i.e. that of examples 3 and 4) has now been replicated by the addition of y_3. However, because some examples are missing, neighbouring examples (i.e. those which differ in the value of irrelevant attribute y_3) share the same classification. This results in an underestimate of the concept's variation compared to the value returned when all examples are available.

Table 1.5 Δ_j *values for various data sets*

Data set	Δ_j	atts (classes)	% error
breast cancer	0.38	4c, 5d (2)	5.28
lymphography	0.78	18d (4)	21.69
primary tumour	0.89	17d (21)	58.5
chess endgame	0.90	39d (2)	8.55
glass	0.55	9c (7)	32.48
hepatitis	0.72	6c, 13d (2)	20.39
auto insurance	0.58	14c, 10d (2)	17.66
diabetes	0.82	8c (2)	25.39
house votes	0.65	16d (2)	5.06

1.8 Dataset analysis

Table 1.5 gives Δ_j values for several UCI data sets [17]. Column 3 details the number of continuous (c) and discrete (d) attributes in the dataset together with the number of classes. Column 4 gives the error rate using C4.5 [18]; all continuous attributes were discretised beforehand using the ChiMerge algorithm [19]. Δ_j suffers from the same problem as Δ—too many irrelevant attributes artificially raise the blurring estimate and make problems appear to be more difficult.

The function seems well behaved for hard problems, such as lymphography, glass and diabetes. However, this leads to a further problem. We have assumed that hard problems have high intrinsic accuracy (i.e. taken together they provide full information on the concept) and that the reason for their difficulty is that some reformulation is required in order for us to learn accurate classifiers, but we are unable to actually prove this until the problem is solved!

There is some evidence to suggest that the high values returned for glass, lymphography and chess endgame are due to poor initial representation. Holte [20] presents the results obtained from C4.5 and 1R (an algorithm which produces one-level decision trees), comparing error rates produced on several UCI datasets. Table 1.6 shows the difference between the error rates of C4.5 (pruned) and those obtained by 1R.

The results show the large difference in error rate between C4.5 and 1R in the chess endgame data set. This indicates that the large blurring value attributed to chess is due to higher-level feature interaction (but is still inflated owing to irrelevant attributes). Lymphography and glass

Table 1.6   1-rule and C4.5 error rate differences

Data set	Error difference (%)
lymphography	6.8
breast cancer	3.3
chess endgame	31.6
glass	9.4
iris	0.3
house votes	0.4

show a slight improvement with deeper decision trees; however Holte obtained similar error rates to Quinlan [18], i.e. deeper decision trees still produced poor classifiers. In the case of glass this could be attributed to the discretisation process. Glass has six class attribute values, so producing a single threshold, i.e. a binary split on a continuous range, will never be able to perfectly separate examples into the six classes. However, 1R divides continuous ranges into several disjoint intervals, so perhaps the poor accuracy obtained on this dataset and reflected by Δ_j means that some reformulation of the ground attributes is required. The glass dataset contains many classes with low *a priori* probability. If a continuous attribute is divided into a range with a high conditional probability with respect to a rarely occurring class (i.e. a high instantaneous information content), then the average information content will be low, and hence the Δ_j value will be higher.

Overestimating owing to irrelevant attributes appears to be the main disadvantage when using information theoretic functions to estimate concept difficulty. Perhaps only adding attributes with blurring values greater than the class average would help to reduce the bias. Possible solutions to these overestimates are discussed further in Sections 1.9, 1.10 and 1.11.

The error difference for the house-votes dataset explains its relatively high Δ_j value given its low error rate. The 1R result was only 0.4% lower than that obtained by C4.5, which indicates that the inflated Δ_j value is due to many irrelevant attributes and not to attribute interaction. Table 1.7 shows a typical type-2 problem: the output is 1 if the input contains an odd number of 1s. However, every conditional probability between a single input and the output is 0.5. This highlights the problem with the J measure, J bound pruning and

Table 1.7   A typical type-2 problem, requiring reformulation of primitive attributes

y_1	y_2	y_3	X
1	1	1	1
1	1	0	0
1	0	1	0
1	0	0	1
0	1	1	0
0	1	0	1
0	0	1	1
0	0	0	0

hence Δ_j. As mentioned previously, we assume that hard problems have high intrinsic accuracy but this cannot be proved until the problem is solved. The J measure is unable to distinguish between irrelevant attributes and noise. The situation where:

$$p(x \mid y) . \log_2 \frac{p(x \mid y)}{p(x)} \approx (1 - p(x \mid y)) . \log_2 \frac{(1 - p(x \mid y))}{(1 - p(x))} \qquad (1.9)$$

can indicate feature interaction or irrelevant features.

1.9 Problems with information-theoretic-based blurring measures

Both Δ and Δ_j suffer from the same problem—irrelevant attributes artificially raise the blurring estimate, i.e. they make problems appear to be more difficult. In extreme cases, where attributes have zero information content, their contribution to the blurring estimate will be a maximum (1.0). There are some possible solutions to this problem:

(i) use background knowledge from a domain expert to highlight relevant and irrelevant attributes, only including relevant attributes when calculating blurring estimates;

(ii) only include attributes with blurring values greater than the class average, as suggested by Rendell and Ragavan [15].

Using background knowledge of which features are likely to be directly or indirectly useful would be a good solution. However, the very nature of the task precludes this—the domains in which we are attempting to learn are poorly understood, so the techniques to be developed should not have to rely on any domain dependent presupplied knowledge, but should be as domain independent as possible.

Only including attributes with blurring values greater than the class average is also problematic. When feature interaction occurs, single attributes can provide little or no information about the class (as is the case with a concept consisting of a $(y_1 \oplus y_2)$-type relation; given a uniform distribution, the transition probabilities of each attribute conditional on each class variable in turn are identical and thus each attribute would give zero instantaneous information, but both attributes are relevant, their utility only becoming obvious when they are combined). Therefore, excluding these low-valued attributes could shift attention away from necessary features.

1.10 Estimating attribute relevance with the RELIEF algorithm

To alleviate the problem of irrelevant attributes when estimating concept difficulty with Δ_j, we need to be able to identify any dependencies between attributes and so separate seemingly irrelevant features (which are relevant but are involved in higher-order relations) from attributes which are noise, i.e. not necessary to identify the underlying concept.

Kira and Rendell [21] developed an algorithm called RELIEF, designed for estimating the quality of attributes, which is able to detect some dependencies between attributes. For example, in parity problems (of varying degree) with a significant proportion of irrelevant attributes, RELIEF correctly identifies the relevant features. The algorithm works on a similar principle to variation; however, in this case each attribute's contribution to the underlying concept's difficulty is highlighted.

RELIEF estimates attributes according to how well their values distinguish between examples which are close to each other. For each example, RELIEF finds its two nearest neighbours, one neighbour from the same class (called the nearest hit) and one from a different class (the nearest miss). The number of seed examples or training instances n is user defined. The basic RELIEF algorithm is outlined below:

set all weights $W[A] := 0.0$;
for $i := 1$ **to** n **do**
  begin
  randomly select an instance R;
  find nearest hit H and nearest miss M;
  for $A := 1$ **to** number-of-attributes **do**
    $W[A] := W[A] - \text{diff}(A, R, H)/n + \text{diff}(A, R, M)/n$;
  end;

where diff(attribute, instance1, instance2) calculates the difference between the values of a particular attribute for two instances. For discrete attributes the difference is either 0, if the values are identical, or 1 if not. For continuous attributes the difference is the actual difference but normalised to the interval [0,1].

The algorithm returns a weight for each attribute; good attributes should have no difference for a nearest hit and should discriminate for a nearest miss. The algorithm is attempting to see whether the fundamental assumption taken by many algorithms holds—are neighbouring instances highly predictive of each other's class membership values?

Kononenko [22] developed an extension of RELIEF called RELIEFF which improves the original algorithm with more reliable probability estimation. Noisy data is handled in a more robust manner, but the original algorithm's time complexity is retained.

The choice of nearest neighbours for each of the n training examples is of great importance. These nearest neighbours produce local estimates of attribute quality and allow some conditional dependencies between attributes to be detected, dependencies which would otherwise be hidden if weights were calculated over all training instances. RELIEFF collects k nearest hits/misses for each training example instead of the single hit/miss used for estimation in the original algorithm. This extension to RELIEF was shown to significantly improve attribute estimates.

1.10.1 Experiments with RELIEFF

As with Kononenko's experiments [22], all testing had k set to ten and n, the number of training examples, equal to 400.

For parity-type problems over four attributes (with eight irrelevant), RELIEF was able to successfully separate relevant from irrelevant attributes (any attributes with final weights less than zero were deemed to be irrelevant). All attributes would have given zero information content when estimated using various information theoretic functions, including information gain and J measure. RELIEFF seems to be a very useful measure when these dependencies exist.

Perez and Rendell [23] give details of several concept types which exhibit extreme interaction, i.e. individual attributes contribute no evidence at all towards class formation (i.e. they are irrelevant according to eqns. 1.2 and 1.3). When measured using Δ_j these data sets returned 1.0 — indicating maximum difficulty with respect to the blurring function.

The concept $F_{cdp}(i, j)$ is defined over 12 Boolean attributes as $\text{odd}(\langle x_i \ldots x_4 \rangle) \wedge [\text{odd}(\langle x_{i+j/2} \ldots x_8 \rangle) + \text{odd}(\langle x_j \ldots x_{12} \rangle)]$. For example, $F_{cdp}(1,9) = \text{odd}(\langle x_1 \ldots x_4 \rangle) \wedge [\text{odd}(\langle x_5 \ldots x_8 \rangle) + \text{odd}(\langle x_9 \ldots x_{12} \rangle)]$ exhibits extreme attribute interaction. Here, all 12 attributes are relevant to the learning task. However, RELIEFF was unable to order the attributes correctly. It was able to weight $x_1 \ldots x_4$ correctly but since this particular disjunct appears in all positive examples (the data set contained no noise) perhaps the inability to correctly order the remaining relevant attributes was due to a lack of data. In this concept (over all 4096 examples), each separate disjunct $[\text{odd}(x_1 \ldots x_4) \wedge \text{odd}(x_5 \ldots x_8)]$ and $[\text{odd}(x_1 \ldots x_4) \wedge \text{odd}(x_9 \ldots x_{12})]$ uniquely covers one third (or 512) of the positive examples (with one third covered by the conjunction).

However, RELIEFF does better on $\text{odd}(\langle x_2 \ldots x_4 \rangle) \wedge [\text{odd}(\langle x_6 \ldots x_8 \rangle) + \text{odd}(\langle x_{10} \ldots x_{12} \rangle)]$, with x_9, x_5 and x_1 correctly indicated as irrelevant; however the algorithm also denotes x_{12} as irrelevant. Finally, with $\text{odd}(\langle x_3 \ldots x_4 \rangle) \wedge [\text{odd}(\langle x_7 \ldots x_8 \rangle) + \text{odd}(\langle x_{11} \ldots x_{12} \rangle)]$, the algorithm achieves perfect separation between relevant and irrelevant attributes.

Clearly the RELIEF approach to detecting attribute interactions suffers when the concept becomes more spread out; as separate disjuncts are defined over a greater number of attributes its performance degrades. But this does not explain why the algorithm is able to detect relevance among attributes $x_1 \ldots x_4$ in $F_{cdp}(1,9)$ but not between the remaining relevant attributes. This could be owing to a lack of data and the amount of interaction present.

When the amount of interaction is reduced RELIEF demonstrates its ability to order attributes correctly. When $F_{cdp}(1,9)$ was altered so that only one disjunct indicated the concept, i.e. $\text{odd}(x_1 \ldots x_4) \wedge \text{odd}(x_5 \ldots x_8)$, the algorithm correctly identified all relevant attributes.

Increased concept dispersion causes increasing variation. At a certain level, given n random examples, the point arrives where:

$$\sum_{i=1}^{n} diff(A, R_i, M_i) < \sum_{i=1}^{n} diff(A, R_i, H_i) \qquad (1.10)$$

i.e. for a given random example, more variation occurs for neighbouring examples of the same class than for examples of differing classes.

The RELIEF function, like variation, relies on local estimates of variance, by examining a number of nearest neighbours. In some experiments, setting this parameter (the number of nearest neighbours examined) too high also causes problems. A scale of closeness can be applied to examples described as 'nearest'; ideally, a nearest neighbour differs from a given example by the value of a single attribute. The implementation of RELIEF used in these experiments collected those neighbours which differed in the value of a single attribute from the random example. If, however, the k parameter was set too high, examples collected in the later stages could differ greatly from the seed example. Some methods employ penalty factors which reduce an example's contribution to the overall estimate in proportion to its distance from the seed example. However, for the data sets used, such a penalty factor was thought to be relatively unimportant, as setting the number of nearest neighbours to ten meant that the neighbours selected differed by only one attribute value from the seed example.

The types of relational dependency between attributes in the synthetic concepts studied here give problems owing to increased variance. Over the entire set of examples, increasing the number of irrelevant attributes (decreasing dispersion or the number of attributes over which the concept is defined) causes the concept to be expanded or replicated throughout a larger space.

For example, each disjunct in $F_{cdp}(3,11)$ is defined over four attributes from 12, and over the entire example space the concept is represented by eight unique instances replicated by the irrelevant attributes. For $F_{cdp}(2,10)$ each disjunct is defined over six relevant attributes defining 32 unique examples replicated by the remaining attributes. However, each disjunct in $F_{cdp}(1,9)$ is defined over eight of the 12 attributes. This level of dispersion results in each disjunct being represented by 128 unique examples, replicated over only four remaining (irrelevant attributes). This level of concept dispersion and the variance it produces causes RELIEF to give unreliable estimates.

As a final experiment a deterministic version of RELIEF, RELIEVED, as described by Kohavi and John[24] was implemented and tested.

RELIEVED differs from the RELIEFF algorithm in two ways:

(i)   every example in the training set is used as a seed;
(ii) when collecting nearest neighbours for a particular seed instance, the algorithm collects all nearest neighbours (examples which differ from the seed example in the value of only a single attribute).

However, even this deterministic version of the RELIEF algorithm was unable to give reliable estimates of attribute relevance. The RELIEVED algorithm produced similar results to the RELIEFF method used in previous experiments.

1.11 Blurring over disjoint subsets

To alleviate some disparities between blurring estimates and accuracies obtained using greedy hill climbing (owing to the presence of many irrelevant attributes), an extension to the Δ_j algorithm was developed.

Greedy splitting algorithms often perform poorly when the biases which they employ are not suited to the target concept (particularly when the source of difficulty is feature interaction). Given that the first split in a decision tree is the most important, the formation of this first decision node and the partitioning which it imposes on the instance space can often greatly ease the apparent difficulty of the problem.

A greedy splitting algorithm selects the best single attribute (using some measure of attribute quality, in our case the J measure), and uses this to form the root node, partitioning the training data into disjoint subsets accordingly. This process is applied recursively to each subset until some stopping criterion is satisfied.

For a discrete k-valued attribute selected to form the root node, the training data is divided into k disjoint subsets. Since the first split is the most important, we measured concept difficulty using Δ_j for each of these subsets (ignoring significant leaf nodes, disregarding any insignificant leaf nodes[8] and measuring over all relevant attributes except the one used to form the root node). These k separate blurring estimates $(\Delta_j^1, \Delta_j^2 \ldots, \Delta_j^k)$ measured over $n-1$ attributes were combined with the original blurring measure (calculated over the entire training set) and the result averaged over all $k+1$ significant sets.

For example, the concepts $C_1 = y_4 + y_3 y_2 y_1$, $C_2 = y_4 + y_2 y_1$ and $C_3 = y_4 y_3 + y_1 y_2$ with four irrelevant attributes, have Δ_j values of 0.8, 0.53 and 0.84, respectively. Concepts C_1 and C_3 have similar Δ_j values despite the fact that C_1 has a gross predictor as part of its definition (i.e. a single

---

[8] We define a leaf node as insignificant if it partitions less than ten per cent of the training data.

Table 1.8 Δ_j and $\bar{\Delta}_j$ values for various data sets

Data set	Δ_j	W	$\bar{\Delta}_j$
breast cancer	0.38	1	0.16
lymphography	0.78	1	0.57
primary tumour	0.89	1	0.82
chess endgame	0.90	16	0.87
hepatitis	0.72	1	0.62
auto insurance	0.58	32	0.57
diabetes	0.82	8	0.83
house votes	0.65	1	0.22

attribute value not conditional on any other). Splitting on y_4, the best attribute produces a leaf node which separates 50 per cent of the training examples, whereas splitting data on the best attribute in C_3 yields impure partitions. The corrected Δ_j values are 0.4, 0.27 and 0.6, respectively.

1.12 Results and discussion

Table 1.8 gives details of blurring results over subsets of data. The last column of the table gives figures for $\bar{\Delta}_j$, the results of averaging Δ_j over the initial instance space and the partitioned space after splitting on the best attribute. The column marked W is the beam width at which the most accurate rules are found (using C4.5). Breast cancer, identified as having little feature interaction, shows a dramatic reduction in Δ_j after the first split, which is confirmed by the low error rate and the fact that the most accurate classifier was found using greedy search (i.e. with a beam width of 1); house votes also follows this pattern. Lymphography and tumour also produce the most accurate classifiers at a beam width of 1. However, error rates are still very high, and tumour has many poorly represented classes which may account for its poor result. Lymphography's Δ_j value does reduce significantly, indicating that the first local decision is the most appropriate. However, the source of difficulty with both these datasets seems to stem from the fact that critical information (i.e. causal variables required to identify the target concept) are missing. For chess endgame the high Δ_j value indicates that the primitive attributes are very poorly correlated with the class attribute, but in this case intrinsic accuracy is high. The first split results in a slight reduction in Δ_j, indicating that the instance space is still very rough and that the best local decision at this point has not eased problem difficulty; this is reflected in that fact that the best classifier is formed at a beam width of 16. Diabetes also requires a more extensive search in order to find the best classifier.

The fact that extensive search fails to produce good hypotheses could be due to the fact that the continuous attributes require reformulation (e.g. if the target concept is based on the absolute difference or the ratio of two primitive attributes). However, the space of potential combinations for continuous attributes is almost infinite. Hepatitis also shows a considerable reduction in Δ_j after the first split. All the continuous attributes return very low individual contributions to the overall value; indicating good correlations; this dataset has only two classes and so a continuous attribute discretised into two ranges could perfectly divide the training examples (binary discretisation for problems with more than two classes will be unable to achieve perfect class separability on the first split). However, the final error rate is still quite high, and this could indicate problems owing to low intrinsic accuracy. Auto insurance gives a relatively low value for Δ_j and approximately the same value after splitting: this indicates that the best local decision is inappropriate. However this does not explain the low value. The auto insurance dataset has a large number of attributes which return individual Δ_j values below the average value (17 out of 24). In addition, their individual values indicate that there is little to differentiate between them. This can cause problems for greedy hill-climbing algorithms as there is little difference between the best and several alternative local decisions.

The $\bar{\Delta}_j$ measure is able to identify problems where greedy search is likely to produce local decisions which will prove to be unfit. Given the initial assumption that the cause of difficulty is higher-order relations and that critical information required to acquire the target concept has been included, the measure seems able to track learning difficulty and predict when more extensive search techniques should be employed. When little or no difference between a particular dataset's Δ_j and $\bar{\Delta}_j$ occurs, the effect of irrelevant attributes on the blurring measure is lessened and the measure is a truer reflection of concept difficulty.

1.13   Summary and future research

Estimating concept difficulty prior to learning has obvious advantages—it allows us to select an appropriate algorithm or bias more suited to acquiring the underlying target concept. Ultimately, this would lead to automatic bias selection based on a combination of factors including estimates on the amount of feature interaction present in the training data.

A number of issues need to be addressed with regard to the application of the Δ_j measure. We can safely say that for a particular dataset, a very low value implies the absence of feature interaction. Likewise, a very high value coupled with an equally high $\bar{\Delta}_j$ measure implies that greedy SBL biases will have difficulty identifying the target concept: the higher the value for Δ_j the more unreliable our assumption of attribute relevance (eqns. 1.2 and 1.3).

At this time, our criterion for weighting the effect of irrelevant attributes is very coarse — if the $\bar{\Delta}_j$ value for a particular dataset drops by more than 50 per cent when compared with its Δ_j value, then we assume that the high value is predominantly owing to the effects of irrelevant attributes and not high degrees of feature interaction.

The Δ_j measure does seem to have more advantages than disadvantages when compared with the alternatives which we have explored. The RELIEF approach gives unreliable estimates when interactions become extreme; in addition, when all attributes are well correlated but not necessary, expert intervention is required to provide a suitable threshold for acceptance. Variation does allow concept difficulty to be quantified when interactions become extreme (as is the case with the synthetic datasets with which we have experimented). However, the results are questionable when estimating from samples. In addition, variation is less closely related to the way in which many algorithms assess candidate hypotheses and so traverse the hypothesis space. Variation uses instance-based evidence, i.e. the closeness of one instance to its nearest neighbour with regards to the predicted attribute, whereas Δ_j uses one-dimensional projections which are often the starting point for building classifiers in many algorithms. Finally, the effect of irrelevant attributes is nonintuitive; irrelevant attributes hinder many algorithms but they actually reduce variation and make the problem appear to be easier.

Further work is required using synthetic datasets of moderate to high difficulty, i.e. mapping $\bar{\Delta}_j$ and Δ_j values to scales of interaction. Experiments on synthetic concepts with varying degrees of interaction, irrelevant attributes and noise are necessary and remain a subject for future research. The $\bar{\Delta}_j$ approach would also be useful as an additional metric for recursive partitioning algorithms. In some domains (for example the auto insurance dataset) the first split provides little information to discriminate between attributes. Calculating the effect of each tentative split on the resulting partitions could give further information on which attribute to select as a root node. This could result in more compact, accurate classifiers.

1.14 References

1 CLARK, A. and THORNTON, C.: 'Trading spaces: computation, representation and the limits of uninformed learning'. Draft BBS article, 1997, ftp://ftp.princeton.edu/pub/harnad/BBS/WWW/bbs.clark.htm
2 NAZAR, K. and BRAMER, M.A.: 'Concept dispersion feature interaction and their effect on particular sources of bias in machine learning'. Proceedings of the 17th SGES international conference on *Knowledge based systems and applied artificial intelligence*, 1997, pp. 7–23
3 UTGOFF, P.E.: Shift of bias for inductive concept learning', *in* MICHAL-SKI, R.S., CARBONELL, J.G. and MITCHELL, T.M. (Eds.): 'Machine learning, an artificial intelligence approach', Volume 2 (Morgan Kaufmann Inc., 1986)
4 QUINLAN, J.R.: 'C4.5: programs for machine learning' (Morgan Kaufmann, San Mateo, CA, 1993)
5 BREIMAN, L., FRIEDMAN, J.H., OLSHEN, R.A. and STONE, C.J.: 'Classification and regression trees' (Belmont, CA, Wadsworth, 1984)
6 RENDELL, L.A.: 'A new basis for state-space learning and a successful implementation', *Artif. Intell.*, 1983, **20**, pp. 369–392
7 RENDELL, L.A. and SESHU, R.: 'Learning hard concepts through constructive induction: framework and rationale', *Comput. Intell.*, 1990, **6**, pp. 247–270
8 HU, Y. and KIBBLER, D.: 'Generation of attributes for learning algorithms'. Proceedings of the 13th national conference on *Artificial intelligence*, 1996, pp. 806–811
9 WNEK, J. and MICHALSKI, R.S.: 'Hypothesis-driven constructive induction in AQ17-HCI: a method and experiments', *Mach. Learn.*, 1994, **14**, pp.139–168
10 VILALTA, R., BLIX, G. and RENDELL, L.A.: 'Global data analysis and the fragmentation problem in decision tree induction', *Lect. Notes Artif. Intell.*, **XXX** (Springer-Verlag, Heidelberg, 1997), pp. 312–326
11 PAGALLO, G: 'Adaptive decision tree algorithms for learning from examples'. Ph.D. thesis, University of California at Santa Cruz, June 1990
12 PAGALLO, G. and HAUSSLER, D.: 'Two algorithms that learn DNF by discovering relevant features'. Proceedings of the sixth international workshop on *Machine learning*, Ithaca, NY, June 1989, pp. 119–123
13 KEARNS, M., LI, M., PITT, L. and VALIANT, L.: 'Recent results on Boolean concept learning'. Proceedings of the fourth international *Machine learning workshop*, 1987, University of California, Irvine, pp. 337–352
14 WATANABE, S.: 'Pattern recognition: human and mechanical' (Wiley, New York, NY, 1985)

15 RENDELL, L. and RAGAVAN, H.: 'Improving the design of induction methods by analysing algorithm functionality and data-based concept complexity'. Proceedings of the 13th international conference on *Artificial intelligence*, 1993, pp. 952–958

16 SMYTH, P. and GOODMAN, R.M.: 'An information theoretic approach to rule induction from databases', *IEEE Trans. Knowl. Data Eng.*, 1992, 4,(4)

17 ftp.ics.uci.edu:/pub/machine-learning-databases/

18 QUINLAN, J.R.: 'Boosting, bagging and C4.5'. Proceedings of the 13th national conference on *Artificial intelligence*, 1996, pp. 725–730

19 KERBER, R.: 'ChiMerge: discretization of numeric attributes'. Proceedings of the 10th national conference on *Artificial intelligence*, 1992, pp. 123–128

20 HOLTE, R.C.: 'Very simple classification rules perform well on most commonly used datasets', *Mach. Learn.*, 1993, 11, pp. 63–91

21 KIRA, K. and RENDELL, L.: 'A practical approach to feature selection'. Proceedings of international conference on *Machine learning*, July 1992, Aberdeen, pp. 249–256

22 KONONENKO, I.: 'Estimating attributes: analysis and extensions of RELIEF'. Proceedings of European conference on *Machine learning*, Catanina, April 1994

23 PEREZ, E. and RENDELL, L.A.: 'Using multidimensional projections to find relations'. Proceedings of XII international conference on *Machine learning*, 1995, Tahoe City, California

24 KOHAVI, R. and JOHN, G.H.: 'Wrappers for feature subset selection', *AIJ special issue on relevance*, 1997

Chapter 2

Analysing outliers by searching for plausible hypotheses

Xiaohui Liu and Gongxian Cheng
Birkbeck College, University of London, UK

2.1 Introduction

The handling of anomalous or outlying observations in a dataset is one of the most important tasks in data preprocessing. It is important for three reasons. First, outlying observations can have a considerable influence on the results of an analysis. Secondly, although outliers are often measurement or recording errors, some of them can represent phenomena of interest, something significant from the viewpoint of the application domain. Thirdly, for many applications, exceptions identified can often lead to the discovery of unexpected knowledge.

One approach to outlier analysis is to identify outliers and decide whether they should be retained or rejected. Many statistical techniques have been proposed to detect outliers and comprehensive texts on this topic are those by Hawkins [1] and Barnet and Lewis [2]. The identification of outliers has also received much attention from the computing community [3–5].

However, there appears to have been much less work on how to decide whether outliers should be retained or rejected. In the statistical community, a commonly adopted strategy when analysing data is to carry out the analysis both including and excluding the suspicious values. If there is little difference in the results obtained, then the outliers have had minimal effect, but if excluding them does have an effect, options need to be sought for analysing these outliers further.

In order to distinguish successfully between noisy outlying data and noise-free outliers, different kinds of information are normally needed. These should not only include various data characteristics and the context in which the outliers occur, but also relevant domain knowledge. The procedure for analysing outliers has been experimentally shown to be subjective, depending on the above mentioned factors [6]. The analyst is normally given this task of judging which suspicious values are obviously impossible and which, although physically possible, should be viewed with caution. However, in the context of data mining where a large number of cases are normally involved, the number of suspicious cases would be sizable too and manual analysis would become insufficient.

In this chapter, we propose an algorithm for outlier analysis. In this approach, outliers detected by statistical methods and the context in which these outliers occur are examined by acquiring and applying relevant domain knowledge. In particular, we try to establish domain-specific hypotheses which may be used to explain the data points.

2.2 Statistical treatment of outliers

An outlier in a set of data is defined as an observation (or subset of observations) which appears to be inconsistent with the remainder of that set of data. The phenomenon of outlying observations is common in real-world data, and outliers exist as part of the experimentalist's reality and the analyst's inescapable responsibility [2].

Outlying observations are not necessarily noisy or erroneous, and they can be genuine members of the main population. In some situations certain outliers may indicate something valuable from application-domain points of view. On the other hand, if outliers are nongenuine members of the population, or contaminants (arising from some other distribution), they may frustrate attempts to draw inferences about the original population. Thus, it is an important task to make the distinction between noise-free and noisy outliers.

The treatment of outliers usually consists of two steps. First, outliers are detected from the dataset. This step is straightforward for a univariate sample; however, specific methods are needed for multivariate or highly-structured data. Fortunately, a number of statistical methods have been developed for this purpose such as those using the subordering principle [7], graphical and pictorial methods [8], principal-components analysis methods [9], the application of simple test statistics [10], and some more formal approach in which a model for the data is provided, and tests of hypotheses that certain observations are outliers are set up against the alternative that they are part of the main body of data [1].

Secondly, outliers are analysed further and there have been two major approaches to this problem. One approach advocates an explicit examination or testing of an outlier with a view to determining whether it should be rejected or taken as a welcome identification of unsuspected factors of practical importance [11]. However, this judgement is extremely difficult to make for statistical methods because noise-free and noisy outliers share similar characteristics from a statistical point of view [2].

In view of the difficulties with explicit examination of outliers, a majority of current statistical work adopts an alternative approach which neither rejects nor welcomes an outlier, but accommodates it [12]. This approach is characterised by the development of a variety of statistical estimation or testing procedures which are robust against, or relatively unaffected by, outliers. In these procedures, outliers them-selves are no longer of prime concern. This approach assumes that outliers are somehow undesirable objects and that their effect or influence ought to be minimised. Unfortunately, this assumption contravenes many practical applications, i.e. outliers can actually represent unsuspected factors of practical importance and can therefore contain valuable information. In these situations, the influence of outliers should be emphasised rather than limited or minimised [5]. For example, outliers in clinical test data can be caused by a patient's behavioural variants, but can also be caused by pathological factors pertaining to the patient [13]. Another example would be suspicious credit card transactions. These transactions may be fraudulent, but can also be legitimate. Any attempt to systematically minimise the influence of outliers without due consideration in these applications can lead to loss of valuable information, often crucial for problem solving.

We are interested in developing the explicit examination approach to outlier management. This type of research in statistics was popular during the early period of the study of outliers, but has received much less attention over the past few decades [2]. However, we believe that this approach deserves more attention than it currently receives: new computational techniques are being developed which are beginning to provide the necessary capability for advancing this important area of research.

2.3 An algorithm for outlier analysis

In this section we propose an algorithm for analysing outliers. The assumed context is that a small set of outliers has been detected using statistical methods for a given set of data points, say X. For example, one may sequentially[1] apply one of the most popular methods, Wilks's multivariate outlier test statistic [14], to detect multiple outliers (see Caroni and Prescott [15] for advantages of this approach). This implies that the outlier set is ordered in that o_1, o_2, . . ., and o_{i-1} must be rejected before o_i can be rejected. In the proposed algorithm we would like to concentrate on how these outliers can be analysed.

One important assumption of the algorithm is that there exists relevant domain knowledge which will help us to understand whether the data distribution in X has specific meanings from application-domain points of view, or whether X conforms to a particular knowledge-based distribution. For example, if data points are the results of a certain medical test, do these results tell us something about the possible disease which the patient under test might have? If data points are a set of symptoms in the form of input and output pairs of a particular electronic circuit, are these pairs indicative of something wrong in the circuit, e.g. components A and B might be faulty?

Of course there are usually a number of competing hypotheses which could explain the data points in X. We may have several different diseases for the medical diagnosis example and a number of possibilities that different components of a circuit might be faulty. That is why we normally need a substantial amount of domain knowledge to enable us to choose the most plausible explanation for the set of data points in hand.

Here is the proposed algorithm for analysing outliers:

Definitions

Let Ω be a p-dimensional sample space. Let $X=\{x_1, x_2, \ldots, x_n\}$ be a set of vectors independently drawn from Ω.
Let $O=\{o_1, o_2, \ldots, o_r\}$ $(1 \leq r < n)$ be an ordered set of outliers in X where $O \subset X$.
Let $\Gamma=\{\Gamma_1, \Gamma_2, \ldots, \Gamma_m\}$ be a set of hypothesised domain properties (or classes).

---

[1] Only a single outlier is detected at a time.

Knowledge-based distributions

Let $P_j(x_i) = p_{ij}$ $(j = 1, \ldots, m)$ be probability distributions corresponding to the hypotheses Γ_j.

Decision making

Determine how many outliers in O should be rejected as follows:
  Input: $O[r]$; $X[n]$; $\Gamma[m]$;
  Output: X_{new} (after rejecting noisy outliers from X);
  Method:
  $i := 0$; $X_{new} := X$;
  repeat
      hypothesis testing: which hypothesis in Γ is the most plausible to explain X_{new};
      if no hypothesis is found with sufficient confidence:
          $i := i + 1$; $X_{new} := X_{new} - \{o_i\}$;
      otherwise:
          algorithm terminates.
  until $i > r$.
  If $i > r$. we do not have a sufficient amount of information to explain
      the outliers in O.

Hypothesis testing

The algorithm uses the maximum-likelihood ratio [16]:

$$R(X; \Gamma_j) = 2 \sum_{i=1}^{n} \log p_{ij} + 2n \log n \qquad (2.1)$$

Eqn. 2.1 provides a likelihood measure of X with respect to each of those hypothesised probability distributions P_j formed by domain knowledge and related data. One can thus conduct a significance test on the distribution P_j for which $R(X; \Gamma_j)$ is maximum.

We make the following remarks regarding the proposed algorithm for analysing outliers.

The algorithm

The first task in the proposed algorithm is to create several knowledge-based hypotheses of data distributions in Ω using domain knowledge and related data. The techniques involved in performing this operation depend on the characteristics of domain knowledge (see below for general discussion and Section 2.4 for examples). Outliers in O can then be analysed as follows. If we manage to find a hypothesis which can adequately explain all the data points in X with sufficient confidence, then we do not reject any outliers. Otherwise, leave the first outlier out of X and see whether a confident hypothesis can be found. If yes, we then believe that the first outlier is a noisy one and that the remaining ones are noise free. If a confident hypothesis is still not formed, let us now try to leave the first two outliers out and see what happens. This procedure carries on until either we find a confident hypothesis or all the outliers have been exhausted in which case we cannot explain the outliers using the knowledge available.

Knowledge-based distribution

The use of domain knowledge to establish hypotheses regarding the data distribution can be achieved by different means, depending largely on how domain knowledge is acquired and which form it takes. For example, if we can obtain these hypotheses either directly from experts, or indirectly from databases (see Section 2.4.1 for an example), this task becomes relatively easy. However, if the knowledge is incomplete, for example, a set of examples provided by a domain expert, machine learning methods [17,18] can be used to extract the structure of the data and form relevant knowledge. This acquired knowledge can then be used to establish those hypotheses (see Section 2.4.2).

In many application domains, we lack quality domain knowledge to create accurate hypotheses regarding how data should be distributed. This is why we try to find the most plausible explanation for a set of data points, rather than to confirm one of the hypotheses with certainty. In general, one may use the training data together with an appropriate probability-density estimation method such as the kernel estimator to establish a probability distribution [19]. Below we give a simple example of how knowledge-based distributions may be estimated in a limited number of events or small dimensional discrete sample space.

Suppose we find a way of assigning data vectors, x_i, from a large dataset to those hypothesised domain classes in Γ. Then each class Γ_j ($j = 1, \ldots, m$) will contain a fixed number of vectors N_j. For each j we can calculate F_{ij}, the frequency that each vector x_i appears in Γ_j. We will then be able to form a knowledge-based probability distribution for each class: $P_j(x_i) = p_{ij}$ where $p_{ij} = F_{ij}/N_j$. Note that x_i need not be individual vectors, but can be a number of mutually exclusive events in Ω.

2.4 Experimental results

The proposed algorithm for analysing outliers has been applied to two sets of visual function test data, responsible to a large extent for diagnosing two blinding diseases, respectively glaucoma and onchocerciasis. Although data vectors for the two applications are similar, the availability of domain knowledge and the corresponding form are remarkably different. Therefore, the procedure for constructing probability models corresponding to hypothesised domain classes also varies for the two applications.

The test data are six-dimensional vectors which represent the visual functions of six locations in the central eccentric region in the retina. An all-nil vector (0,0,0,0,0,0) corresponds to nothing seen at all locations; an all-one vector indicates that the subject under test is normal. For each test there are ten repeated measurements of the six testing locations, thereby producing ten six-dimensional vectors.

2.4.1 *Case I: onchocerciasis*

There are 546 available visual function test records (5460 data vectors) for detecting onchocerciasis, which were collected in Africa. A subset of these records is used to help construct the knowledge-based hypotheses of how data are distributed, and others are used to evaluate the performance of the algorithm.

Knowledge regarding this disease is stored in a diagnostic database, which contains detailed diagnostic results for each test record. This appears to be a simple case where we could take advantage of the implicit domain knowledge hidden in the diagnostic database. As each test record has been classified into one of the diagnostic groups, one may simply assign all the vectors within that record to the diagnostic group. After processing all the test records in this way, we can use the simple procedure as described in Section 2.3 (knowledge-based distribution discussion) to establish the probability models for all the onchocerciasis diagnostic groups.

The proposed algorithm is then applied to this set of data and results are summarised below. Outliers detected by Wilks's statistic constitute 5.3 per cent of all the data points. Among these outliers, 30.0 per cent are considered to be noisy ones, 13.8 per cent are taken as noise-free outliers and the remaining 56.2 per cent cannot be

Table 2.1   Diagnostic groups

Groups	Meanings
group 1	early sign of upper hemifield damage
group 2	probable upper hemifield damage
group 3	probable lower hemifield damage
group 4	early sign of lower hemifield damage
group 5	severe overall damage

explained by the domain knowledge. Although this result can clearly be improved if more relevant domain knowledge is available, the deletion of the noisy outliers from the dataset does seem to improve the diagnostic results, as described in Section 2.5.

2.4.2   Case II: glaucoma

There are a total of 431 available glaucomatous test records (the corresponding subjects were either glaucoma patients or glaucoma suspects). In this section we describe work involved in applying the proposed algorithm to these test data.

2.4.2.1 Domain knowledge

Unfortunately, in this application we do not have the type of ready-to-use knowledge that we had in the case of onchocerciasis to classify data vectors into one or more hypothesised domain classes. A potential remedy would be to ask domain experts to come up with several diagnostic groups and to try to classify as many data vectors as possible into those groups. As a result, five diagnostic groups were created (see Table 2.1). However, only 42 per cent of all the possible data vectors were classified with certainty by one glaucoma specialist. The domain knowledge in the form of these incomplete examples from the expert needs to be generalised for us to be able to apply the algorithm most effectively. We have used Quinlan's C4.5 [18] for this purpose as described below.

2.4.2.2 Generalising from examples using C4.5

We have used C4.5 to construct decision trees using the above described examples. Having tried the different options that C4.5

offers, such as varying degrees of pruning and windowing, the results were somewhat disappointing: the best classifier that we can find is the one which can correctly classify all the members of the training set, but the corresponding tree size is 23, and unseen error estimate is around 25 per cent.

One particular attempt to make C4.5 produce better trees has met with some success. As described in Quinlan [18], C4.5 considers tests on attributes individually. It does not consider the effects of combinations of attributes as this would lead to a combinatorial explosion in computational time. Classification of many of the typical vectors in the diagnostic groups for glaucoma might, however, benefit from this approach; a human being would look at case (0,0,0,0,0,0) and say 'nothing seen — must be group 5' and not, for example, 'nothing seen at location 1, nothing seen at location 2, etc. — must be group 5'. An approach which coerced C4.5 into examining overall attributes of vectors in addition to individual attributes offered considerable possibilities for improving classification. We shall call attributes that contain information regarding the nature of the whole vector 'overall attributes'.

In particular, two overall attributes for this data set are considered: number seen and group indicator. Number seen refers to the number of locations in a vector at which the stimulus was observed.

It is clear from Table 2.1 that vectors in groups 1 and 2 tend to have more locations seen within the upper hemifield than those within the lower hemifield, and the opposite is true for vectors in groups 3 and 4. Group indicator was derived by counting the number of locations seen in the upper hemifield and subtracting this figure from the number in the lower hemifield. Thus, negative values are generally indicative of vectors in groups 1 and 2 and positive values are more likely to be associated with vectors in groups 3 and 4.

We can create a new series of training sets by including these two overall attributes in the associated vectors. C4.5 is then applied to these training sets and the results obtained are very encouraging. We are now able to produce a classifier that can correctly classify all the members of the training set, and the tree size is reduced to 14 with the unseen error estimate down to 15 per cent. This is an improvement of around 40 per cent both in terms of tree size and error estimate over the results (23 and 25 per cent were the respective figures) obtained from not using overall attributes.

In short, we have described ways of using domain-specific knowledge (overall attributes) to make C4.5 produce better decision trees for glaucomatous test vectors. The best classifier generated from this process can then be applied to glaucomatous test records to assign data vectors to diagnostic groups and to form hypotheses regarding how data are distributed using the same procedure as described in Section 2.3.

2.4.2.3 Applying the algorithm

Here are the results of applying the algorithm to glaucomatous test records: among the outliers detected which constitute 8.0 per cent of all the data points, 30.4 per cent are considered as noisy, 12.0 per cent are taken to be noise free and the remaining 57.6 per cent cannot be explained by the domain knowledge. The fact that only 42.4 per cent of the outliers can be explained indicates that more quality knowledge regarding how glaucoma manifests itself on the test data is required. However, the deletion of the noisy outliers from the glaucomatous dataset does considerably improve the diagnostic results, as described in Section 2.5.

2.5 Evaluation

The algorithm is based on the notion that if outliers and the context in which they occur (those associated data points) can be adequately explained using domain knowledge, then these outliers should be considered to be noise free ones. This notion can be extended further in that if a set of data points (with outliers) can be explained using domain knowledge as a result of leaving certain outliers out, then those outliers are noisy. The algorithm may be applied to those domains where repeated measurements of data points can be made and where there is a sufficient amount of relevant knowledge. Although this knowledge need not be complete, it should be enough to allow a sensible generalisation.

It should be pointed out that it is always possible that we simply do not have sufficient amounts of quality domain knowledge to be able to explain certain outliers, as demonstrated in the experimental results from the two applications. For example, the diagnostic groups created for glaucomatous patients may not be the optimal classification; or it might be even possible that one important diagnostic group, which has not been observed before, has been missed out. A careful study of those vectors which cannot be explained by present domain theories may lead to useful findings such as those described above. Further work is being carried out along this direction.

Below we report on the results of evaluating performance of the algorithm on the two applications. We have used the receiver operator characteristic (ROC) analysis as a comparative criterion. The purpose of the ROC is to determine a complete range of discriminating performance of a decision system in terms of its fault-detection rate against false-alarm rate. In diagnostic applications, by varying a decision threshold, we can obtain a series of different detection rates and false alarms over a group of subjects with or without the disease [20]. Thus, one can plot an ROC curve using these two parameters as two axes. On the one end of the threshold, the diagnostic system would become more conservative with fewer detections but also fewer false alarms; on the other end of the threshold, the system would become more sensitive with more detections and also more false alarms.

The decision threshold used here for discriminating between normal and abnormal subjects is the average percentage of positive responses within a test. Figure 2.1 is the ROC plot for a set of onchocerciasis test records (63 onchocerciasis patients' records and 77 normal subjects' data). These 63 onchocerciasis records are different from those used to construct the knowledge-based hypotheses

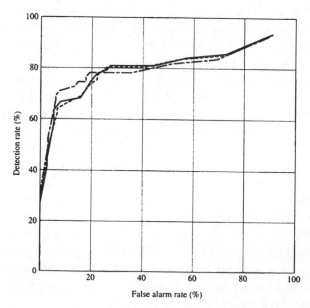

Figure 2.1   Onchocerciasis ROC results

discussed in Section 2.4.1. The solid curve represents the results of using the original onchocerciasis test records to perform diagnosis, the evenly-dashed curve is for the results of the same set of test records except that all the outliers have been deleted, and the other curve depicts the results for the same records except that only those noisy outliers have been taken out.

There seems to be not much difference between the three curves except in the box bounded by 0 and 20 per cent false-alarm rate, 60 and 80 per cent detection rate. The curves in this box happen to be the most significant as this normally reflects the practical decision compromise between the two measurements—trying to achieve as high a detection rate as possible, while at the same time trying to keep the false-alarm rate down. Judging from this point of view, the set of test data without noisy outliers outperforms the other two datasets.

Figure 2.2 is the ROC plot for a set of glaucomatous test records (157 unused glaucoma patients' records against 77 normal subjects' data). The interpretations of the three curves are the same as for onchocerciasis records. One can see clearly that the set of test data without noisy outliers consistently yields better results (higher detection rate and lower false-alarm rate) than either the original test data (nothing is taken out) or the outlier-free test data.

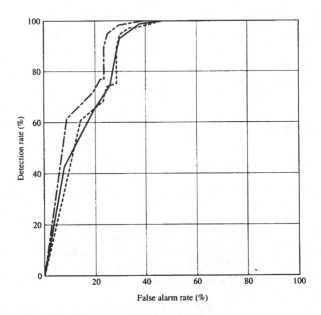

Figure 2.2   Glaucoma ROC results

2.6 Concluding remarks

Real-world data are typically characterised by outlying or unrepresentative observations. An effective way of preprocessing these data is usually needed before using them for a variety of problem-solving activities.

In this chapter we have proposed an algorithm for outlier analysis. Early experiments have demonstrated its promise in distinguishing between noise-free and noisy outliers. Following Liu *et al.* [13], this is a further attempt to model real measurements, namely how measurements should be distributed in a domain of interest. The difficulty in applying this approach is the requirement for sufficient, high-quality, relevant domain knowledge. For those applications where such knowledge regarding the distribution of real measurements is lacking, we have recently suggested another way of analysing outliers, using knowledge regarding our understanding of noisy data points instead [21].

2.7 Acknowledgments

We would like to thank Dr. John Wu and Professor Barrie Jones for being our domain experts and Michael Hickman for additional programming support. The data were provided by the Moorfields Eye Hospital and the International Centre for Eye Health, London. The work reported in this chapter is in part supported by the British Council for Prevention of Blindness. Finally, we thank two anonymous referees for their helpful comments.

2.8 References

1 HAWKINS, D.M.: 'Identification of outliers' (Chapman and Hall, London, 1980)
2 BARNET, V. and LEWIS, T.: '*Outliers in statistical data*' (John Wiley & Sons, 1994)
3 KNORR, E. and NG, R.: 'A unified notion of outliers: properties and computation'. Proceedings of 3rd international conference on *Knowledge discovery and data mining, KDD-97*, 1997, pp. 219–222
4 LIU, X., CHENG, G. and WU, J.X.: 'Identifying the measurement noise in glaucomatous testing: an artificial neural network approach', *Artif. Intell. Med.*, 1994, **6**, pp. 401–416
5 MATIC, N., GUYON, I., BOTTOU, L., DENKER, J. and VAPNIK, V.: 'Computer aided cleaning of large databases for character recognition'.

Proceedings of the 11th international conference on *Pattern recognition*, 1992, **2**, pp. 330–333

6 COLLETT, D. and LEWIS, T.: 'The subjective nature of outlier rejection procedures', *Appl. Stat.*, 1976, **25**, pp. 228–237

7 BARNET, V.: 'The ordering of multivariate data (with discussion)', *J. Roy. Statist. Soc. A*, 1976, **139**, pp. 318–354

8 KLEINER, B. and HARTIGAN, J.A.: 'Representing points in many dimensions by trees and castles (with discussion)', *J. Am. Stat. Assoc.*, 1981, **76**, pp. 260–276

9 HAWKINS, D.M.: 'The detection of errors in multivariate data using principal components', *J. Am. Stat. Assoc.*, 1974, **69**, pp. 340–344

10 GNANADESIKAN, R. and KETTENRING, J.R.: 'Robust estimates, residuals and outlier detection with multi-response data', *Biometrics*, 1972, **28**, pp. 81–124

11 GRUBBS, F.E.: 'Sample criteria for testing outlying observations', *Ann. Math. Stat.*, 1950, **21**, pp. 27–58

12 HUBER, P. J.: '*Robust statistics*' (John Wiley & Sons, 1981)

13 LIU, X., CHENG G. and WU, J.: 'Noise and uncertainty management in intelligent data modeling'. Proceedings of the 12th national conference on *Artificial intelligence, AAAI-94*, Seattle, 1994, pp. 263–268

14 WILKS, S.S.: 'Multivariate statistical outliers', *Sankhya: The Indian Journal of Statistics*, 1963, **25**, pp. 407–426

15 CARONI, C. and PRESCOTT, P.: 'Sequential application of Wilks's multivariate outlier test', *Appl. Stat.*, 1992, **41**, pp. 355–364

16 KALBFLEISCH, J.G.: 'Probability and statistical inference II' (Springer-Verlag, 1979)

17 MICHALSKI, R.S., CARBONELL, J.G. and MITCHELL, T.M.: 'Machine learning: an artificial intelligence approach' (Morgan Kaufmann, 1986)

18 QUINLAN, R.: 'C4.5: programs for machine learning' (Morgan Kaufmann, 1993)

19 SILVERMAN, B.W.: 'Density estimation for statistics and data analysis', (Chapman and Hall, 1986)

20 HENKELMAN, R.M., KAY, I. and BRONSKILL, M.J.: 'Receiver operator characteristic (ROC) analysis without ground truth', *Medical Decision Making*, 1990, **10**, pp. 24–29

21 WU, J., CHENG, G. and LIU, X.: 'Reasoning about outliers by modelling noisy data', *in* 'Advances in intelligent data analysis (IDA-97), vol. LNCS 1280' (Springer–Verlag, London, 1997) pp. 549–558

Chapter 3

Attribute-value distribution as a technique for increasing the efficiency of data mining

David McSherry

University of Ulster, Northern Ireland

3.1 Introduction

Often in data mining the objective is the discovery of classification rules, for example for assessing the creditworthiness of customers or predicting their loyalty to a product [1–3]. The target dataset is often a table (e.g. a relational database table) in which one column is the outcome of interest and the remaining columns are attributes which may affect the outcome. A typical classification rule has one or more conditions on the left-hand side (LHS), and a single outcome class on the right-hand side (RHS). A probabilistic rule states the probability of the outcome class given its conditions, and an exact rule holds for all instances in the dataset.

Often the size of the target dataset is such that the number of rules which could be discovered is very large. Various measures for ranking the discovered rules in order of potential interest have been proposed. Quantitative measures of rule interest include:

$$p(E)\,(p(H|E) - p(H))$$

where E and H are the LHS and RHS of a discovered rule [4] and the information-theoretic J measure used in ITRULE [5]. The support for a discovered rule is the proportion of instances in the dataset which satisfy both its LHS and its RHS. One algorithm for rule discovery in which the assessment of rule interest is primarily qualitative is XCAVATOR [6,7]. This chapter is also primarily concerned with qualitative aspects of rule interest, such as whether every condition of a rule increases the probability of the outcome class on its RHS.

Increasing the efficiency of rule discovery is a major focus of research interest in data mining. Strategies available to the data miner include data sampling [9], knowledge-guided discovery [3], parallelising the discovery process [10] and attribute reduction [11]. Another strategy is to target a restricted class of rules, such as exact or almost exact rules [4], rules with a limited number of conditions [5] or rules in which each condition eliminates a competing outcome class [12].

This chapter presents an approach to rule discovery in which the strategy of targeting a restricted class of rules is combined with a technique for their efficient discovery called attribute-value distribution (AVD). In AVD, attribute values are distributed among the outcome classes in the dataset in such a way that the attribute values associated with an outcome class are those which are most likely, on a heuristic basis, to appear as conditions of a discovered rule with this outcome class on the RHS. The resulting partition of attribute values in the dataset provides a natural decomposition of the discovery process into separate subtasks, one for each outcome class. An algorithm for the discovery of all exact rules with the associated outcome class on the RHS is applied within each attribute-value partition. Finally, the rules discovered in the separate partitions are pooled to provide the overall results of the discovery process.

The rules discovered by AVD are exact rules with additional properties determined by the heuristic used to distribute attribute values among the outcome classes in the dataset. One such heuristic leads to the discovery of rules in which each condition, on its own, increases the probability of the outcome class on the RHS. Another leads to the discovery of rules in which each condition is more likely in the outcome class on the RHS than in any competing outcome class. The relationship between these properties is examined in the following section, and the properties are shown to be equivalent when there are only two outcome classes in the dataset.

The contact-lens data, which provide a source of examples throughout this chapter, are based on a simplified version of the optician's real-world problem of selecting a suitable type of contact lens, if any, for an adult spectacle wearer [8]. Outcome classes in the dataset are no contact lenses, soft contact lenses and hard contact lenses. The attributes are spectacle prescription, age, astigmatism and tear-production rate. Table 3.1 shows the conditional probabilities of their values in each outcome class.

Table 3.1   Conditional probabilities of attribute values in the contact-lens data [8]

| | Contact-lens type | | |
	none	soft	hard
Spectacle prescription:			
myope	0.47	0.40	0.75
hypermetrope	0.53	0.60	0.25
Age:			
young	0.27	0.40	0.50
prepresbyopic	0.33	0.40	0.25
presbyopic	0.40	0.20	0.25
Astigmatism:			
present	0.53	0.00	1.00
absent	0.47	1.00	0.00
Tear production rate:			
normal	0.20	1.00	1.00
reduced	0.80	0.00	0.00

3.2 Targeting a restricted class of rules

The decision to target a restricted class of rules may be motivated either by the need to increase the efficiency of the discovery process or a requirement for the discovery of a certain type of rule which is of interest to the data miner [6]. For example, it is not necessarily the case that every condition of a discovered rule, on its own, increases the probability of the outcome class on its RHS. The following is one of the rules induced from the contact lens data by the machine-learning algorithm PRISM [8]:

   if astigmatism=absent
   and age=presbyopic
   and spectacle prescription=myope
   then no contact lenses

Since the prior probabilities of no contact lenses, soft contact lenses and hard contact lenses in the dataset are 0.63, 0.21 and 0.17, respectively, it follows from Table 3.1 and Bayes' theorem that:

$$p(\text{no contact lenses} \mid \text{astigmatism=absent}) =$$

$$\frac{0.63 \times 0.47}{0.63 \times 0.47 + 0.21 \times 1 + 0.17 \times 0} = 0.58$$

The first condition of the example rule therefore reduces the probability of no contact lenses. In fact, the only condition in the rule which, on its own, increases the probability of no contact lenses is (age=presbyopic). The rule does not therefore qualify as a β rule according to the following definition.

Definition 3.1: An attribute value E will be called a β feature of an outcome class H if $p(H|E) > p(H)$. An exact rule in which every condition is a β feature of the outcome class on its RHS will be called a β rule.

Depending on the application, the conditions of β rules may be interesting discoveries in their own right. However, if the majority of the rules in a data set are β rules, the reduction in discovery effort obtained by focusing on their discovery may not be significant. A greater reduction in discovery effort can be obtained by focusing on a smaller class of rules such as the α rules defined below.

Definition 3.2: An attribute value E will be called an α feature of an outcome class H if E is more likely in H than in any competing outcome class. An exact rule in which every condition is an α feature of the outcome class on its RHS will be called an α rule.

It can be seen from Table 3.1 that the conditional probabilities of (spectacle prescription=hypermetrope) in no contact lenses, soft contact lenses and hard contact lenses are 0.53, 0.60 and 0.25, respectively. Since it is more likely in soft contact lenses than in no contact lenses or hard contact lenses, (spectacle prescription=hypermetrope) is an α feature of soft contact lenses. Similarly, (astigmatism=absent) is an α feature of soft contact lenses. In practice, an attribute value which would otherwise qualify as an α feature of an outcome class H may be equally likely in one or more of the competing outcome classes. Such an attribute value will be called an α feature of H provided it is more likely in H than in one of the competing outcome classes. An attribute value may therefore be an α feature of more than one outcome class. For example, (tear production rate=normal) is an α feature of both soft contact lenses and hard contact lenses.

The relevance of α features in classification and diagnosis can be seen from the following theorem, adapted from a result in diagnostic reasoning which states that a symptom will increase the probability of a disease if it is more likely in that disease than in any other disease [13].

Theorem 3.1: If E is an α feature of an outcome class H_1, then E is also a β feature of H_1.

Proof: If E is an α feature of H_1, then $p(E|H_1) > p(E|H_i)$ for $2 \leq i \leq r$, where $H_2, \ldots, H_r$ are the other outcome classes in the dataset. It follows from Bayes' theorem that:

$$p(H_1|E) = \frac{p(H_1)\ p(E|H_1)}{\Sigma_{i=1}^{r}\ p(H_i)\ p(E|H_i)} > \frac{p(H_1)\ p(E|H_1)}{\Sigma_{i=1}^{r}\ p(H_i)\ p(E|H_1)} = p(H_1)$$

and so E is a β feature of H.

In general, however, a β feature of an outcome class H need not be an α feature of H. For example, (astigmatism=present) can be shown to increase the probability of no contact lenses and is therefore a β feature of no contact lenses. However, it is not an α feature of no contact lenses as it is more likely in hard contact lenses than in no contact lenses. Being more likely in a particular outcome class than in any competing outcome class is therefore a sufficient but not a necessary condition for an attribute value to increase the probability of the outcome class. However, as the following theorem shows, it is a necessary condition if there are only two distinct outcomes in the dataset. It follows that α rules and β rules are equivalent in such a dataset.

Theorem 3.2: In a dataset with only two outcome classes, an attribute value E is an α feature of an outcome class H_1 if and only if it is a β feature of H_1.

Proof: Since any α feature of H_1 is also a β feature of H_1 by theorem 3.1, it suffices to show that any β feature of H_1 is also an α feature of H_1. If E is an attribute value which is not an α feature of H_1, then $p(E|H_2) \geq p(E|H_1)$, where H_2 is the other outcome class in the dataset. By an argument similar to that used in theorem 3.1, it follows that $p(H_2|E) \geq p(H_2)$. Thus:

$$p(H_1|E) = 1 - p(H_2|E) \leq 1 - p(H_2) = p(H_1)$$

and so E is not a β feature of H_1. It follows as required that any β feature of H_1 must also be an α feature of H_1.

3.3 Discovery effort and yield

The complexity of rule discovery arises from the fact that the number of possible rules in a given dataset, all of which must be examined in exhaustive rule discovery, may be very large. It can be seen from the following theorem that the number of possible rules in a given dataset is approximately:

$$r((k+1)^m - 1)$$

where r is the number of outcome classes, m is the number of attributes and k is the average number of values of each attribute.

Theorem 3.3: In a given dataset, the number of possible rules of the form *if E then H*, where E is an attribute-value pair, or conjunction of attribute-value pairs, is:

$$r((k_1 + 1)(k_2 + 1) \ldots (k_m + 1) - 1)$$

where r is the number of outcome classes in the dataset, m is the number of attributes and $k_1, k_2, \ldots, k_m$ are the numbers of values of the attributes.

Proof: Let $a_1, a_2, \ldots, a_m$ be the attributes in the dataset. For $1 \leq j \leq m$, there are k_j possible ways in which a_j can appear on the LHS of a rule. Another possibility is that it does not appear in the rule. The number of possible rule left-hand sides is therefore:

$$(k_1 + 1)(k_2 + 1) \ldots (k_m + 1)$$

One of the possibilities, however, is not valid as the LHS of a rule, since there cannot be a rule with no conditions. The number of possible, and valid, rule left-hand sides is therefore:

$$(k_1 + 1)(k_2 + 1) \ldots (k_m + 1) - 1$$

Since the number of possible rule right-hand sides is r, it follows as required that the number of possible rules is:

$$r((k_1 + 1)(k_2 + 1) \ldots (k_m + 1) - 1)$$

Although the worst-case complexity of rule discovery is exponential in the number of attributes, the average complexity of a given algorithm will depend on its implementation. For example, the worst-case scenario rarely occurs in ITRULE, which uses bounds on the attainable information to determine whether further specialisation of a candidate rule is worthwhile [5].

The complexity of an algorithm, although very useful as a measure of its computational efficiency, gives no other indication of its effectiveness in the task for which it is designed. Criteria of particular relevance in the evaluation of an algorithm which targets a restricted class of rules are the proportion of rules in the dataset discovered by the algorithm, and the amount by which the computational effort is reduced in comparison with exhaustive rule discovery.

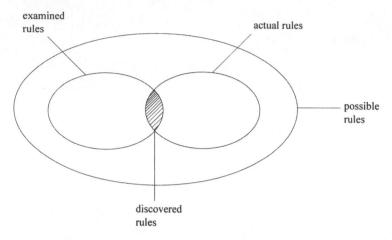

Figure 3.1   Targeting a restricted class of rules involves a trade off between discovery effort and discovery yield

The number of actual rules in a dataset is usually much smaller than the number of possible rules. An actual rule is one with an LHS which is satisfied by at least one instance in the dataset and, in the case of an exact rule, with an RHS which is satisfied by all instances which satisfy its LHS. As Figure 3.1 illustrates, targeting a restricted class of rules involves a trade off between discovery effort, as measured by the proportion of possible rules examined, and discovery yield, as measured by the proportion of actual rules discovered. The discovery effort is reduced because only a subset of possible rules in the dataset is examined. Inevitably, the discovery yield is also reduced. In discovery algorithms which target a restricted class of rules, the aim of algorithm design is therefore to maximise discovery yield while minimising discovery effort. Empirical criteria for the evaluation of discovery algorithms which target a restricted class of rules are formally defined below.

Definition 3.3: When an algorithm for the discovery of a restricted class of rules is applied to a dataset, the discovery effort and yield are:

$$\text{effort} = \frac{\text{no. of rules examined}}{\text{no. of possible rules}}$$

$$\text{yield} = \frac{\text{no. of rules discovered}}{\text{no. of actual rules}}$$

Measured as a proportion of the computational effort required for exhaustive rule discovery, the discovery effort is independent of the size of the dataset. In exhaustive rule discovery, the discovery effort, expressed as a percentage, is 100 per cent. The discovery yield is also 100 per cent.

3.4 Attribute-value distribution

In rule discovery by AVD, attribute values are distributed among the outcome classes in the dataset in such a way that the values allocated to each outcome class are those which are most likely, on a heuristic basis, to appear as conditions of discovered rules with this outcome class on the RHS. The resulting partition of attribute values in the dataset provides a natural decomposition of the discovery process into subtasks, one for each outcome class. An algorithm for the discovery of all exact rules with the associated outcome class on the RHS is applied within each attribute-value partition. Finally, the rules discovered in the separate attribute-value partitions are pooled to provide the overall results of the discovery process.

The properties of the rules discovered by AVD are determined by the heuristic used to distribute attribute values among outcome classes in the dataset. One possible heuristic is to allocate each attribute value E to the outcome class H for which $p(E|H)$ is maximum. In the attribute-value partitions produced by this heuristic, the attribute values associated with an outcome class are the α features of the outcome class. This heuristic therefore leads to the discovery of all α rules in the dataset and will be called the α heuristic.

Another possible heuristic is to allocate each attribute value E to each outcome class H such that $p(H|E) > p(H)$. Since it is not unusual for an attribute value to increase the probability of more than one outcome class, there is likely to be considerable overlap between the attribute-value partitions produced by this heuristic. In this case, the attribute values associated with an outcome class are the β features of the outcome class. The second heuristic therefore leads to the discovery of all β rules in the dataset and will be called the β heuristic.

The following theorem provides an approximate method for predicting the effort required for rule discovery by AVD based on the α heuristic.

Theorem 3.4: In rule discovery by AVD based on the α heuristic, the expected discovery effort is approximately:

$$\lambda(r,m,k) = \frac{r\left(\left(\dfrac{k}{r}+1\right)^m - 1\right)}{(k+1)^m - 1}$$

where r is the number of outcome classes in the dataset, m is the number of attributes and k is the average number of values of each attribute.

Proof: Let $a_1, a_2, \ldots, a_m$ be the attributes in the dataset and let $k_1, k_2, \ldots, k_m$, respectively, be the numbers of values of these attributes. Let $P_1, P_2, \ldots, P_r$ be the attribute-value partitions of the dataset produced by AVD. For $1 \leq j \leq m$ and $1 \leq i \leq r$, the number of values of a_j which can be expected to be allocated by the α heuristic to partition P_i is k_j/r. The average of the expected numbers of values of the m attributes in P_i, for $1 \leq i \leq r$, is therefore:

$$\frac{1}{mr}\sum_{j=1}^{m} k_j = \frac{k}{r}$$

Although only rules with H on the RHS are targeted in the partition corresponding to an outcome class H, the rules in a given partition may include rules for any outcome class. By theorem 3.3, the number of possible rules in each partition will therefore be approximately:

$$r\left(\left(\frac{k}{r}+1\right)^m - 1\right)$$

In rule discovery by AVD based on the α heuristic, the total number of rules examined will therefore be approximately:

$$r^2\left(\left(\frac{k}{r}+1\right)^m - 1\right)$$

By theorem 3.3, the number of possible rules in the complete dataset is approximately:

$$r((k+1)^m - 1)$$

It follows as required that the expected discovery effort is approximately:

$$\frac{r\left(\left(\dfrac{k}{r}+1\right)^{m}-1\right)}{(k+1)^{m}-1}$$

The discovery effort predicted by the theorem is an approximation because attribute values in the dataset are assumed to be evenly distributed among the outcome classes, and each attribute value to be distributed by the α heuristic to the partition for a single outcome class. In practice, the attribute values may be unevenly distributed and it is possible that an attribute value may be an α feature of two or more outcome classes. Such an attribute value must be allocated to the partitions for all the outcome classes for which it is an α feature, thereby increasing the number of rules to be examined in rule discovery by AVD.

For example, in a dataset with ten binary attributes and two outcome classes, the expected discovery effort is approximately:

$$\lambda(2,\,10,\,2) = \frac{2(2^{10}-1)}{3^{10}-1} = 0.03$$

or three per cent.

The effort required in rule discovery by AVD based on the β heuristic is more difficult to predict. However, because of the greater tendency of the β heuristic to allocate the same attribute value to more than one outcome class, the discovery effort is likely to be greater than that required in AVD based on the α heuristic.

3.5 Experimental results

In this section, the results of rule discovery in the contact-lens data by AVD based on the α and β heuristics are compared. The results of rule discovery by AVD in a real-world dataset with two outcome classes are also presented.

3.5.1 The contact-lens data

Attribute-value partitions of the contact-lens data produced by AVD based on the α heuristic are shown in Table 3.2. From Table 3.1, for example, the outcome class in which the conditional probability of (spectacle prescription = hypermetrope) is maximum is soft contact lenses. This attribute value is therefore allocated by the α heuristic to the attribute-value partition for soft contact lenses. Of the three values

Table 3.2   Attribute-value partitions of the contact-lens data based on the α heuristic

Target outcome class	Attributes	Associated value(s)	No. of possible rules
No contact lenses	tear production rate	reduced	9
	age	presbyopic	
Soft contact lenses	tear production rate	normal	45
	age	prepresbyopic	
	astigmatism	absent	
	spectacle prescription	hypermetrope	
Hard contact lenses	tear production rate	normal	45
	age	young	
	astigmatism	present	
	spectacle prescription	myope	

of age, (age=young) is most likely in hard contact lenses, (age=prepresbyopic) in soft contact lenses and (age = presbyopic) in no contact lenses.

The attribute values in the partition for no contact lenses are (tear production rate=reduced) and (age=presbyopic). Since (tear production=normal) is equally likely in soft contact lenses and hard contact lenses, it is allocated to the attribute-value partitions for both outcome classes. Table 3.2 also shows the number of possible rules in each attribute-value partition. For example, each of the four attributes in the partition for hard contact lenses has just one value. By theorem 3.3, the number of possible rules in this partition is therefore:

$$3 \times (2^4 - 1) = 45$$

Similarly, the numbers of possible rules in the partitions for soft contact lenses and no contact lenses are 45 and 9. The total number of rules to be examined in rule discovery by AVD based on the α heuristic is therefore 99. In the original dataset, one attribute has three values and the other three attributes are binary attributes. By theorem 3.3, the number of possible rules in the original dataset is therefore:

$$3 \times (4 \times 3 \times 3 \times 3 - 1) = 321$$

The effort required for rule discovery by AVD based on the α heuristic is therefore:

$$\text{effort} = \frac{\text{no. of rules examined}}{\text{no. of possible rules}} = \frac{99}{321}$$

or 31 per cent. Among the four attributes in the contact-lens data, the average number of values per attribute is 2.25. According to theorem 3.4, the expected discovery effort is therefore:

$$\lambda(r, m, k) = \frac{r\left(\left(\frac{k}{r}+1\right)^m - 1\right)}{(k+1)^m - 1} = \frac{3\left(\left(\frac{2.25}{3}+1\right)^4 - 1\right)}{(2.25+1)^4 - 1} = 0.23$$

or 23 per cent. Theorem 3.4 therefore provides a reasonable approximation of the actual discovery effort of 31 per cent in this experiment, despite the unbalanced distribution of attribute values among the outcome classes and allocation of (tear production rate=normal) to two of the four partitions.

The following five rules, consisting of all α rules in the dataset, were discovered in the contact-lens data by AVD based on the α heuristic. The figure in brackets after each rule is the proportion of instances in the dataset which support the rule:

Rule 1 if (tear production rate=reduced) then no contact lenses (0.50)

Rule 2 if (astigmatism=absent) and (tear production rate=normal) and (spectacle prescription=hypermetrope) then soft contact lenses (0.13)

Rule 3 if (astigmatism=present) and (tear production rate=normal) and (spectacle prescription=myope) then hard contact lenses (0.13)

Rule 4 if (astigmatism=absent) and (tear production rate=normal) and (age=prepresbyopic) then soft contact lenses (0.08)

Rule 5 if (astigmatism=present) and (tear production rate=normal) and (age=young) then hard contact lenses (0.08)

The complete set of rules in the contact-lens data, as first induced by the machine-learning algorithm PRISM, consists of nine rules [8]. In this experiment, the yield for rule discovery by AVD based on the α heuristic is therefore:

$$\text{yield} = \frac{\text{no. of rules discovered}}{\text{no. of actual rules}} = \frac{5}{9}$$

or 56 per cent.

The four rules in the contact-lens data which AVD based on the α heuristic failed to discover are shown below. Each of the undiscovered rules has at least one condition which does not appear in the attribute-value partition for the outcome class on its RHS. In fact, none of the conditions of Rule 8 is an α feature of no contact lenses:

Rule 6 if (astigmatism=absent) and (age=presbyopic) and (spectacle prescription=myope) then no contact lenses (0.08)

Rule 7 if (astigmatism=present) and (age=presbyopic) and (spectacle prescription=hypermetrope) then no contact lenses (0.08)

Rule 8 if (astigmatism=present) and (age=prepresbyopic) and (spectacle prescription=hypermetrope) then no contact lenses (0.08)

Rule 9 if (astigmatism=absent) and (tear production rate=normal) and (age=young) then soft contact lenses (0.08)

Rule 9 is not an α rule since (age=young) is more likely in hard contact lenses than in soft contact lenses and therefore not an α feature of soft contact lenses. However, (age=young) can be shown to increase the probability of soft contact lenses and is therefore a β feature of soft contact lenses. Since its other two conditions are α features of soft contact lenses, and therefore β features by theorem 3.1, Rule 9 is a β rule. Similarly, Rule 7 is a β rule. Both rules must therefore be discovered by AVD based on the β heuristic.

As noted in Section 3.2, neither (astigmatism=absent) nor (spectacle prescription=myope) increases the probability of no contact lenses, so Rule 6 is not a β rule. Attribute-value partitions of the contact lens data produced by AVD based on the β heuristic are shown in Table 3.3. Since the partition for no contact lenses does not include (age=prepresbyopic), Rule 8 is not a β rule. By theorem 3.1, the rules discovered by AVD based on the β heuristic include all α rules in the dataset. The rules discovered by AVD based on the β heuristic are therefore Rule 1, Rule 2, Rule 3, Rule 4, Rule 5, Rule 7 and Rule 9. The discovery yield for AVD based on the β heuristic is therefore:

$$\text{yield} = \frac{\text{no. of rules discovered}}{\text{no. of actual rules}} = \frac{7}{9}$$

or 78 per cent.

In the partition for soft contact lenses produced by the β heuristic there are three attributes with one value and one attribute with two values. By theorem 3.3, the number of possible rules in this partition is therefore:

$$3 \times (2 \times 2 \times 2 \times 3 - 1) = 69$$

The attribute-value partition for hard contact lenses produced by the β heuristic is the same as that produced by the α heuristic, so the

Table 3.3 Attribute-value partitions of the contact-lens data based on the β heuristic

Target outcome class	Attributes	Associated value(s)	No. of possible rules
No contact lenses	tear production rate age astigmatism spectacle prescription	reduced presbyopic present hypermetrope	45
Soft contact lenses	tear production rate age astigmatism spectacle prescription	normal young prepresbyopic absent hypermetrope	69
Hard contact lenses	tear production rate age astigmatism spectacle prescription	normal young present myope	45

number of possible rules in this partition is again 45. The number of possible rules in the new partition for no contact lenses, which has two additional attribute values, is also 45. The total number of rules to be examined in AVD based on the β heuristic is therefore 159. The discovery effort required in this case is therefore:

$$\text{effort} = \frac{\text{no. of rules examined}}{\text{no. of possible rules}} = \frac{159}{321}$$

or 50 per cent.

None of the rules which AVD based on the α heuristic fails to discover is more strongly supported than one that is discovered. The average support for the discovered α rules is 18 per cent compared with 14 per cent for the complete set of rules. The average support for the β rules discovered by AVD based on the β heuristic is 15 per cent. The experimental results for the contact-lens data, summarised in Table 3.4, show that for a fraction of the computational effort required for exhaustive rule discovery, AVD based on the α heuristic provides a reasonable yield both in terms of the percentage of actual rules discovered and average strength of support for the discovered rules. Although the yield for AVD based on the β heuristic is higher, the discovery effort required is greater and the discovered rules are less strongly supported on average.

Table 3.4   Comparison of exhaustive rule discovery and rule discovery by AVD based on the α and β heuristics in the contact-lens data

	Discovery yield (%)	Discovery effort (%)	Average rule support (%)
Exhaustive rule discovery	100	100	14
AVD based on α heuristic	56	31	18
AVD based on β heuristic	78	50	15

3.5.2 The project-outcome dataset

The project-outcome dataset was collected as part of an investigation of factors which influence the outcome of final-year projects in computer science [14]. To avoid fragmentation of the data, which would weaken the support for discovered rules, continuous attributes in the dataset were transformed to binary attributes based on the ranges of values considered most appropriate and meaningful. For example, the ranges used to transform the student's average mark in the second year were 0–59 and 60+, corresponding to honours-degree classifications of up to and including 2.2 and 2.1 or better. Similarly, the outcomes to be predicted correspond to project marks in the ranges 0–59 and 60+.

Since the size of the project-outcome dataset is such that exhaustive rule discovery does not present a problem, the discovery effort required and yield provided by AVD in comparison with exhaustive rule discovery can be precisely determined by experiment. The attributes in the dataset are the project application area (with eight values), the programming language used (with six values), the method by which the project was allocated to the student (with three values) and five binary attributes. By theorem 3.3, the number of possible rules in the dataset is therefore:

$$2 \times (9 \times 7 \times 4 \times 3 \times 3 \times 3 \times 3 \times 3 - 1) = 122\ 470$$

By theorem 3.2, the α and β heuristics are equivalent for the project-outcome dataset as there are only two outcome classes in the dataset. The α heuristic, which allocates each attribute value to the outcome class in which its conditional probability is greatest, remains the easier to apply of the two heuristics. Following AVD based on the α heuristic, the numbers of possible rules in the partitions for the outcome classes 0–59 and 60+ are 2046 and 4606, respectively. The effort required for rule discovery by AVD is therefore:

Table 3.5   *Comparison of exhaustive rule discovery and rule discovery by AVD based on the α heuristic in the project-outcome dataset*

	Discovery yield (%)	Discovery effort (%)	Average rule support (%)
Exhaustive rule discovery	100	100	3
AVD based on α heuristic	33	5	4

$$\text{effort} = \frac{\text{no. of rules examined}}{\text{no. of possible rules}} = \frac{6652}{122\,470} = 0.05$$

or five per cent.

As shown by exhaustive rule discovery, the number of actual rules in the project-outcome dataset is 126 [14]. In rule discovery by AVD based on the α heuristic, 42 rules were discovered. In this experiment, the discovery yield for AVD is therefore:

$$\text{yield} = \frac{\text{no. of rules discovered}}{\text{no. of actual rules}} = \frac{42}{126} = 0.33$$

or 33 per cent.

The 42 rules discovered by AVD included the four most strongly supported rules in the dataset. The results of the experiment are summarised in Table 3.5. AVD based on the α heuristic (equivalent to the β heuristic for this dataset) provided a discovery yield of 33 per cent for a discovery effort of only five per cent. The average support for the discovered rules was four per cent compared with three per cent for exhaustive rule discovery.

Among the eight attributes in the project-outcome dataset, the average number of values per attribute is 3.375. According to theorem 3.4, the expected effort in rule discovery by AVD based on the α heuristic is therefore:

$$\lambda(2, 8, 3.375) = \frac{r\left(\left(\frac{k}{r}+1\right)^m - 1\right)}{(k+1)^m - 1} = \frac{2\left(\left(\frac{3.375}{2}+1\right)^8 - 1\right)}{(3.375+1)^8 - 1} = 0.04$$

or four per cent. Theorem 3.4 therefore provides a good approximation of the actual discovery effort of five per cent in this experiment.

3.6 Discussion and conclusions

An approach to rule discovery has been presented in which the strategy of targeting a restricted class of rules is combined with a technique for their efficient discovery. Attribute values in the dataset are distributed among the outcome classes in the dataset in such a way that the attribute values associated with an outcome class are more likely, on a heuristic basis, to appear as conditions of a discovered rule with this outcome class on the RHS. The discovered rules are exact rules with additional properties depending on the heuristic used to distribute attribute values among outcome classes in the dataset.

One such heuristic, called the β heuristic, leads to the discovery of rules in which each condition, on its own, increases the probability of the outcome class on the RHS. Another heuristic, called the α heuristic, leads to the discovery of rules in which each condition is more likely in the outcome class on the RHS than in any competing class. The two heuristics, and resulting sets of discovered rules, have been shown to be equivalent when there are only two outcome classes in the dataset. A method for estimating the effort required in rule discovery by AVD based on the α heuristic has been presented.

Ideally, a heuristic for AVD should be a good predictor of attribute values which are likely to appear as the conditions of discovered rules, and produce attribute-value partitions with a minimum of overlap. The first property is necessary to ensure an acceptable discovery yield and the second to ensure a worthwhile reduction in discovery effort. Both heuristics examined in this chapter appear to be good predictors of attribute values which are likely to appear as conditions of discovered rules. However, the α heuristic has a greater tendency to allocate each attribute value to a single outcome class, thereby providing a greater reduction in discovery effort.

Experimental results indicate that the reduction in discovery yield is well compensated for by the reduction in discovery effort provided by AVD. The discovered rules also appear to be more strongly supported on average than those which are not discovered. Further efficiency gains are possible by parallelising the discovery process, since AVD produces a natural decomposition of the discovery task into subtasks which can be independently executed on parallel processors. Issues to be addressed by further research include an investigation of the yield produced by AVD, and reliability of the formula for the estimation of discovery effort, in datasets with large numbers of attributes.

3.7 References

1 SHORTLAND, R.J. and SCARFE, R.T.: 'Data mining applications in BT', *BT Technol. J.*, 1994, **12**, pp. 17–22

2 SIMOUDIS, E. *et al.*: 'Developing customer vulnerability models using data mining techniques'. Proceedings of *Intelligent data analysis 95*, Baden-Baden, Germany, August 1995, pp. 181–185

3 NELSON, C.: 'Improving customer retention with knowledge guided data mining', *BCS Specialist Group on Expert Systems Newsletter*, 1995, (33), pp. 15–20

4 PIATETSKY-SHAPIRO, G.: 'Discovery, analysis and presentation of strong rules', *in* PIATETSKY-SHAPIRO, G., and FRAWLEY, W.J. (eds.): 'Knowledge discovery in databases (AAAI Press, Menlo Park, CA, 1991) pp. 229–248

5 SMYTH, P. and GOODMAN, R.M.: 'Rule induction using information theory', *in* PIATETSKY-SHAPIRO, G., and FRAWLEY, W.J. (eds.): 'Knowledge discovery in databases' (AAAI Press, Menlo Park, CA, 1991) pp. 159–176

6 McSHERRY, D.: 'Qualitative assessment of rule interest in data mining', Proceedings of *Expert systems 96*, Cambridge, England, December 1996, pp. 204–215

7 McSHERRY, D.: 'Hypothetico-deductive data mining', *Applied Stochastic Models and Data Analysis*, 1998, **13**, pp. 415–422

8 CENDROWSKA, J.: 'PRISM: an algorithm for inducing modular rules', *Int. J. Man-Mach. Stud.*, 1987, **27**, pp. 349–370

9 FRAWLEY, W.J., PIATETSKY-SHAPIRO, G. and MATHEUS, C.J.: 'Knowledge discovery in databases: an overview', *in* PIATETSKY-SHAPIRO, G. and FRAWLEY, W.J. (eds.): 'Knowledge discovery in databases' (AAAI Press, Menlo Park, CA, 1991) pp. 1–27

10 THOMPSON, S. and BRAMER, M.A.: 'Parallel knowledge discovery: a review of existing techniques'. Colloquium on *Knowledge discovery and data mining*, Digest 96/198 (Institution of Electrical Engineers, London, 1996) pp. 5/1–5

11 ZIARKO, W.: 'Discovery, analysis, and representation of data dependencies in databases', *in* PIATETSKY-SHAPIRO, G. and FRAWLEY, W.J. (eds.): 'Knowledge discovery in databases' (AAAI Press, Menlo Park, CA, 1991) pp. 195–209

12 McSHERRY, D.: 'Knowledge discovery by inspection', special issue on knowledge discovery and its applications to business decision making, *Decis. Support Syst.*, 1997, **21**, pp. 43–47.

13 McSHERRY, D.: 'Intelligent dialogue based on statistical models of clinical decision making', *Statistics in Medicine*, 1986, **12**, pp. 497–502

14 McSHERRY, D. and STRINGER, K.: 'A data mining approach to the analysis of student project outcomes'. Proceedings of the fifth annual conference on the *Teaching of computing*, Dublin, August 1997, pp. 154–156

Chapter 4
Using background knowledge with attribute-oriented data mining

Mary Shapcott, Sally McClean and Bryan Scotney
University of Ulster, Northern Ireland

4.1 Introduction

Real-world databases typically contain large amounts of incomplete and noisy data: there may be only partial information about the values of fields in records, the fields can be missing completely from some records and data may come from different sources with different units of measurement and different coding conventions [1–3]. This is particularly likely to be true when the data were originally collected for different purposes, as is often the case in data warehousing. The provision of tools to handle such imperfections in data has been identified as a challenging area for knowledge discovery in databases [4]. Previous work has provided some methods of handling such data using machine learning or statistical methods to predict likely values to replace the missing or noisy values [5].

The information kept explicitly in database tables is, of course, not the only information that the users have about the data which is stored. A domain expert often has background knowledge about the database. This background knowledge acts to constrain the space of patterns which the data-mining process can explore. Two effects result from constraints due to background knowledge. First, the pattern space is smaller, and this limits the number of patterns which need to be compared for their interestingness. Secondly, the measure of interestingness changes. A pattern which results merely from the requirement to satisfy the constraints is not of interest in the constrained database, whereas it might have been of interest in the unconstrained database.

In previous work [6] the authors have defined a type of generalised data model which allows many types of imprecise and noisy data to be described. Frequently, data are imprecise, i.e. we are not certain about the specific value of an attribute but only that it takes a value which is a member of a set of possible values. Such data have previously been discussed as a basis of attribute-oriented induction for data mining [7]. This approach has been shown to provide a powerful methodology for the extraction of different kinds of patterns from relational databases. This data model in which we allow attributes to be set valued, to have partial values, also allows us to describe data from a concept hierarchy very succinctly.

In this chapter we outline how functionality can be provided for a generalised data model of imprecision in the presence of real-world background information. The real-world background information has an impact in two main areas.

First, we can use rules which might represent integrity constraints, concept hierarchies or other knowledge specified by the domain expert, to reengineer the database by assigning missing or unaccept-able outlying data to subsets of the attribute domain. For example, we may know that Tracy Brown belongs to the technical staff, and that all technical staff are either programmers or systems analysts. We can reassign Tracy's job title to be the subset {programmer, systems analyst}. Similarly, we may know that the value of the attribute job_title is null for the tuple relating to employee John Smith, but know from the attribute salary that John Smith earns £23 000. Then, domain knowledge in the form of integrity constraints might tell us that only a programmer's salary scale is between £20 000 and £25 000. A logic programming algorithm can derive the result that John Smith is a programmer, and we then impute this value to the attribute job_title of tuple John Smith in the reengineered database. In such a manner we may use the background knowledge to replace many of the null or outlying data in the original database.

Secondly, having reengineered the database, we can use the rules again, for attribute-valued data mining. Using the example already quoted, we should hardly be surprised to discover a pattern which indicates that all employees with salaries of £24 000 happen to be programmers. In other words, we wish to take existing background knowledge into account when assessing the interestingness of patterns. In this chapter we show how background knowledge can be incorpo-rated into the data-mining process so that only truly interesting patterns are discovered.

4.2 Partial value model

Parsons [8] has provided a recent survey of various approaches to handling imperfect information in data and knowledge bases. In this chapter we use a generalised data model to describe imprecise data. The data model includes the standard relational data model as a submodel.

First, we generalise the relational model to cater for imprecision in data as follows.

4.2.1 Definition: partial value

Consider tuple t, in relation R, and the value of attribute A, which is defined on a finite domain, D, which consists of the k values $\{v_1, \ldots v_k\}$. Assume that the true value of A is known to be one of a subset, $S = \{v_r, \ldots v_s\}$ of h elements of D. The subset S is called a partial value of attribute A in tuple t.

Partial values cater for imprecision in data. The generalised data model allows attributes with finite domains to have partial values. An attribute which can have partial values is called an imprecise attribute. Attributes which cannot have partial values are called precise attributes.

4.2.2 Definition: partial-value relation

A partial-value relation is a generalised form of database relation in which the attribute values of a tuple can be partial values.

4.2.3 Example

Consider the (artificial) example relation, employee, in Table 4.1. The attribute job_title has the domain $D=\{$senior manager, junior manager, senior programmer, junior programmer, trainee$\}$. Fred is known to be some kind of manager. In the tuple describing the employee, Fred, the attribute job_title has the partial value {junior manager, senior manager}. In other tuples, such as Joey, Sheila, Margaret and Sean, the value of job_title is precise.

The partial value concept takes care of null values quite nicely. If the null value denotes an unknown value of the attribute then the domain set, D, can be substituted for the null. Hence, for tuples Nuala, Niall and David in Table 4.1, the value null should be understood to mean

Table 4.1   A partial-value relation: employee (m – male, f – female; salary in pounds)

Name	Sex	Job_title	Salary
Fred	m	{junior manager; senior manager}	{20 000}
Michael	m	{junior programmer; trainee}	{28 000}
Joey	m	{manager}	{35 000}
Sheila	f	{trainee}	{15 000}
Nuala	f	null	{25 000}
Margaret	f	{manager}	{42 000}
Niall	m	null	{14 500}
Sean	m	{programmer}	{NULL}
David	m	null	{28 000}
Roisin	f	{trainee; programmer}	{16 000}

the domain set, $D=$\{senior manager, junior manager, senior programmer, junior programmer, trainee\}.

4.2.4 Aggregation

Previous work on databases containing partial-value relations has concentrated on defining the analogues of standard relational operators such as select, project and join [9]. These operators return relations as their results. However, in applications such as data mining it is often necessary to define aggregate operators, such as sum, count and average — operators which return numerical measures, describing the properties of the data as a whole. In work already mentioned [6] the authors have defined aggregate operators for imprecise databases, and here we give a summary of the general results. We start by defining two aggregate operators for precise databases: the simple count operator and the simple aggregate operator.

4.2.5 Definition: simple count operator

Let R be a relation and A be a precise attribute of R with finite domain, D. Assume that the cardinality of D is k. The simple count operator, count($R.A$), returns a vector of k integers, one integer for each element v_i of domain D. In other words:

$$\text{count}(R.A) = (n_1, \ldots, n_i, \ldots n_k)$$

and

$$n_i = \sum_{r=1}^{m} I(t_r.A = v_i)$$

where I is an indicator function, returning 1 if the tuple r has value v_i for attribute A, 0 otherwise. $t_r.A$ denotes the value of attribute A in tuple r. There are m tuples in relation R.

Note that the simple count operator corresponds to the count operator in SQL.

4.2.6 Example

In Table 4.1, relation employee has precise attribute, sex, with domain:

$$D = \{v_1, v_2\} = \{\text{male, female}\}$$

The application of the simple count operator to sex in employee yields:

$$\text{count}(\text{employee}.\text{sex}) = (6, 4)$$

4.2.7 Definition: simple aggregate operator

The simple aggregate operator is very similar to the simple count operator, but returns proportions, rather than counts. Let R, A and D be as before. The simple aggregate operator, $\text{sagg}(R.A)$, returns a vector of k real numbers, one real for each value of domain D:

$$\text{sagg}(R.A) = (\pi_1, \pi_2, \ldots, \pi_i, \ldots \pi_k)$$

where:

$$\pi_i = \frac{n_i}{\sum_{p=1}^{k} n_p}$$

4.2.8 Example

From Table 4.1 we obtain:

$$\text{sagg}(\text{employee}.\text{sex}) = (0.6, 0.4)$$

Intuitively, $\text{sagg}(R.A)$ returns the proportions of each of the values of attribute A that occur in R. Interestingly, it appears that there is no direct analogy for sagg in SQL.

4.2.9 Aggregation of partial values

We now define a generalised operator which returns the proportions of values of an imprecise attribute. This operator, which we call a partial-value aggregate operator, pvagg, cannot be defined in a direct formula, but is obtained as the result of an iterative scheme. Using pvagg its companion operator, pvcount, is easily derived.

4.2.10 Definition: partial value aggregate operator

Let R be a partial-value relation. Assume that attribute A has partial values. Assume that the domain, D, of A is $\{v_1, v_2, \ldots, v_k\}$. Denote the value of A in the rth tuple by the set S_r. Furthermore, define the table q_{ir} by the following rule:

$$q_{ir} = 1 \text{ if } v_i \text{ belongs to } S_r$$

$$q_{ir} = 0 \text{ if } v_i \text{ does not belong to } S_r$$

In other words, q_{ir} is a mask function, masking out all the attribute values that do not belong to S_r.

The partial-value aggregate operator, pvagg, operates on attribute A to yield a vector-valued function:

$$\text{pvagg}(R.A) = (\pi_1, \pi_2, \ldots, \pi_k)$$

where the values π_i are computed from an iterative scheme.

If the estimated value of π_i after the $(t-1)$th iteration is denoted by $\pi_i^{(t-1)}$, then the value of π_i after t iterations is:

$$\pi_i^{(t)} = \frac{\pi_i^{(t-1)}}{m} \sum_{r=1}^{m} \frac{q_{ir}}{\sum_{u=1}^{k} \pi_u^{(t-1)} q_{ur}}$$

4.2.11 Example

Consider Table 4.2 (possibly a derived view in the database), of partial-value relation eview with the attribute job_title.

The subsets, and the corresponding indicator values are:

$S_1 = \{$junior programmer$\}$, $q_{11} = 0$, $q_{21} = 1$, $q_{31} = 0$

$S_2 = \{$junior programmer, junior manager$\}$, $q_{12} = 0$, $q_{22} = 1$, $q_{32} = 1$

$S_3 = \{$junior manager$\}$, $q_{13} = 0$, $q_{23} = 0$, $q_{33} = 1$

And the iterative scheme for pvagg(eview.job_title) $= (\pi_1, \pi_2, \pi_3)$ is:

Table 4.2   Eview — a partial-value relation

Name	Sex	Job_title	Salary
Zaphod	m	{junior programmer}	{20 000}
Lenin	m	{junior programmer; junior manager}	{28 000}
Susie	f	{junior manager}	{35 000}

Assume that here the attribute domain of job_title is {trainee, junior programmer, junior manager}.

$$\pi_1^{(t)} = \frac{\pi_1^{(t-1)}(0)}{3}$$

$$\pi_2^{(t)} = \frac{\pi_2^{(t-1)}}{3} \left(\frac{1}{\pi_2^{(t-1)}} + \frac{1}{(\pi_2^{(t-1)} + \pi_3^{(t-1)})} \right)$$

$$\pi_3^{(t)} = \frac{\pi_3^{(t-1)}}{3} \left(\frac{1}{(\pi_2^{(t-1)} + \pi_3^{(t-1)})} + \frac{1}{\pi_3^{(t-1)}} \right)$$

By iteration we obtain $\pi_1 = 0$, $\pi_2 = 0.5$ and $\pi_3 = 0.5$. This is what we would have expected intuitively from the symmetrical nature of the data, but it is always comforting to have intuition confirmed by calculation.

Note that intuition is also rewarded in the case of sagg. It can be shown that sagg is a special case of pvagg, applying to the situation where all tuple values are precise [6].

4.2.12 Definition: partial-value count operator

Letting all terms be as already described, the partial-value count operator pvcount, is derived from the partial-value aggregate operator by multiplying pvagg by m, the number of tuples in the table:

$$\text{pvcount}(R.A) = (n_1, \ldots, n_i, \ldots n_k)$$

where

$$n_i = m\,\pi_i$$

4.2.13 Theoretical framework

The equations that define the aggregation minimise the Kullback–Leibler information divergence between the aggregated probability distribution $\{\pi_i\}$ and the data $\{S_r\}$. This is equivalent to maximising the likelihood of the model given the data.

The Kullback–Leibler information divergence between two distributions $p = (p_1, \ldots, p_n)$ and $q = (q_1, \ldots, q_n)$ is defined as:

$$D(p \| q) = \sum_j p_j \log(p_j/q_j)$$

Here, minimising Kullback–Leibler information divergence is maximising W:

$$W = \sum_{r=1}^{m} \log(\sum_{i=1}^{k} q_{ir}\pi_i)$$

subject to:

$$\sum_{i=1}^{k} \pi_i = 1$$

The problem belongs to the general class of linear inverse problems [10]. The algorithm used here is known as the EM (expectation-maximisation) algorithm. The EM algorithm converges monotonically but possibly slowly as shown by Wu [11].

4.3 Reengineering the database—the role of background knowledge

Having defined partial-value relations, we now go on to discuss the role of background knowledge.

In this chapter we consider two main forms of background knowledge that can be used in the extended data-mining process: concept hierarchies and database integrity constraints.

4.3.1 Concept hierarchies

In real-world databases it is often the case that an attribute has a natural concept hierarchy. The first kind of background knowledge that we envisage consists of a set of user-defined predicates which define a concept hierarchy. For example, the attribute job_title may have the concept hierarchy shown in Figure 4.1.

From the Figure we can see that a manager is either a junior manager or a senior manager. Similarly a junior member of staff could

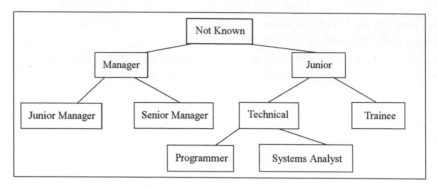

Figure 4.1   Concept hierarchy for attribute job_title

be any one of the three basic types of programmer, systems analyst or trainee. It is possible to express the concept hierarchy in the form of rules and, using a logic programming language, to replace an instance of a high-level concept with the subset consisting of its descendants which are leaf nodes. For example, with Prolog the rules could be of the form:

included(programmer, technical).
included(systems_analyst, technical).

. . . and so on, for the other nodes of the hierarchy. We can also define a recursive relation, descendant:

descendant(X, Y) :- included(X, Y).
descendant(X, Z) :- descendant(X,Y), included(Y, Z).
leaf(X) :- not(descendant(Y, X)).

leaf_descendant(X, Y) := descendant(X, Y), leaf(X).

Assume that the initial database table has the values for the job_title attribute given by the nodes of the hierarchy in Figure 4.1. We scan the table and reengineer the database by replacing every instance, *y*, of job_title by its set of leaf descendants (that is, repeatedly apply the query:

leaf_descendant(X, y).

until no more answers are received).

Note that even if the initial relation is crisp, this procedure creates a partial-value relation. Of course, we have not prevented the database designer from specifying a partial-value relation—the user is at liberty to specify subsets such as {senior manager, programmer} if he or she wishes.

4.3.2 Database-integrity constraints

Modern database management systems (DBMS) typically allow the database manager to define integrity constraints [12]. An integrity constraint, which is a predicate that is a statement about the properties of the database, enables the database manager to prevent users from modifying the database in undesirable ways. There are different types of integrity constraint. A table-based constraint refers to attributes which are all in the same tuple. For example, a table of parts on order might require that the delivery date of an item is later than the order date. A referential integrity constraint ensures that references to foreign keys always point to objects which exist in the database—for example that a supplier referred to in an order is still dealing with the company. More complex constraints can be defined using triggers; the trigger construct lets the user perform a tentative update of the database and then apply an SQL SELECT statement to test if the update violates integrity. The SELECT statement checks the database to see if there is a nonempty answer to a query concerning an undesirable state. If there is an answer, the DBMS abandons the tentative update; if there is no answer then the update is committed to the database.

In this chapter we concentrate on table-based constraints. These constraints can be defined in SQL using the 'check' key word. The database manager can incorporate them into the definition of a table, or define them explicitly. For example, in Oracle, an employee table can be created as shown below:

create table employee (job_title character(10), salary number(7),
employee_id character(10), sex character(1),
check (not (job_title ='trainee' and salary >= 12 000)))

The check constraint specifies that trainees must have salaries below £12 000.

Other rules can also be expressed using check conditions. A check condition for a given database table *R* is created as follows.

4.3.3 Definition: simple comparison predicate

Let A_j be an attribute of *R*, with domain D_j. Assume that v_j^i belongs to the domain D_j. Let op be an operator: = for any domain, $<$, $>$, $\geq$, $\leq$ if the domain can be ordered.

Then a simple comparison predicate is an expression of the form:

$$A_j \text{ op } v_j^i$$

4.3.4 Examples of simple comparison predicates

salary > 1000
job_title = 'trainee'

4.3.5 Definition: table-based predicate

Simple comparison predicates can be combined using AND, OR, NOT and brackets to construct more complex predicates, using the usual rules for logical connectives.

Table-based predicates are constructed recursively using two rules as follows:
(i)   A simple comparison predicate is a table-based predicate.
(ii) If *P*, *Q* are table-based predicates then so are: *P* AND *Q*, *P* OR *Q*, NOT *P* and (*P*).

Brackets are used in order to establish precedence where necessary. The expected rules of distribution apply. Thus, (*P* AND *Q*) OR *R* is equivalent to (*P* OR *R*) AND (*Q* OR *R*).

4.3.6 Example of a table-based predicate

salary > 12 000 AND (NOT (job_title = 'trainee'))

Table-based predicates can be used as check conditions.

4.3.7 Expression of rules as table-based predicates

If_then-type rules can be expressed with table-based predicates. We may simply use the fact that:

$$A \rightarrow B \text{ and } (\text{NOT } A) \text{ OR } B$$

are equivalent in order to transform if–then rules.

For example, assume that we have a rule that if an employee is a systems analyst then she or he has a salary of over £20 000, and that the rule is expressed thus:

job_title = 'systems analyst' → salary > 20 000.

This can be transformed into the table-based predicate:

(NOT (job_title = 'systems analyst')) OR (salary > 20 000).

4.3.8 Reengineering the database

We now show how to prune the database with the two forms of background knowledge described above. Assume that Table 4.3 is a summary of an employee table in which there are just two attributes:

Table 4.3 Raw table before reengineering

Category	Salary	Job_title	Frequency
1	{10 000}	trainee	100
2	{10 000}	manager	150
3	{15 000}	trainee	170
4	{15 000}	programmer	150
5	{15 000}	junior manager	444
6	{25 000}	programmer	125
7	{25 000}	systems analyst	310
8	{25 000; 35 000}	junior manager	213
9	{25 000}	senior manager	400
10	{35 000}	systems analyst	120
11	{35 000}	senior manager	40
12	{15 000; 35 000}	{programmer; junior manager}	100
13	{10 000}	{trainee; junior manager}	72
14	{10 000; 15 000}	{trainee; junior manager}	63
15	{25 000; 35 000}	manager	43

salary and job_title. A certain amount of work has already been done on the table. Tuples which have the same entries for salary and job_title have been aggregated and the frequency column contains the number of each type of tuple. The leftmost column, category, is merely a labelling device so that the different rows of the table can be distinguished.

4.3.8.1 Reengineering the database — using the concept hierarchy

Assume that the concept hierarchy is the hierarchy appearing in Figure 4.1. In rows 2 and 15 we can replace the entry manager with the subset {junior manager, senior manager}.

4.3.8.2 Reengineering the database — using integrity constraints

Assume that the database has the following four integrity constraints, expressed as rules:

Rule 1:
NOT (job_title = 'trainee' AND salary $\geq$ 20 000)

Rule 2:
(job_title = 'systems analyst' OR job_title = 'senior manager') $\rightarrow$ salary > 20 000

Table 4.4   Mask table

	Trainee	Programmer	Systems analyst	Junior manager	Senior manager
10k	1^1	0	0	1^2	0
15k	1^3	1^4	0	1^5	0
25k	0	1^6	1^7	1^8	1^9
35k	0	0	1^{10}	0	1^{11}

Rule 3:

job_title = 'technical' → salary < 30 000

Rule 4:

salary = 10 000 → (job_title = 'trainee' OR job_title = 'junior manager')

We can use the rules to create a mask table, shown in Table 4.4. The Table shows allowable combinations of salary and job_title, where a figure 1 indicates an allowable combination and a zero indicates a combination of salary and job_title that is not allowed by the rules. (The superscripts refer to the row number in the aggregated table, Table 4.3.)

Comparing each row of the aggregated table against the mask table, we see that we can eliminate one of the entries in row 8. This is because junior managers are not allowed a salary of £35 000. Similarly, in row 2, because the salary is known to be £10 000, we must eliminate the senior manager entry from the job_title subset. In row 12 we can eliminate the 35k entry for the junior manager, because the maximum salary for a junior manager is £25 000.

Having pruned Table 4.4 we end up with a new table, Table 4.5, shown below (for the time being the reader should ignore the second column, labelled 'Subsets'). Although in this particular case we have only simplified the Table slightly, we hope that we have illustrated the essentials of the reengineering process.

4.4 Multiattribute count operators

The single-attribute count operator can be generalised to multiple attributes. Instead of a single attribute we now consider the cross product of attributes $A = A_1 \times \ldots A_j \ldots \times A_n$.

If the values of domain D_j are given by the list of attribute values:

$$\{v_1^{(j)}, v_2^{(j)}, \ldots, v_{k_j}^{(j)}\}$$

Table 4.5 Reengineered table

Category	Subsets	Salary	Job_title	Frequency
1	{1}	{10 000}	{trainee}	100
2	{2}	{10 000}	{junior manager}	150
3	{3}	{15 000}	{trainee}	170
4	{4}	{15 000}	{programmer}	150
5	{5}	{15 000}	{junior manager}	444
6	{6}	{25 000}	{programmer}	125
7	{7}	{25 000}	{systems analyst}	310
8	{8}	{25 000}	{junior manager}	213
9	{9}	{25 000}	{senior manager}	400
10	{10}	{35 000}	{systems analyst}	120
11	{11}	{35 000}	{senior manager}	40
12	{4, 5}	{15 000}	{programmer; junior manager}	100
13	{1, 2}	{10 000}	{trainee; junior manager}	72
14	{1, 2, 3, 5}	{10 000; 15 000}	{trainee; junior manager}	63
15	{8, 9, 11}	{25 000; 35 000}	{junior manager; senior manager}	43

then the cross product has the domain $D = D_1 \times \ldots \times D_j \times \ldots \times D_n$ and the values of D are of the form:

$$\{v_{a_1}^{(1)}, \; v_{a_2}^{(2)}, \ldots, v_{a_j}^{(j)}, \ldots, v_{a_n}^{(n)}\}$$

where $a_j \in \{1, \ldots, k_j\}$.

In other words, the number of values an index, a_j, can take depends on the size of the domain.

4.4.1 Example

From Table 4.3, consider the two-attribute domain $D = \text{salary} \times \text{job\_title}$. There are four values of salary and five values of job_title, giving twenty pairs in D of the form (10K, trainee), (10K, programmer) . . ., (35K, senior manager).

Just as with the single-attribute case, we can consider subsets of the domain, where a subset consists of a set of tuples. If a particular tuple has subsets $S_1, S_2, \ldots, S_j, \ldots, S_n$ as its partial values, then we cross-multiply the subsets to obtain a set of tuples in the extended domain.

4.4.2 Example

Consider row 14 in Table 4.3. Attribute 1 has subset {10K, 15K} as its partial value, and attribute 2 has subset {trainee, junior manager} as its partial value. We cross-multiply S_1 and S_2 and obtain the following set S in the extended domain:

$S=\{(10\text{K, trainee}), (10\text{K, junior manager}), (15\text{K, trainee}), (15\text{K, junior manager})\}$

4.4.3 Example

Consider the mask table, Table 4.4. Each cell in the mask table corresponds to a singleton subset of the extended domain — to crisp values of the data.

Because the mask table precludes certain attribute pairs, these pairs need not be considered in the computation of the partial value aggregates for the multiattribute case. We are left with only eleven admissible pairs in the example.

The second column, labelled 'Subsets', shows the subsets which result from the two-attribute analysis applied to the reengineered table. We have not shown the pairs in the subsets explicitly, but have replaced them by the numbering system from the mask table. Note that, in row 15, the cross product of the partial values yields four pairs, but one of them (junior manager, 35K) is excluded by the mask table and hence does not appear in the subset column.

$$\pi_1^{(t)} = \frac{1}{2500}\left(100 + \frac{72\pi_1^{(t-1)}}{(\pi_1^{(t-1)} + \pi_2^{(t-1)})} + \frac{63\pi_1^{(t-1)}}{(\pi_1^{(t-1)} + \pi_2^{(t-1)} + \pi_3^{(t-1)} + \pi_5^{(t-1)})}\right)$$

$$\pi_2^{(t)} = \frac{1}{2500}\left(150 + \frac{72\pi_2^{(t-1)}}{(\pi_1^{(t-1)} + \pi_2^{(t-1)})} + \frac{63\pi_2^{(t-1)}}{(\pi_1^{(t-1)} + \pi_2^{(t-1)} + \pi_3^{(t-1)} + \pi_5^{(t-1)})}\right)$$

$$\pi_3^{(t)} = \frac{1}{2500}\left(170 + \frac{63\pi_3^{(t-1)}}{(\pi_1^{(t-1)} + \pi_2^{(t-1)} + \pi_3^{(t-1)} + \pi_5^{(t-1)})}\right)$$

$$\pi_4^{(t)} = \frac{1}{2500}\left(150 + \frac{100\pi_4^{(t-1)}}{(\pi_4^{(t-1)} + \pi_5^{(t-1)})}\right)$$

. . .

$$\pi_{11}^{(n)} = \frac{1}{2500}\left(40 + \frac{43\pi_{11}^{(n-1)}}{(\pi_8^{(n-1)} + \pi_9^{(n-1)}) + \pi_{11}^{(n-1)}}\right)$$

We apply the iterative formula repeatedly, and obtain the following result, shown in Table 4.6. Table 4.6 is a two-dimensional table showing

Table 4.6 Iterative solution for salary×job_title: π_{ij} *(i=row, j=column)*

	Trainee	Programmer	Systems analyst	Junior manager	Senior manager	$\pi_{i.}$
10k	0.055	0.000	0.000	0.082	0.000	0.137
15k	0.072	0.070	0.000	0.221	0.000	0.363
25k	0.000	0.050	0.124	0.091	0.171	0.435
35k	0.000	0.000	0.048	0.000	0.017	0.065
$\pi_{.j}$	0.127	0.120	0.172	0.394	0.188	1.000

the results of the partial-value aggregate operator when applied to the multiattribute domain salary×job_title. The value for π_i is shown in the cell which it subscripts in the mask table. For example, the cell (25K, systems analyst) contains π_7. Note the column and row totals, in the bottom row and right-hand column, respectively. Their purpose will be explained in the next section.

4.4.4 Quasi-independence

In the previous section we showed how to compute the generalised partial-value aggregate, pvagg, for multiattribute data. The output can be arranged in the form of a multidimensional table, where each cell corresponds to an element of the cross product of the domains. The cells are numbered in exactly the way in which we have already numbered them. The table is a contingency table. The multi-dimensional table is the cube defined in online analytical processing for multidimensional data, restricted to the case where proportions only are stored. Where there are two attributes the table is a crosstabulation of proportions and is sometimes called a pivot table in spreadsheet jargon.

Because of the existence of integrity constraints, some of the cells in the contingency table are constrained to be zero. In the statistical literature [13] they are called structural zeros.

In the data-mining process the data miner is not interested in discovering patterns in the data which result from the existence of structural zeros but, rather, is interested in patterns which deviate from a notional default configuration, that is, the simplest configuration in accordance with the structural zeros.

An appropriate default configuration turns out to be one in which the attributes are quasi-independent.

In such a configuration the formula for the nonzero probability aggregate (where i_j is the index to the value of attribute j), is:

$$\mu_{i_1 \ldots i_j \ldots i_n} = \mu_{i_1} \times \mu_{i_2} \ldots \times \mu_{i_n}$$

(Note that the variable μ_j is considered to be different from:

$$\mu_{i_1 \ldots i_j \ldots i_n}$$

because it has one subscript and refers to a single label.)

We cannot compute the values of μ_j from an explicit formula, but instead we must use an iterative algorithm. The iterative algorithm takes the computed values of pvagg as input and outputs the values of μ_j that are the maximum-likelihood estimators [13].

Let us consider the two-dimensional case in detail. Relabel π_i by replacing i with the appropriate pair ij from the mask table. It is convenient to define the following shorthand notation for sums:

$$\pi_{i.} = \sum_{j=1}^{k_2} \pi_{ij}$$

and

$$\pi_{.j} = \sum_{i=1}^{k_1} \pi_{ij}$$

where the dot (.) notation is used to denote summation.

We need to use the mask table, Table 4.4. Denote the value of cell (i, j) in the mask table by M_{ij}. The matrix M_{ij} is binary valued—0 or 1 as shown in Table 4.4.

Also define a normalising factor:

$$\| \pi \| = \sum_{i=1}^{k_1} \sum_{j=1}^{k_2} \pi_{.j} \pi_{i.} M_{ij}$$

Use these terms to define the starting values of an iterative scheme [14]:

$$\mu_{ij}^{(0)} = \frac{1}{\| \pi \|} M_{ij} \pi_{i.} \pi_{.j}$$

The iterative scheme has alternating steps; even steps deal with rows, odd steps deal with columns.

If the step number, t, is even then compute:

$$\mu_{i.}^{(t+1)} = \sum_{j=1}^{k_2} \mu_{ij}^{(t)}$$

Table 4.7   Quasi-independence model predictions of proportions

	Trainee	Programmer	Systems analyst	Junior manager	Senior manager	$\pi_{i.}$
10k	0.041	0.000	0.000	0.095	0.000	0.137
15k	0.086	0.079	0.000	0.198	0.000	0.363
25k	0.000	0.040	0.141	0.101	0.154	0.435
35k	0.000	0.000	0.031	0.000	0.034	0.065
$\pi_{.j}$	0.127	0.120	0.172	0.394	0.188	1.000

and estimate:

$$\mu_{ij}^{(t+1)} = \mu_{ij}^{(t)} \times \frac{\pi_{i.}}{\mu_{i.}^{(t+1)}}$$

If t is odd then compute:

$$\mu_{.j}^{(t+1)} = \sum_{i=1}^{k_j} \mu_{ij}^{(t)}$$

and estimate:

$$\mu_{ij}^{(t+1)} = \mu_{ij}^{(t)} \times \frac{\pi_{.j}}{\mu_{.j}^{(t+1)}}$$

4.4.5 Example

The iterative scheme was applied using the row and column totals in Table 4.6 and the proportions were estimated as shown in Table 4.7.

4.4.6 Interestingness

We now define the interestingness, I_{ij}, of a given cell value π_{ij} to be:

$$I_{ij} = \frac{\pi_{ij} - \mu_{ij}}{\pi_{ij}}$$

The rationale for using this formula is that the numerator is large for a large deviation from the default configuration, and the deviation is scaled by the expected frequency of occurrence, so that the relative deviation is used for interestingness. Note that, in the case where there

Table 4.8   Interestingness—I_{ij}

	Trainee	Programmer	Systems analyst	Junior manager	Senior manager
10k	0.245	n/a	n/a	− 0.163	n/a
15k	− 0.186	− 0.139	n/a	0.105	n/a
25k	n/a	0.194	− 0.136	− 0.108	0.099
35k	n/a	n/a	0.352	n/a	− 0.990

are no structural zeros, the interestingness is an index of the deviation from independence.

4.4.7 Example

Applying the formula above to Tables 4.6 and 4.7, we obtain a table of the interestingness, Table 4.8.

Examining Table 4.8 we conclude that, for this organisation, there are fewer senior managers earning the top salary scale of £35 000 than we might expect from the quasi-independence model.

4.5 Related work

There is a large amount of literature on statistical databases and the summarisation problem, such as that described by Malvestuto [15–17]. Uncertainty and lack of knowledge are problems in the integration of distributed databases [18] and the data mining of distributed databases [19–21].

In other work [6] not described here, the authors have extended the partial-value model to include the notion of probabilistic partial values. As well as defining partial values, it is also possible to define uncertainty concerning data: a user may ascribe chances or probabilities to values of an attribute rather than be prepared to confirm that a particular value holds. For example, a medical practitioner may be prepared to give odds that a patient is suffering from appendicitis, but not wish to confirm the diagnosis absolutely. It is important that appropriate functionality is provided to handle the generalised database.

In the probabilistic partial-value data model there can be several partial values in a cell. The database assigns to each of these a probability. Many of the results for aggregrates described here carry over quite nicely.

DeMichiel [22] and Chen and Tseng [23] described an extended relational model in which the tuples consisted of partial values. A relation consisting of tuples with probabilistic partial values was defined by Tseng *et al.* [24] and termed a probabilistic partial relation. We have extended this data model to an extended relational-database model based on a partial probability distribution. Barbará *et al.* [25], who introduced the term 'probability data model' (PDM), proposed an equivalent data model. They also provided some extended relational operators such as project and join for use in conjunction with this model.

We note in passing that the model described here is similar to that described by Bell *et al.* [9] which uses Dempster–Shafer mass functions where we use probabilities. Such data have also been discussed in the context of knowledge discovery by Dhar and Tuzhilin [26]. It is clear that partial probability distributions will provide useful mechanisms for representing imprecise and uncertain information in similar circumstances to those discussed by Bell *et al.* [9]. However, in addition, a probability data model provides us with powerful data manipulation and analysis capabilities which in turn provide a framework suitable for rule induction and knowledge discovery.

4.6 Conclusions

There have been two major themes in this chapter: partial values and database background knowledge.

First, we have shown that the partial-value data model is a useful extension to the relational-database model. As well as increasing the expressivity of the data model, partial values allow the data miner to deal with concept hierarchies rigorously. We have shown how an iterative procedure allows us to calculate aggregate proportions for a database table. The use of this iterative procedure is well founded in statistical theory, being a maximum-likelihood estimator. It is possible that the Newton–Raphson procedure described by Jamshidian and Jennrich [27] will provide a means of speeding up the solution of the maximum-likelihood equations.

Secondly, we have demonstrated how it is possible to use background knowledge about the database. We have indicated how to reengineer the database using logic programming and integrity constraints. The aggregation algorithms were extended to the multi-attribute case and we have shown how they are computed in the case where integrity constraints limit the allowed combinations of attribute values.

We were then able to show how to pick out interesting patterns in the database: this approach applies both to the partial-value data model and to the standard data model.

The approach outlined looks very promising. Currently, we are working on an implementation strategy for partial values and their aggregation. Statistical theory is able to handle sampling errors as well as telling us how to compute the maximum-likelihood estimators which we have described in this chapter. This will allow us to compute rule strengths in a rigorous fashion.

We also intend to generalise the theory to allow more complex relationships to be discovered, such as the independence or dependence of sets of variables. The effect of more complex integrity constraints also warrants investigation.

4.7 Acknowledgments

This work was partially funded by IDARESA (ESPRIT project no. 20478) and partially funded by ADDSIA (ESPRIT project no. 22950) which are both part of EUROSTAT's DOSIS (Development of Statistical Information Systems) initiative.

The authors would like to thank Jagjot Anand for help with Oracle integrity constraints.

4.8 References

1 DAO, S. and PERRY, B.: 'Applying a data miner to heterogeneous schema integration'. Proceedings of the first international conference on *Knowledge discovery and data mining*, 1995, AAAI Press, Montreal, pp. 63–68
2 GUYON, I., MATIC N. and VAPNIK, V.: 'Discovering informative patterns and data cleansing', *in* FAYYAD, U.M., PIATETSKY-SHAPIRO, G., SMYTH, P. and UTHURUSAY, R. (eds.): 'Advances in knowledge discovery' (AAAI Press/The MIT Press, 1996) pp. 181–203
3 LAKSHMINARAYAN, K., HARP, S., GOLDMAN, R. and SAMAD, T.: 'Imputation of missing data using machine learning techniques'. Proceedings of second international conference on *Knowledge discovery and data mining*, 1996, Portland, Oregon, pp. 140–145.
4 FAYYAD, U.M., PIATETSKY-SHAPIRO, G. and SMYTH, P.: 'From data mining to knowledge discovery', *in* FAYYAD, U.M., PIATETSKY-SHAPIRO, G., SMYTH, P. and UTHURUSAY, R. (eds.): 'Advances in knowledge discovery' (AAAI Press/The MIT Press, 1996) pp. 181–203

5 FROESCHL, K.A. and PAPAGEORGIOU, H.: 'IDARESA deliverable 1.4: harmonized structure for time series data'. Eurostat, ESPRIT project 20478, 1997

6 McCLEAN, S.I., SCOTNEY, B.W. and SHAPCOTT, C.M.: 'Aggregation of imprecise and uncertain information in databases'. Proceedings of the fourth international conference on *Knowledge discovery and data mining*, AAAI Press, New York, 1998, pp. 269–273

7 HAN, J. and FU, Y.: 'Attribute-oriented induction in data mining', *in* FAYYAD, U.M., PIATETSKY-SHAPIRO, G., SMYTH, P. and UTHURUSAY, R. (eds.): 'Advances in knowledge discovery' (AAAI Press/The MIT Press, 1996) pp. 399–421

8 PARSONS, S.: 'Current approaches to handling imperfect information in data and knowledge bases', *IEEE Trans. Knowl. Data Eng.*, 1996, **8**, pp. 353–372

9 BELL, D.A., GUAN J.W. and LEE, S.K.: 'Generalized union and project operations for pooling uncertain and imprecise information', *Data Knowl. Eng.*, 1996, **18**, pp. 89–117

10 VARDI, Y. and LEE, D.: 'From image deblurring to optimal investments: maximum likelihood solutions for positive linear inverse problems (with discussion)', *J. R. Statist. Soc. B*, 1993, pp. 569–612

11 WU, C.F.J.: 'On the convergence properties of the EM algorithm', *The Annals of Statistics*, 1983, **11**, (1), pp. 95–103

12 CANNAN, S.J. and OTTEN, G.A.M.: 'SQL—the standard handbook' (McGraw-Hill Book Company, Maidenhead, England, 1992)

13 HABERMAN, S.J.: 'Analysis of qualitative data, volume 2' (Academic Press, New York, 1979)

14 CAUSSINUS, H.: 'Contribution à l'analyse statistique des tableaux des corrélations', *Ann. Fac. Sci. Univ. Toulouse*, 1965, **29**, pp. 97–115

15 MALVESTUTO, F.M.: 'The derivation problem for summary data'. Proceedings of the ACM-SIGMOD conference on *Management of data*, New York, 1988, pp. 87–96

16 MALVESTUTO, F.M. and MOSCARINI, M.: 'Query evaluability in statistical databases', *IEEE Trans. Knowl. Data Eng.*, 1990, **2**, pp. 425–430

17 MALVESTUTO, F.M.: 'A universal-scheme approach to statistical databases containing homogeneous summary tables', *ACM Trans. Database Syst.*, 1993, **18**, pp. 678–708

18 McCLEAN, S.I. and SCOTNEY, B.W.: 'Deriving statistical aggregates for knowledge discovery in distributed databases'. Proceedings of *Expert systems '96* Cambridge, BCS, 1996, pp. 245–254

19 RIBEIRO, J.S., KAUFMAN, K.A. and KERSCHBERG, L.: 'Knowledge discovery from multiple databases'. Proceedings of the first international conference on *Knowledge discovery and data mining*, AAAI Press, 1995, pp. 240–245

20 SCOTNEY, B.W. and McCLEAN, S.I.: 'Efficient knowledge discovery through the integration of heterogeneous data', *Inf. Softw. Technol.*, 1999, **41**, (2)

21 SCOTNEY, B.W., McCLEAN, S.I. and RODGERS, M.C.: 'Optimal and efficient integration of heterogeneous summary tables in a distributed database', *Data Knowl. Eng.*, 1999

22 DeMICHIEL L.G.: 'Resolving database incompatibility: an approach to performing relational operations over mismatched domains', *IEEE Trans. Knowl. Data Eng.*, 1989, **4**, pp. 485–493

23 CHEN, A.L.P. and TSENG, F.S.C.: 'Evaluating aggregate operations over imprecise data', *IEEE Trans. Knowl. Data Eng.*, 1996, **8**, pp. 273–284

24 TSENG, F.S.C., CHEN, A.L.P. and YANG, W.-P.: 'Answering heterogeneous database queries with degrees of uncertainty', *Distrib. Parallel Databases*, 1993, **1**, pp. 281–302

25 BARBARÁ, D., GARCIA-MOLINA, H. and PORTER, D.: 'The management of probabilistic data', *IEEE Trans. Knowl. Data Eng.*, 1992, **4**, pp. 487–501

26 DHAR, V. and TUZHILIN, A.: 'Abstract-driven pattern discovery in databases', *IEEE Trans. Knowl. Data Eng.*, 1993, **6**, pp. 926–938

27 JAMSHIDIAN, J.M. and JENNRICH, R.I.: 'Acceleration of the EM algorithm by using quasi-Newton methods', *J. R. Statist. Soc. B*, 1997, **59**, pp. 569–587

Chapter 5

A development framework for temporal data mining

Xiaodong Chen
Manchester Metropolitan University, UK

Ilias Petrounias
UMIST, UK

5.1 Introduction

Data mining is a field which potentially offers nonexplicitly stored knowledge for a particular application domain. In most application areas that have been studied for data mining, the time at which something happened is also known and recorded (e.g. the date and time when a point-of-sale transaction took place, or a patient's temperature was taken). Most existing approaches, however, take a static view of an application domain so that the discovered knowledge is considered to be valid indefinitely on the time line. If data mining is to be used as a vehicle for better decision making, the existing approaches will in most cases lead into not very significant or interesting results. Consider, for example, a possible association between butter and bread (i.e. people who buy butter also buy bread) among the transactions of a supermarket. If someone looks at all transactions that are available, say for the past ten years, that association might be—with a certain possibility—true. If, however, the highest concentration of people who bought butter and bread can be found up to five years ago, then the discovery of the association is not significant for the present and the future of the supermarket organisation. Similarly, if someone looks at the rule 'over a year 50 per cent of people buy umbrellas', this may be true. But if the periodic pattern 'during autumn 85 per cent of people buy umbrellas' is true, then it is certainly more interesting to a company making or selling umbrellas, since it also indicates when and how often the highest concentration of people buying umbrellas can be found.

Over the past decades, a great amount of temporal data has been stored in different databases. Examples range from transaction databases in the healthcare and insurance, patient-record, stock-exchange and consumer-goods market sectors, to scientific databases in geophysics and astronomy areas. Although the field of temporal databases is not very old and commercial DBMSs offer very limited temporal support, the history of data in many of the above and other domains has been kept in some form or another. In many application domains, temporal data are now being viewed as rich sources of information from which time-related knowledge can be derived, so as to help understand the past and/or plan for the future. For example, in stock-market databases, we may find that 'over the last six months some stocks rose by five per cent when the financial index dropped by ten per cent'. In retail applications one may also be interested in a rule which states that 'during the summer customers who buy bread and butter also buy milk', and in the medical domain it may be discovered that 'some patients experience nausea for about an hour followed by headache after each meal'. It has been recognised recently [1–6] that potential temporal patterns or rules should be investigated and discovered from temporal databases since they can provide accurate information about an evolving rather than a static business domain. The growth of research and applications of temporal databases [7,8] has motivated an urgent need for temporal data mining.

Temporal data mining can be defined as: *a set of approaches and techniques to deal with the problem of knowledge discovery from temporal data or databases*. It is expected that the discovered temporal knowledge by temporal data mining can initiate business process change and redevelopment activities in order for an organisation to adapt to changes within its operating area.

The work presented in this chapter is focused on a framework for temporal data mining, aiming to sketch out an outline for the investigation into temporal data mining approaches and techniques. Since the process of knowledge discovery consists of several interactive and iterative stages [9], powerful languages are expected to be used for expressing different *ad hoc* data-mining tasks [10]. As a part of the framework, an SQL-like mining language is also proposed. With this language, any temporal data-mining task can easily be expressed.

5.2 Analysis and representation of temporal features

An analysis of time and the extension of traditional approaches with periodic time will facilitate an understanding of temporal features of knowledge hidden in temporal databases and lead the way to reveal the potential requirements for temporal data mining. The main points in the support for time-varying data in databases refer to the semantics of time which are used and their suitability for describing an application domain. There are several aspects that have to be taken into consideration and these are outlined in this section.

5.2.1 Time domain

Most of the approaches that have appeared in the literature regard time as being represented by an arbitrary set of instants or points with a total order. This means that time is linear and that it advances from the past to the future in a step-by-step fashion. With this linear model of time, the question is whether time should be modelled as discrete, dense or continuous elements. There are several reasons for choosing a discrete time representation [8]. First, although time is generally perceived to be continuous, this cannot be represented when one tries to map it onto finite state machines like computers. Any implementation of a data model with a temporal dimension will of necessity have to have some discrete encoding of time [11]. Secondly, the measures of time are inherently imprecise [12,13]. The occurrences of events are generally minuted by clocking instruments in terms of intervals (even with very small granularity), instead of time points. Moreover, in most natural language, the time is often interpreted as a period during which something occurs. For example, 'an event occurring at 4:30 p.m.' does not usually mean that the event occurred at the time point associated with 4:30 p.m., but at some time in the time period (perhaps minute) associated with 4:30 p.m. [12,14]. Hence, events, even so-called instantaneous events, can best be measured as having occurred during a time period, which can be modelled as a discrete time value on the time line.

In the discrete, linear model of time, an instant can be represented by a chronon, which is a nondecomposable time interval of some fixed, minimal duration, in which an event takes place. Depending on different applications, the granularity of a chronon is different. For example, it might be a second, minute, hour, day etc. A time line is a totally ordered set of chronons and an interval may be represented by a set of contiguous chronons.

5.2.2 *Calendar expression of time*

To represent temporal features of information, calendar time expressions are used in this chapter on the basis of previously proposed notions [15,16]. A calendar unit is referred to as a set of consecutive intervals, which is defined according to a specific calendar (e.g., the Gregorian calendar, the Muslim calendar or the financial calendar). Some examples of calendar units are days, months and years in the Gregorian calendar, which represent the sets of all the days, all the months and all the years, respectively. Other examples are terms and academic years in the academic calendar. These express the sets of all the terms and all the academic years, respectively, on the basis of the academic calendar. Starting from a zero point, each interval of a calendar unit is successively given a natural number, which is called index of the interval. For example, assuming that the granularity of an instant (or a chronon) is day and that the zero point is the beginning of the Christian era, the time interval between January 1 1997 and December 31 1997 is an interval of years, numbered by 1997. Currently, some commercial DBMSs provide support for dates and time. However, they usually support conventional calendar units, such as hours, days, weeks, months and years, in the Gregorian calendar. Special calendar units in application-dependent calendars should be defined by designers in application systems with some suggested calendar expression language [15–18]. Here, it is presumed that every calendar unit in the calendar-unit set is well defined.

Given two calendar units U and V, U is a subunit of V, denoted by $U < V$, if each interval v of V is exactly covered by several consecutive intervals, $u_1, u_2, \ldots, u_n$, of U, such that $v = u_1 \cup u_2 \cup \ldots \cup u_n$ and $n > 1$. For example, 'days' is a subunit of 'weeks', 'months' and 'years', and 'months' is a subunit of 'years'. For any two calendar units U and V with $U < V$, V can be regarded as a reference calendar unit of U. With respect to a reference calendar unit, each interval of a calendar unit is given a number or a name (if applicable) to express the ordinal number of this interval within an interval of the reference calendar unit. This number or name is called reference number or reference name relative to the reference calendar unit. For instance, the interval between July 1 1997 and July 31 1997 is an interval of the calendar unit 'months' and its reference number and name relative to 'years' are 7 and July, respectively.

Before defining time expressions, two functions, index function and reference function, are introduced:

1 Let T be the set of all instants and U be the set of all calendar units: we define index function as $f_{index}: T \times U \to N^+$, where for $\forall t \in T$ and $\forall U \in U$, $f_{index}(t, U)$ is the index of u, such that $t \in u$ and $u \in U$. Following from the previous example, the value of f_{index}(July 1 1997, years) is 1997 since July 1 1997 belongs to the interval [January 1 1997, December 31 1997] which is an interval of the calendar unit 'years' with the index of 1997.

2 Let T be the set of all instants and U be the set of all calendar units: we define reference function as $f_{reference}: T \times U \times U \to N^+$, where for $\forall t \in T$ and $\forall U$, $V \in U$, $f_{reference}(t, U, V)$ is the reference number of u relative to V, such that $t \in u$, $u \in U$ and $U < V$. We have, for example, $f_{reference}$(July 1 1997, months, years) = 7 since July 1 1997 belongs to the interval [July 1 1997, July 31 1997] which is an interval of the calendar unit 'months' and has a reference number relative to the calendar unit 'years' of 7.

Definition 5.1: A calendar interval expression is defined as:

$$CI := \prod_{i=1}^{m} U_i(r_i)$$

where $m \geq 1$; $\forall i \in \{1, \ldots, m\}, U_i \in U$ and $r_i \in N^+$; $\forall i \in \{1, \ldots, m-1\}$, $U_{i+1} < U_i$.

A calendar interval expression CI represents a specific interval of the calendar unit U_m and its interpretation is defined as:

$$\Phi(CI) = \{t | (t \in T) \text{ and } (f_{index}(t, U_1) = r_1) \text{ and }$$
$$(\forall i \in \{2, \ldots, m\}, f_{reference}(t, U_i, U_{i-1}) = r_i)\}$$

For example, the expression years(1990) · months(6) · days(15) represents the interval June 15 1990 of days and the expression years(1993) · months(5) the interval May 1993 of 'months'.

Five interval operators can be introduced to extend the ability to express time intervals and are interpreted as follows:

$\Phi(\text{during } CI) = \Phi(CI)$
$\Phi(\text{starts\_from } CI) = \{t | (t \in T) \text{ and } (\exists t' \in \Phi(CI), t' \leq t)\}$;
$\Phi(\text{finishes\_by } CI) = \{t | (t \in T) \text{ and } (\exists t'' \in \Phi(CI), t \leq t'')\}$;
$\Phi(\text{after } CI) = \{t | (t \in T) \text{ and } (\forall t' \in \Phi(CI), t' < t)\}$;
$\Phi(\text{before } CI) = \{t | (t \in T) \text{ and } (\forall t'' \in \Phi(CI), t < t'')\}$;

For example, 'starts_from years(1993) · months(5)' indicates the time interval which includes the time of not earlier than May 1993 and 'before years(1996) · months(8)' indicates the time interval covering the time before August 1996.

Definition 5.2: An arbitrary contiguous time interval can be expressed by the conjunction of the above extended interval expressions with the interpretation as follows:

$$\Phi(EI_1 \text{ and } EI_2) = \Phi(EI_1) \cap \Phi(EI_2)$$

For example, 'starts_from years(1993) · months(5)' and 'finishes_by years(1996) · months(8)' represents the interval between May 1993 and August 1996.

5.2.3 Periodicity of time

The notion of periodicity [19,20] is an important temporal feature in the real world. A series of repeated occurrences of a certain type of event at regular intervals is described as a periodic event, which exists in many temporal applications.

Definition 5.3: A periodic expression is defined as:

$$PT := U_0 \cdot \prod_{i=1}^{m-1} U_i(r_i) \cdot U_m(a_m : b_m)$$

where $m \geq 1$; $\forall i \in \{0, \ldots, m\}$, $U_i \in U$; $\forall i \in \{0, \ldots, m-1\}$, $U_{i+1} < U_i$; $\forall i \in \{1, \ldots, m-1\}$, r_i, a_m, $b_m \in N^+$. A periodic expression PT represents a periodic time, which is a set of intervals.

The interpretation of a periodic expression is denoted by $\Phi(PT) = \{p_1, p_2, \ldots, p_j, \ldots\}$ such that:

$$\forall j > 0,\ p_j = \{t | (t \in T) \text{ and } (f_{\text{index}}(t, U_0) = j) \text{ and } (\forall i \in \{1, \ldots, m-1\}, f_{\text{reference}}(t, U_i, U_{i-1}) = r_i) \text{ and } (a_m \leq f_{\text{reference}}(t, U_m, U_{m-1}) \leq b_m)\}$$

Here, the definition of the periodic time is consistent with the first notion of the periodicity discussed by Tuzhilin and Clifford [19]. Each periodic time is related to a basic calendar unit, called a cycle unit and denoted by U_0. Each interval of a periodic time is called a periodic interval, which is a subset of an interval of the cycle unit and has the same position in its correspondent cycles. Table 5.1 lists some examples of periodic time and their descriptions.

As we may notice, the above periodic expression describes a set of all relevant intervals along the time line (or within the time domain). In

Table 5.1   Examples of periodic times

Expressions	Descriptions
years · months (7:9)	summertime of each year
months · days (25:25)	the twenty-fifth day of every month
weeks · days(2) · hours (12:13)	Monday lunch time (assuming a week starting from Sunday) of every week
academic years · terms (3) · weeks (5:8)	5th to 8th weeks of summer term of each academic year
3_shift workdays · shift (1:1)	the first shift of every three-shift work day

many applications, we may only be interested in some periodic intervals during a contiguous time period, that constitute a limited periodic time which is represented by a limited periodic expression.

Definition 5.4: A limited periodic expression is the combination of a periodic expression and a general interval expression. The interpretation of a limited periodic expression is defined as:

$$\Phi(PT \circ GI) = \{p | \exists p' \in \Phi(PT), p = p' \cap \Phi(GI) \text{ and } p \neq \varnothing\}$$

For example, the twenty-fifth day of every month in 1995 can be expressed as:

$$\text{months} \cdot \text{days}(25:25) \text{ during years}(1995)$$

and the Monday lunch time of every week during the time period before August 1996 represented as:

$$\text{weeks} \cdot \text{days}(2) \cdot \text{hours}(12:13) \text{ before years}(1996) \cdot \text{months}(8)$$

Furthermore, the following are two other examples of periodic time with more complex limitations:

$$\text{years} \cdot \text{months}(7:9) \text{ after years}(1990) \text{ and before years}(1995)$$

describes the summer time of each year from 1990 to 1995, and:

$$\text{academic years} \cdot \text{terms}(3) \cdot \text{weeks}(5:8)$$
$$\text{after years}(1990) \cdot \text{months}(9) \text{ and before years}(1996) \cdot \text{months}(8)$$

represents the fifth to eighth weeks of summer terms of each academic year during the time period between September 1990 and August 1998.

5.2.4 Time dimensions in temporal databases

The issues concerning the concepts of time which are to be supported by temporal databases mainly refer to the dimensions of time that are supported. So far, there are three main orthogonal kinds of time which a data model may support: valid time, transaction time and user-defined time [8]. Valid time concerns modelling a time-varying reality; it is the time at which something happened or existed in the real world. Transaction time, on the other hand, concerns the storage of information in the database. User-defined time is an uninterpreted domain for which the data model supports the operations of input, output, and perhaps comparison. As the name implies, the semantics of the user-defined time are provided by the user or application program. An additional dimension of time that exists in reality is the time at which a particular decision has been taken [21]. This dimension—orthogonal to the previously-mentioned dimensions—is referred to as decision time and is equally important, especially at the enterprise level, to enable people to reason about decisions that have been taken. It should also be considered separately, because the time at which a decision about a change is taken in the real world is different from the time at which this change actually takes place and from the time that it is recorded. Currently, only user-defined time is supported by commercial DBMSs. However, both valid time and transaction time are supported by the proposed temporal query language TSQL2 [22] and will be included in the future SQL3 standard.

In temporal databases, a data object (e.g., an attribute value or a tuple) may be associated with a time instant or a time interval, depending on whether it expresses an event or a state. A time instant can be represented by a time stamp with an associated scale (e.g., minute, hour, day or month), and a time interval can be implemented by the composition of two instant time stamps and the constraint that the starting time stamp equals or precedes the ending time stamp. An event is an instance of temporal data which happens during an instant in time. Each recorded event is associated with a time stamp to record the time instant during which the event occurs. In TSQL2, a table which implements the event model is called an event table and can be used in some application fields such as sales, other financial transactions, inventory transfers, bookings and new hires. A state is an instance of temporal data which exists or is satisfied over a period of time. Each recorded state is time stamped with an interval to record the time during which that state exists. In TSQL2, a table which implements the state model is called a state table, and it can be used in other application areas such as customer credit ratings, insurance policies, account balances, bills of material, personnel records etc.

5.3 Potential knowledge and temporal data mining problems

There are many different forms of knowledge that potentially can be extracted from databases with temporal data mining and these are presented below. The second part of the Section concentrates on the problem of mining temporal patterns.

5.3.1 Forms of potential temporal knowledge

Many studies on knowledge discovery and data mining have been pursued in the fields of artificial intelligence, statistics and databases [9]. The forms of potential knowledge that have been identified in the literature can be mainly classified as follows:

5.3.1.1 Inducted rules

Generally, an inducted rule is a description for a subset of data in the database. There are various types of inducted rule that can be learnt from the content of databases. For example, a characteristic rule [23] can be regarded as an assertion which describes the characteristics of a concept satisfied by all of the relevant data in the database and is generalised from these data with the help of a known concept hierarchy. A classification rule describes the common properties among a known or clustered class of objects in terms of attributes of the objects, which can be inducted by supervised learning (e.g. decision-tree induction) or unsupervised learning (e.g. conceptual clustering) and can be used to predict the class of a new object [24].

5.3.1.2 Trends and deviation

Trends are particularly important knowledge forms in time-series data, which characterise the upward or downward fluctuations in series of data over a period of time. The fluctuations may be linear or exponential and can usually be highlighted in the form of lines or curves. In time-series databases with data at lots of time points, people often need help in uncovering data trends. For example, stock-market analysts want to know if a stock is moving up or down and retail managers want to know if their sales figures are improving. In real-world application, trends are also often used to predicate the expected data values which may form the references of deviation analysis [25]. Significant differences between measured values in the time-related data and corresponding references can be used for recommending to people the actions to be taken in order to get possible benefits.

5.3.1.3 Similar patterns

Similar patterns are time sequences which match a given sequence or shape, exactly or approximately [26,27], and exist in large quantities in time-series databases. In stock-price databases, for instance, there might be many patterns which are similar to some technical analysis shape, such as 'panic reversal', 'double top reversal' or 'head & shoulder reversal' [28]. In financial and marketing applications, similar patterns can help us to find companies with stock prices which move similarly, or identify companies which have similar sales patterns. In scientific databases, we might find past days in which the solar magnetic wind showed patterns similar to today's pattern so as to help in predictions of the earth's magnetic field [29].

5.3.1.4 Event relationships

An event relationship is a totally or partially ordinal set of events, which is frequently present in the time-series data. There are several different event relationships identified in various application areas. A sequential pattern [30] is an item or event sequence that is frequently buried low in the transaction sequence in the retailing domain. An example of such a pattern is that '70 per cent of customers first bought a PC, then a CD-ROM and then a modem'. In the medical domain, causal relationships [31], such as some symptoms or diseases typically preceding certain other symptoms or diseases, may be hidden in patient record databases. Moreover, frequent episodes in telecommunication-network alarm databases were identified by Mannila *et al.* [32] and can be presented by arbitrary directed acyclic graphs (DAG). An episode can also be generalised as an event structure [33] which consists of a set of event variables with temporal constraints among these variables, and may appear frequently in the stock-market applications. Finally, the association [34] can also be regarded as a special kind of event relationship, where one event occurs at the same time as another.

5.3.2 Associating knowledge with temporal features

In real-world applications, the knowledge which is used for helping decision making is always time varying. However, most of the existing data-mining approaches depend on the assumption that discovered knowledge is valid indefinitely [3], so that temporal features of the knowledge are not taken into account in the mining models or processes. As a result of this, people who expect to use the discovered knowledge may not know when it became valid, or whether it is still valid in the present or if it will be valid sometime in the future. Obviously, this will limit the usability of the discovered knowledge. For supporting better decision making, it is desirable to associate some temporal features with the interesting patterns or rules. For example, in stock-market databases, the interesting event relationship that 'some stocks rise by five per cent when the financial index drops from ten to 20 per cent', could just hold 'over the last four months'. In retail applications, we may be more interested in the association that 'customers who buy bread and butter also buy milk during summer'. There are several temporal aspects that can be associated with patterns to describe temporal knowledge. The major concerns in this chapter are the valid period and the periodicity of patterns.

Definition 5.5: A temporal pattern is a triplet <patt, periodicexp, intervalexp>, where patt is a general pattern which may be a trend, a classification rule, an association, a causal relationship etc., periodicexp is a periodic time expression or a special symbol p_null with $\Phi(p\_null)$ being $\{T\}$ and intervalexp is a general interval expression or a special symbol i_null with $\Phi(i\_null)$ being T. It expresses that patt holds during each interval in $\Phi(\text{periodicexp} \circ \text{intervalexp})$. T is the time domain.

For any temporal pattern of the form <patt, periodicexp, intervalexp>, if periodicexp is p_null and intervalexp is not i_null, the expression represents a pattern which refers to an absolute time interval $\Phi(\text{intervalexp})$; if periodicexp is not p_null and intervalexp is i_null, it represents a periodic pattern without any time limitation; if neither periodicexp is p_null nor intervalexp is i_null, it represents a periodic pattern which is valid during the time interval $\Phi(\text{intervalexp})$; otherwise, it represents a nontemporal pattern. The following are some examples of temporal patterns that refer to absolute time intervals or periodic times:

- <'(emp,=),(rank,<)⟹(salary,≤)',   *p*_null,   starts_from   years (1992) · months(3)   and   finishes_by   years(1993) · months(7) >:   it describes that during the period between March 1992 and July 1993, if an employee's rank increases then his/her salary does not decrease;
- <'hikingboots ⟹ outerwear',   years · months(4:6),   starts_from years(1990) and finishes_by years(1995) >: it shows that every spring during 1990 to 1995 the shoppers who buy hiking boots, also want outerwear at the same time;
- <'nausea → headache', days · hours(6:8), *i*_null>: it indicates that the patients with some certain disease feel nausea, followed by headaches from 6 to 8 o'clock every morning. The '→' is used in this case to describe a sequence rather than an association as was the case in the previous examples.

5.3.3 Temporal mining problems

The essential task of temporal data mining is finding useful knowledge from temporal data. Any form of potential pattern as discussed in Section 5.3.1 may be discovered from temporal data and any mining approach is aimed at solving the problem of finding patterns of a certain type. To extract temporal features, time values need to be used. In the context of temporal databases, data may be stamped with time values in different time dimensions as discussed in Section 5.2.4. Obviously, the time dimension of discovered temporal patterns depends on the dimension of the time values with which the used data is stamped. For simplicity, time values associating with data are generally called time stamps, no matter whether they are user-defined, valid, transaction or decision time.

Definition 5.6: Given a set D of time-stamped data over a time domain T, we use $D(p)$ to denote a subset of D, which contains all data with time stamps belonging to time interval p. We define:

- <patt, periodicexp, intervalexp> holds during interval p, $p \in \Phi$(periodicexp ° intervalexp), if patt satisfies all relevant thresholds in $D(p)$;
- <patt, periodicexp, intervalexp> satisfies all relevant thresholds with respect to the frequency $f\%$ in the dataset D if <patt,

periodicexp, intervalexp> holds during not less than $f\%$ of intervals in Φ(periodicexp ° intervalexp).

In the above definition, the relevant thresholds are given in terms of the forms of interesting patterns. Different thresholds have been suggested to be used for different forms of patterns in the literature [9]. The notion of frequency is introduced for measuring the proportion of the intervals, during which patt satisfies all relevant thresholds, to the intervals in Φ(periodicexp ° intervalexp). It is required that the frequency of any discovered temporal pattern <patt, periodicexp, intervalexp> should not be smaller than the user-specified minimum frequency which is a fraction within [0,1]. In the case where $|\Phi$(periodicexp ° intervalexp)$|=1$, Φ(periodicexp ° interva-lexp) just includes a single interval so that any non-zero minimum frequency has the same meaning, that is, patt must satisfy all the relevant thresholds during this single interval.

Definition 5.7: Given a time-stamped dataset D over a time domain T, the problem of mining temporal patterns of a certain type is to discover all patterns of the form <patt, periodicexp, intervalexp> in D which satisfy all the user-specified thresholds with respect to the user-specified minimum frequency min_$f\%$, with some given conditions.

   Ideally, it might be expected that all possibly hidden patterns of a certain type can be discovered without any known temporal features of patterns. From a practical point of view, however, something with some known temporal features might be required. For example:

* mining all patterns of a certain type during a specific time interval;
* mining all patterns of a certain type with a specific periodicity;
* mining all patterns of a certain type with a specific periodicity during a specific time interval.

On the other hand, people might also be interested in looking for temporal features of some specific pattern. For example:

* finding all contiguous time intervals during which a specific pattern holds;

- finding all periodicities of a specific pattern during a specific time interval;
- finding all limited periodicities of a specific pattern.

5.4 A framework for temporal data mining

5.4.1 A temporal mining language

From the point of view of database systems, knowledge discovery is the process of interactively and iteratively querying patterns. To a greater or lesser extent, data mining is both application dependent and user dependent. To find useful knowledge, the user of a KDD system has to select the relevant data subset, identify suitable classes of patterns and define good criteria for interestingness of the patterns. Therefore, it is important that KDD systems supply users with flexible and powerful descriptive languages to express data-mining tasks. Since SQL has been used almost exclusively as a query language owing to the extensive use of relational DBMSs in organisations, it is practically reasonable to develop SQL-like data mining languages [10,35,36], although some logic-based approaches have also been proposed [37]. In this Section, a temporal query and mining language (TQML) is presented, being focused on the needs and requirements for querying a database for the mining of temporal patterns and aimed at expressing several aspects of temporal data mining tasks:

- *query demand*: not all data in the database give contribution to a specific data-mining task. Data relevant to a specific data-mining task need to be selected from the database, according to the application requirement. The traditional query mechanism should be extended to supply the support for specific features, such as nested relations and temporal queries;
- *mining demand:* many different forms of knowledge, such as trends, classification rules, association rules etc., have been identified, and they may be extracted from databases, based on different models and algorithms. For different applications and different pattern forms, mining users may also use different criteria to measure the interestingness of discovered patterns and limit the search space;
- *representation demand*: the discovered knowledge may be shown in different forms, such as productions, tables, graphs etc.

The structure of the TQML language is briefly defined as follows in the BNF grammar:

```
1    <TQML> ::=
2      mine <pattern-form-descriptor> ( all I <specific-pattern> )
3         with periodicity ( all I omission I <periodic-expression> )
4         during interval ( all I t_domain I <interval-expression> )
5         [ having thresholds <threshold-expression-list> ]
6         [ shown as <display-form> ]
7      in
8         select <relevant-attribute-list> [ , <time-attribute> ]
9         from <relation-list>
10        [ where <condition-expression>]
11        [ group by <group-attribute-list> [ having <condition-
           expression> ] ]
```

A mining task in TQML consists of the mining-target section (lines 2–6) and the data-query section (lines 8–11). In the above definition, <pattern-form-descriptor> points out the form of patterns which users may be interested in, and this may be 'trend', 'classification', 'association', 'causality' etc. The option that follows indicates whether all of the possible patterns should be found or whether the temporal features of a specific pattern should be extracted. The periodicity of patterns can be expressed by with-periodicity (option), where an 'all' shows that all possible periodic patterns or the periodicities of the specific pattern are expected, an 'omission' shows that the periodicity of patterns is not of interest and <periodic-expression> gives the periodicity of the expected patterns. The during-interval (option) can be used for describing the valid period of patterns, where 'all' shows that all contiguous time intervals during which patterns (periodic or nonperiodic) may exist are expected to be extracted, 't_domain' makes the assumption that the expected patterns are valid indefinitely and <interval-expression> indicates the specific time period in which users are interested.

Thresholds, relevant to different forms of expected pattern, can be stated in the having-threshold clause and presentation demands can be stated in the shown-as clause. Note that the granularity of the time interval should be considered as one of the criteria, if people want to extract the contiguous time intervals during which a specific pattern exists.

The data that are relevant to the data-mining task can be stated in the select-from-where-group clause. The select subclause indicates attributes which are relevant to the mining task. The attribute in <relevant-attribute-list> may be an attribute that exists in the tables appearing in the from clause, an aggregate function (such as max, sum etc.) or a set function which forms an attribute of a nested relation.

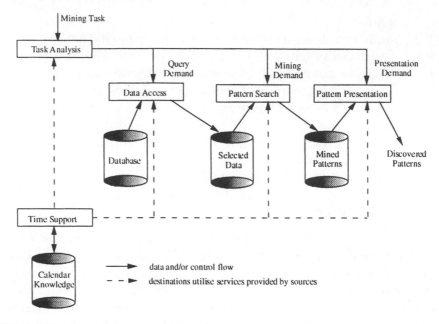

Figure 5.1   Prototype system architecture

Each attribute in <relevant-attribute-list> may also be followed by a descriptor, which is relevant to a specific mining model for a certain type of pattern in which the mining user is interested. The <time-attribute> indicates the time dimension which users are concerned with in the database, such as transaction-time, valid-time, decision-time or user-defined-time, as defined in the temporal databases literature [22]. The from-where clause has the same syntax and semantics as SQL92, constituting a basic query to collect the set of relevant data. The where subclause can also contain time-related conditions, and the selected data may be grouped by <group-attribute-list>, being presented in the form which mining algorithms expect. The having clause can be used to filter the groups which users want to consider.

5.4.2 System architecture

Figure 5.1 shows an architecture for mining temporal patterns in temporal databases which includes five modules.

Task analysis: The task-analysis module syntactically and semantically analyses the mining task which is submitted by data-mining users and expressed in the temporal query and mining language, TQML. This module generates the query for relevant data, which is represented in an SQL-like intermediate language and will be processed by the data-access module. It also extracts relevant information according to the patterns expected by the user, such as the form of patterns and thresholds, and generates the internal representation of the mining problem according to different mining models. During the course of analysis, it calls the time-support module to construct the time expression by handling time-related components in the mining task. Based on the results of analysis, it successively invokes the data-access, pattern-search and pattern-presentation modules with query demand, mining demand and presentation demand, respectively.

Data access: With the query demand generated by the task-analysis module, the data-access module queries the database to select data that are relevant to the mining task and organises the selected data in the format which is required by the mining algorithms. The input of this module is the query demand in SQL-like intermediate language, which is generated from both the mining-target and data-query parts in the mining-task description in TQML. The data-access module uses services supplied by the time-support module to interpret time-related components such as periodic predicates and interval-comparison predicates in the query demand.

Pattern search: According to the mining demand, the pattern-search module chooses and runs the relevant algorithm which will pass through the selected data to search for interesting patterns. The mining demand indicates the kind of knowledge that the user wants to find, and specifies the thresholds given by the user. With these demands and the dataset selected by the data-access module, the pattern-search module executes the algorithm and stores the searched patterns in the internal form in a pattern base.

The design of search algorithms for temporal patterns is one of the crucial issues in temporal data mining; the overall discussion on search algorithms for temporal patterns is beyond the scope of this chapter. The description of a pair of algorithms for mining temporal association rules will be presented in the next Section. In many cases, where only specific temporal features are interesting, the search performance is reasonable. However, the performance of search algorithms attempting to identify all possible temporal patterns (especially, periodic patterns) may be worse than the performance of an algorithm which does not take into account the time component. Special techniques for different mining problems and models need to be used for improving the search performance.

Pattern presentation: In terms of different presentation demands, the pattern-presentation module displays the discovered knowledge in different forms. For example, the patterns may be expressed as productions, tables, graphs etc. Sometimes, the module may present rules with their thresholds.

Time support: This is a key module for supporting the processing of temporal aspects in data mining. It supplies time support for all other modules. Any expression in the temporal query and mining language will be passed to the time-support module in order to identify temporal aspects in the mining task. All other modules utilise its services when they need to deal with a time issue, such as constructing time expressions for task analysis, evaluating periodic predicates and interval-comparison predicates when accessing data and interpreting time expressions while performing pattern searching etc. The time-support module maintains and uses the calendar knowledge base which includes definitions of all relevant calendars.

5.5 An example: discovery of temporal association rules

As an example of generic temporal patterns, temporal association rules are presented in this Section, along with their search algorithms.

5.5.1 Mining problem

Investigation of the problem of finding association rules [34] was motivated by analyses of sales data, which are usually recorded in transaction databases. Given a set of transactions, where each transaction is a set of items, an association rule is an expression of the form $X \Rightarrow Y$, where X and Y are sets of items, and indicates that the presence of X in a transaction will imply the presence of Y in the same transaction.

Consider a supermarket database where the set of items purchased by a customer is stored as a transaction. A possible example of the association rule is: '60 per cent of transactions that contain bread and butter also contain milk; 30 per cent of all transactions contain both of these items.' Here, 60 per cent is called the confidence of the rule and 30 per cent the support of the rule. The meaning of this rule is that customers who purchase bread and butter also buy milk. The problem of mining association rules is defined as the attempt to find all association rules which satisfy the user-specified minimum support and minimum confidence. This problem has been extended for discovering temporal association rules [5].

Let $I=\{i_1, i_2, \ldots, i_n\}$ be a set of literals which are called items. A set of items $X \subset I$ is called an itemset. Let D be a set of time-stamped transactions. Each time-stamped transaction S is a triplet <tid, itemset, timestamp>, where S.tid is the transaction identifier, S.itemset is a set of items such that S.itemset$\subseteq I$, and S.timestamp is an instant (or a chronon) with which the transaction S is stamped, such that S.timestamp$\in T$. We say a transaction S contains an itemset X if $X \subseteq S$.itemset.

Definition 5.8: A temporal association rule is, in accordance with the definition of temporal patterns, a triplet <assorule, periodicexp, intervalexp>, where assorule is an implication of the form $X \Rightarrow Y$ such that $X \subset I$, $Y \subset I$ and $X \cap Y = \emptyset$, periodicexp is a periodic expression and intervalexp is an interval expression. We define:

- the rule has confidence c % during interval p_i, $p_i \in \Phi$(periodicexp° intervalexp), if not less than c % of transactions in $D(p_i)$ that contain X also contain Y;
- the rule has support s % during interval p_i, $p_i \in \Phi$(periodicexp°intervalexp), if not less than s % of transactions in $D(p_i)$ contain $X \cup Y$;
- the rule has confidence c % and support s % with respect to the frequency f % in the transaction set D (or, say, in the database D) if it has confidence c % and support s % during not less than f % of intervals in Φ(periodicexp°intervalexp).

Definition 5.9: Given a set D of time-stamped transactions over a time domain T, a periodic expression periodicexp, and an interval expression intervalexp, the problem of mining temporal association rules is to discover all rules of the form <$X \Rightarrow Y$, periodicexp, intervalexp> in D which satisfy the user-specified minimum support min_s % and confidence min_c % with respect to the user-specified minimum frequency min_f%.

Here, the mining problem is restricted to finding association rules with a specific periodicity and a specific time period.

In the above definition, the notion of frequency is used for measuring the proportion of the intervals, during which $X \Rightarrow Y$ satisfies minimum support and minimum confidence, to the intervals in Φ(periodicex°intervalexp). It is required that the frequency of any temporal association rule <$X \Rightarrow Y$, periodicexp, intervalexp> should not be smaller than the user-specified minimum frequency.

---

items

item-no   item-name   brand   category   retail-price

purchase

trans-no   trans-time   customer   item-no   qty   amount

Figure 5.2   Relation schemes in sales database

5.5.2 Description of mining tasks in TQML

Consider a sales database containing two relations, items and purchase, as shown in Figure 5.2. The following is an example of a mining task for finding all periodic association rules which convey purchase patterns every summer (assuming that summer starts from the sixth month of each year) between June 1992 and May 1997, with the thresholds of support, confidence and frequency being 0.6, 0.75 and 0.8, respectively. In this example, we are only concerned with items for which retail prices are not less than £10 and transactions in which the number of purchased items is greater than three.

> mine association_rule (all)
> with periodicity(years · months(6:8))
> during interval(starts_from years(1992) · months(6) and finishes_
> by years(1997) · months(5))
> having thresholds support=0.6, confidence=0.75, frequency=0.8
> in
>   select trans-no: TID, set(item-name): itemset, trans-time:time-stamp
>   from purchase, items
>   where   purchase.item-no=items.item-no   and   items.retail-price≥£10
>   group by purchase.trans-no having count(*)>3

In the above example, the select-from-where-group part expresses a basic data query demand. The result of the data query is a nested relation, forming the dataset which is relevant to this mining task. TID and itemset are descriptors which indicate the trans-no and set(item-name) as the TID and itemset, respectively, in the mining model for temporal associations. The trans-time in the database is chosen as the time stamp.

5.5.3 Search algorithms

For simplicity, a general time expression periodicexp $\circ$ intervalexp is denoted as P and the set of all time expressions as $\mathbf{P}$ below. The concept of a large itemset [34] is extended as follows:

Definition 5.10: The support of an itemset during a time interval p in transaction set D is the number of transactions, which contain this itemset, in $D(p)$. An itemset is large during a time interval p if the ratio of its support during this time interval p to the number of transactions that occur during the time interval p is not less than min_s%. An itemset is large with respect to a time expression P if it is large during not less than min_f% of intervals in $\Phi(P)$, and it is called a large itemset relative to P.

Similar to the method presented by Agrawal and Srikant [34], the problem of discovering temporal association rules can be solved in two steps: finding all itemsets which are large with respect to the time expression P and using the large itemsets found to generate rules. A pair of algorithms, FLTIS (finding large temporal item sets) and GTAR (generating temporal association rules), is used in these two steps and presented below.

Algorithm FLTIS is an extension of the Apriori algorithm in [34], which was based on the fact that any subset of a large itemset must be large. The candidate itemsets having k items can be generated by joining large itemsets having $k-1$ items, and deleting those which contain any subset that is not large. This basic idea is also suitable for finding large itemsets relative to a specific time expression.

To describe the algorithm, each transaction in a time stamped transaction set (or database) D is expressed by a triplet <tid, timestamp, itemset>. The term time stamp can be used to represent any of the different types of time identified in Section 5.2 (transaction, valid, decision or user-defined time). The number of items in an itemset is defined as the size of this itemset. An itemset of size k is called a k-itemset.

The FLTIS algorithm is presented in Figure 5.3, where L_k and C_k are, respectively, extended to denote sets of large k-itemsets and candidate potential large k-itemset, relative to the time expression, P. Each itemset in L_k or C_k is associated with two related fields:

- support list: support$[p_1]$, support$[p_2]$, . . . , support$[p_i]$, . . . , where p_i $\in \Phi(P)$, and support$[p_i]$ expresses the support of this itemset during interval p_i;
- frequency: the count of intervals during which this itemset is large.

```
(1)     for (each transaction s ∈ D) do
(2)       if (∃pᵢ ∈ Φ(P), s.timestamp ∈ pᵢ) {
(3)         R[pᵢ]++;
(4)         for (∀item ∈ s.itemset)d {
(5)           itemset={item};
(6)           if (itemset ∈ C₁)
(7)             C₁[itemset].support[pᵢ]++;
(8)           else {
(9)             C₁=C₁ ∪ {itemset};
(10)            C₁[itemset]. support[pᵢ]=1;
(11)          }
(12)        }
(13)     }
(14)    for (∀itemset ∈ C₁) do {
(15)      C₁[itemset].frequency=0;
(16)      for (∀ pᵢ ∈ Φ(P)) do
(17)        if (C₁[itemset].support[pᵢ]/R[pᵢ]≥ min_s%) C₁[itemset].frequency++;
(18)    }
(19)    L₁={itemset ∈ C₁|C₁[itemset].frequency/|Φ(P)|≥ min_f%};
(20)    for (k=2; L_{k−1} ≠ φ; k++) do {
(21)      C_k=get_candidate_set(L_{k−1});  //apriori-gen algorithm in [34]
(22)      for (each transaction s ∈ D) do
(23)        if (∃pᵢ ∈ Φ(P), s.timestamp ∈ pᵢ) {
(24)          C_t=get_subsets(C_k, s.itemset);  //subset algorithm in [34]
(25)          for (∀w ∈ C_t) do C_k[w].support[pᵢ]++;
(26)        }
(27)      for (∀itemset ∈ C_k) do {
(28)        C_k[itemset].frequency=0;
(29)        for (∀ pᵢ ∈ Φ(P)) do
(30)          if (C_k[itemset].support[pᵢ]/R[pᵢ]≥ min_s%)
                    C_k[itemset].frequency++;
(31)      }
(32)      L_k={ itemset ∈ C_k | C_k[itemset].frequency/ | Φ(P) | ≥ min_f%};
(33)    }
```

Figure 5.3   Algorithm FLTIS

The algorithm starts from finding large 1-itemsets and takes all items occurring in the database as potentially large 1-itemsets. Lines 1–13 in the algorithm make a pass over the database to count the number of transactions and the occurrences of candidate 1-itemsets during different intervals. We use $R[p_i]$, where $p_i \in \Phi(P)$ and $P \in P$, to count the transactions with timestamps which are within the interval p_i. Lines 14–19 calculate the frequency of all candidate 1-itemsets and select the itemsets satisfying minimum frequency as large 1-itemsets. $|\Phi(P)|$ expresses the number of intervals in $\Phi(P)$.

Among the iterations between line 20 and line 33 in the algorithm, the large $(k-1)$-itemsets are first used to generate candidate k-itemsets according to the Apriori-gen algorithm in [34]. The supports of all candidate k-itemsets during different intervals are then computed by

```
(1)    procedure genrules(   l_k:large k-itemset relative to P,
(2)                           a_m: large m-itemset relative to P,
(3)                           m: size of a_m)
(4)    {
(5)    A={a_{m-1}|a_{m-1} ⊂ a_m and the size of a_{m-1}=m − 1};
(6)    for (∀ a_{m-1} ∈ A) do {
(7)       frequency=0;
(8)       for (∀ p_i ∈ Φ(P)) do {
(9)          confidence[p_i]=l_k.support[p_i]/a_{m-1}.support[p_i];
(10)         support[p_i]=l_k.support[p_i]/R[p_i];
(11)         if (confidence[p_i] ≥ min_c% and support[p_i] ≥ min_s%)
(12)            frequency++;
(13)      }
(14)      if (frequency/|Φ(P)| ≥ min_f%) {
(15)         output the rule < a_{m-1} ⇒ (l_k − a_{m-1}), P > with frequency;
(16)         if (m − 1 > 1) call genrules (l_k, a_{m-1}, m − 1);
(17)      }
(18)   }}
```

Figure 5.4   Algorithm GTAR

passing over the database. Using the subset algorithm in [34], line 24 chooses those itemsets existing in transaction s which occurs during an interval in $\Phi(P)$ from the set of candidate k-itemsets. As shown in line 25, each of these chosen itemsets contributes to its support related to the interval during which transaction s occurs.

Finally, the frequencies of all candidate k-itemsets are calculated, and the itemsets satisfying minimum frequency are selected as large k-itemsets. The iteration continues until no new large itemsets are found.

To generate temporal association rules, we consider every large itemset Z relative to the time expression P. For each nonempty subset X of Z, $<X \Rightarrow (Z-X), P>$ is a potential rule the support and confidence of which during an interval p_i in $\Phi(P)$ are the ratio of the support of Z during p_i to the number of transactions in $D(p_i)$ and the ratio of the support of Z to the support of X during p_i, respectively. A rule of the form $<X \Rightarrow (Z-X), P>$ is generated if its support is not smaller than min_s % and its confidence is not smaller than min_c %, during not less than min_f % of intervals of P. Based on the algorithm in [34], a recursive algorithm GTAR for generating possible temporal association rules from a large k-itemset relative to the time expression P is shown in Figure 5.4. For finding all temporal association rules relative to a time expression P, we can simply scan all the large itemsets relative to P and for each of them call the genrules procedure in algorithm GTAR.

5.6 Conclusion and future research direction

With the growth of research on temporal databases and the possibility of inclusion of temporal support in SQL3, more attention is being paid to temporal data mining owing to the value of temporal data. We argue that temporal aspects of potential knowledge hidden in temporal databases are very important since they can provide companies or organisations with accurate information about their evolving business domains for decision-making purposes. Until now there has been little work reported which has been directed to the discovery of temporal patterns with temporal features. An attempt of this chapter is to set out a framework for investigation into the approaches and techniques for mining temporal patterns.

Temporal patterns has been defined in this chapter by associating general patterns with temporal features which are represented by calendar time expressions. Two different aspects of temporal features of patterns are identified: the valid period and periodicity of patterns. For evaluating the significance and interestingness of mined temporal patterns, the minimum frequency is introduced as the threshold which can be specified by users in terms of different requirements. Different mining problems for different applications have been addressed. An architecture for temporal data mining was also presented in order to show all the components required for solving the mining problem of temporal patterns. The presented mining language is an effective tool for expressing different kinds of temporal data-mining task addressed within the framework. The language can accommodate all different types of time which have been identified in the temporal-database literature. The problem of mining temporal association rules has been discussed in detail, demonstrating a specific case of temporal data mining within the proposed framework.

Current work concentrates mainly on the implementation of the temporal discovery language and the extension of calendar support beyond that of the Gregorian calendar, in order to supply the essential support for temporal data-mining tasks. Further research needs to be undertaken to seek different search techniques for different forms of expected pattern with temporal features.

5.7 References

1 GOLAN, R. and EDWARDS, D.: 'Temporal rules discovery using data-logic/R+ with stock market data'. Proceedings of the international

workshop on *Rough set and knowledge*, (RSKD'93), Banff, Alberta, Canada, pp. 74–81

2 SARAEE, M. and THEODOULIDIS, B.: 'Knowledge discovery in temporal databases'. Proceedings of IEE colloquium on *Knowledge discovery in databases*, 1995, pp. 1–4

3 RAINSFORD, C.P. and RODDICK, J.F.: 'Temporal data mining in information systems: a model'. Proceedings of 7th Australasian conference on *Information systems*, Hobart, Tasmania, 1996, pp. 545–553

4 WIJSEN, J. and MEERSMAN, R.: 'On the complexity of mining temporal trends'. SIGMOD'97 workshop on research issues on *Data mining and knowledge discovery* (DMKD'97), May 1997

5 CHEN, X., PETROUNIAS, I. and HEATHFIELD, H.: 'Discovering temporal association rules in temporal databases. Proceedings of international workshop on *Issues and applications of database technology* (IADT'98), Berlin, Germany, July 1998

6 WEISS, S. and INDURKHYA, N.: 'Predictive data mining' (Morgan Kaufmann Publishers, Inc., San Francisco, USA, 1998)

7 TANSEL, A., CLIFFORD J., GADIA, S., JAJODIA, S., SEGEV, A. and SNODGRASS, R.: 'Temporal databases: theory, design and implementation' (Benjamin/Cummings, Redwood City, CA, 1994)

8 SNODGRASS, R.T.: 'Temporal databases' *in* 'Advanced database systems' (Morgan Kaufmann Publishers, Inc., San Francisco, California, 1997) part 2

9 FAYYAD, U., PIATETSKY-SHAPIRO, G., SMYTH, P. and UTHURUSAMY, R.: 'Advances in knowledge discovery and data mining' (The AAAI Press/ The MIT Press, 1996)

10 IMIELINSKI, T. and MANNILA, H.: 'A database perspective on knowledge discovery', *CACM*, 1996, **39** (11)

11 SNODGRASS, R.: 'The temporal language TQuel', *ACM Trans. Database Syst.*, 1987, **12**, (2), pp. 247–298

12 ANDERSON, T.: 'Modelling time at the conceptual level'. Proceedings of international conference on *Databases: improving usability and responsiveness*, Jerusalem, Israel, June 1982, pp. 273–297

13 CLIFFORD, J. and TANSEL, A.U.: 'On an algebra for historical relational databases: two views'. Proceedings of the ACM SIGMOD international conference on *Management of data*, Austin, Texas, May 1985, pp. 247–265

14 CLIFFORD, J. and RAO, A.: 'A simple, general structure for temporal domains'. Proceedings of the IFIP 8/WG8.1 working conference on *Temporal aspects in information systems*, Sophia Antipolis, France, May 1987

15 NIEZETTE, M. and STEVENNE, J.M.: 'An efficient symbolic representation of periodic time'. Proceedings of the 1st international conference on *Information and knowledge management*, Baltimore, Maryland, 1992

16 CUKIERMAN, D. and DELGRANDE, J.: 'A language to express time intervals and repetition'. Proceedings of the international workshop on *Temporal representation and reasoning* (TIME-95), Florida, USA, April 1995

17 SOO, M.D. and SNODGRASS, R.T.: 'Multiple calendar support for conventional database management systems'. Technical report TR-92-07, Department of Computer Science, University of Arizona, 1992

18 CHANDRA, R., SEGEV, A. and STONEBRAKER, M.: 'Implementing calendars and temporal rules in next generation databases'. Proceedings of the international conference on *Data engineering*, 1994
19 TUZHILIN, A. and CLIFFORD, J.: 'On periodicity in temporal databases', *Inf. Syst.*, 1995, **20**, (8), pp. 619–639
20 KERAVNOU, E.: 'Temporal abstraction of medical data: deriving periodicity'. Proceedings of workshop on *Intelligent data analysis in medicine and pharmacology*, Budapest, Hungary, August 1996
21 PETROUNIAS, I.: 'A conceptual development framework for temporal information systems'. Proceedings of 16th international conference on *Conceptual modelling* (ER'97), Los Angeles, CA, USA, November 1997
22 SNODGRASS, R.T. (ed.), AHN, I., ARIAV, G., BATORY, D.S., CLIFFORD, J., DYRESON, C.E., ELMASRI, R., GRANDI, F., JENSEN, C.S., KAEFER, W., KLINE, N., KULKANRI, K., LEUNG, C.Y.T., LORENTZOS, N., RODDICK, J.F., SEGEV, A., SOO, M.D. and SRIPADA, S.M.: 'The TSQL2 temporal query language' (Kluwer Academic, Norwell, MA, 1995)
23 HAN, J., CAI, Y. and CERCONE, N.: 'Knowledge discovery in databases: an attribute-oriented approach'. Proceedings of the 18th international conference on *Very large databases*, British Columbia, Canada, 1992
24 HOLSHEIMER, H. and SIEBES, A.: 'Data mining: the search for knowledge in databases'. CWI technical report CS-R9406, 1994
25 MATHEUS, C.J., PIATETSKY-SHAPIRO, G., and McNEILL, D.: 'Selecting and reporting what is interesting: the KEFIR application to healthcare data' *in* FAYYAD, U.M. PIATETSKY-SHAPIRO, G., SMYTH, P. and UTHURUSAMY, R. (eds.) 'Advances in knowledge discovery and data mining' (AAAI Press/The MIT Press, 1996) pp. 495–514
26 AGRAWAL, R., FALOUTSOS, C. and SWAMI, A.: 'Efficient similarity search in sequence databases'. Proceedings of the 4th international conference on *Foundations of data organisation and algorithms*, Chicago, Oct. 1993
27 FALOUTSOS, C., RANGANTHAN, M. and MANOLOPOULOS, Y.: 'Fast subsequence matching in time-series databases'. Proceedings of ACM-SIGMOD international conference on *Management of data*, Minneapolis, MN, May 1994, pp. 419–429
28 BERNDT, D.J. and CLIFFORD, J.: 'Finding patterns in time series: a dynamic programming approach' *in* FAYYAD, U.M., PIATETSKY-SHA-PIRO, G, SMYTH, P. and UTHURUSAMY, R. (eds.): 'Advances in knowledge discovery and data mining' (AAAI Press/The MIT Press, 1996), pp. 229–248
29 AGRAWAL, R., LIN, K., SAWHNEY, H.S. and SHIM, K.: 'Fast similarity search in the presence of noise, scaling and translation in time-series databases'. Proceedings of the 21st international conference on *Very large databases*, Zurich, Switzerland, September 1995
30 AGRAWAL, R. and SRIKANT, R.: 'Mining sequential patterns'. Proceedings of the international conference on *Data engineering*, (ICDE), Taipei, Taiwan, March 1995
31 LONG, J.M., IRANI, E.A. and SLAGLE, J.R.: 'Automating the discovery of causal relationships in a medical records database' *in*

PIATETSKY-SHAPIRO, G. and FRAWLEY, W. (eds): Knowledge discovery in databases (AAAI Press, Menlo Park, CA, 1991), pp. 465–476

32 MANNILA, H., TOIVONEN, H. and VERKAMO, A.V.: 'Discovering frequent episodes in sequences'. First international conference on *Knowledge discovery and data mining*, (KDD'95), Montreal, Canada, August 1995, pp. 210–215

33 BETTINI, C., WANG, X.S. and JAJODIA, S.: 'Testing complex temporal relationship involving multiple granularities and its application to data mining'. Proceedings of ACM SIGACT-SIGMOD-SIGART symposium on *Principles of database systems*, 1996

34 AGRAWAL, R. and SRIKANT, R.: 'Fast algorithms for mining association rules'. IBM Research Report RJ9839, IBM Almaden Research Center, California, 1994

35 HAN, J., FU, Y., KOPERSKI, K., WANG, W. and ZAIANE, O.: 'DMQL: a data mining query language for relational databases'. SIGMOD'96 workshop on *Research issues on data mining and knowledge discovery*, (DMKD'96), Montreal, Canada, June 1996

36 MEO, R., PSAILE, G. and CERI, S.: 'A new SQL-like operator for mining association rules'. Proceedings of 22nd international conference on *Very large data bases*, (VLDB'96), Bombay, India, 1996

37 SHEN, W-M., ONG, K., MITBANDER, B. and ZANIOLO, C.: 'Metaqueries for data mining' *in* FAYYAD, U.M., *et al.*, (eds.): 'Advances in knowledge discovery and data mining' (AAAI Press/The MIT Press, 1996)

38 ALLEN, J.: 'Maintaining knowledge about temporal intervals', *Commun. ACM*, 1983, **26**(11)

Chapter 6
An integrated architecture for OLAP and data mining

Zhengxin Chen
University of Nebraska at Omaha, USA

Most chapters of this book present specific approaches or applications related to data mining. Unlike these studies, in this chapter we discuss unique features of data mining in the data-warehousing environment where online analysis processing (OLAP) takes place. We focus on the complementary roles of OLAP and data mining in the overall process of intelligent data analysis for decision-support queries. We start with a discussion on the intrinsic mismatch between OLAP and data mining at granularity/aggregation levels, including different types of query which can be answered, different semantics of rules which can be discovered and different heuristics which may be used. From this discussion we point out that there are at least two different ways of combining OLAP and data mining:

(i) incorporating data mining into an existing OLAP engine (that is, OLAP techniques and data-mining techniques are inter-twined together to analyse the same data);

(ii) incorporating the previous result of data mining as intensional historical data for current data analysis (here, the term intensional is used in the same sense as in intensional databases).

We introduce a feedback sandwich model (revised from Parsaye's recent proposals) to capture both types of combination. The top layer and the bottom layer of this model indicate premining and (conventional) data mining, respectively, and the filling part of the sandwich is the combined OLAP/data-mining engine. The intuition behind this model is that the flavour of data mining from the historical data (at the bottom layer) can enhance the taste of the filling (namely, OLAP and its extended functions for data mining on current/historical data). In addition, an integrated architecture for integrated OLAP/data mining is proposed. Several specific issues are further discussed to illustrate the use of this model and the proposed architecture. Among other things, we show how intensional historical data can provide useful hindsight for OLAP, including how to aid OLAP in selecting views to be materialised, and how to determine the schema for constructing materialised views which can be used for further data mining.

6.1 Introduction

Decision-support queries are *ad hoc* user queries in various business applications. In these applications, current and historical data are comprehensively analysed and explored, identifying useful trends and creating summaries of the data, in order to support high-level decision making in a data-warehousing environment [1,2]. A class of stylised queries typically involves group-by and aggregation operators. Applications dominated by such queries are referred to as online analysis processing (OLAP) [3].

Recently, the importance of integrating OLAP and data mining has been widely addressed by database practitioners from industry's perspectives, e.g. [4–6]. As a reply from academia for this practical need, studies on multiple-level data mining [7,8] can be viewed as a step closer to the goal of this integration. The various ways of mining knowledge at multiple concept levels, such as progressive deepening, progressive generalisation and interactive up-and-down, bear significant similarities to OLAP operations (such as roll-up and drill-down). More recently, research papers on integrated OLAP and data mining have started emerging, particularly from Han and his research group on the issue of incorporating data cubes into data-mining techniques [9–11]. However, the integration of OLAP and data mining is not limited to data cubes, and many other important aspects should also be studied.

In this chapter, rather than presenting new algorithms for integrated OLAP and data mining, we focus on the different and complementary roles of OLAP and data mining in the overall process of intelligent data analysis in data-warehousing environments; that is, we examine how to put together different aspects of OLAP and data mining.

6.2 Preliminaries

6.2.1 Decision-support queries

Decision-support queries comprehensively analyse/explore current and historical data, identify useful trends and create summaries of data to support high-level decision making for knowledge workers (executives, managers, analysts) [3]. There are three classes of data-analysis tool [2]:

(i)   *complex queries*: tools which support traditional SQL-style queries, but designed to support complex queries efficiently; relational DBMSs optimised for decision support applications;

(ii) *OLAP*: tools which support a class of stylised query which typically involves group-by and aggregation operators; applications dominated by such queries are called online analytic processing, or OLAP; these systems support a query style in which the data is best thought of as a multidimensional array, and are influenced by end-user tools such as spreadsheets, in addition to database query languages; OLAP systems work in a mostly-read environment;

(iii) *data mining (intelligent exploratory data analysis)*: discovery of interesting patterns in the data.

6.2.2 Data warehousing

Data warehousing provides an effective approach to dealing with complex decision-support queries over data from multiple sites. A data warehouse is a subject-oriented, integrated, time-varying, nonvolatile collection of data that is used primarily in organisational decision making [12]. The key to the data-warehousing approach is to create a copy of (or a derived copy) all the data at some one location, and to use that copy rather than the individual sources. Data warehouses contain consolidated data from many sources (different business units), spanning long time periods and augmented with summary information. Warehouses are much larger than other kinds of database, sizes are much larger, typical workloads involve *ad hoc*, fairly complex queries, and fast response times are important. Since decision support often is the goal of data warehousing, clearly warehouses may be tuned for decision support, and perhaps *vice versa*.

A typical data-warehousing architecture consists of the following:

• data marts are departmental subsets focused on selected subjects;

- back-end and front-end tools and utilities;
- metadata: the system catalogues associated with a warehouse are very large, and are often stored and managed in a separate database called a metadata repository.

Decision-support functions in a data warehouse involve hundreds of complex aggregate queries over large volumes of data. To meet the performance demands so that fast answers can be provided, virtually all OLAP products resort to some degree of these aggregates.

According to popular opinion [13], a data warehouse is usually based on relational technology, and OLAP uses a multidimensional view of aggregate data to provide quick access to strategic information for further analysis. A data warehouse stores tactical information that answers 'who?' and 'what?' questions about past events. OLAP systems go beyond these questions; they are able to answer 'what if?' and 'why?' questions. A typical OLAP calculation is more complex than simply summarising data.

6.2.3 Basics of OLAP

OLAP or multidimensional analysis is a method of viewing aggregate data called measurements (e.g. sales, expenses etc.) along a set of dimensions such as product, brand, stored, month, city and state etc. An OLAP typically consists of three conceptual tokens:

(i)   *dimension:* each dimension is described by a set of attributes;
(ii) *measure:* each of the numeric measures depends on a set of dimensions, which provide the context for that measure; the dimensions together are assumed to uniquely determine the measure and, therefore, the multidimensional data views a measure as a value in the multidimensional space of dimensions;
(iii) *domain hierarchy:* for example, country, state and city form a domain hierarchy.

There are several basic approaches to implementing an OLAP; for convenience of discussion, in this chapter we generally assume that ROLAP (relational OLAP) is used, where the aggregations are stored with the relational system itself.

The two most well known operations for OLAP queries are:

- *roll-up:* this operation takes the current data object and performs a further group-by on one of the dimensions; for example, given total sale by day, we can ask for total sale by month;

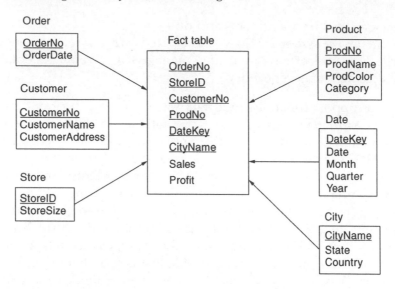

Figure 6.1   A star schema

- *drill-down:* as the converse of roll-up, this operation tries to get more detailed presentation for example, given total sale by model, we can ask for total sale by model by year.

Other operations include pivot (result is called a crosstabulation), slice (equality selection, reducing the dimensionality of data), dice (range selection) etc.

6.2.4 Star schema

Most data warehouses use star schemas to represent the multi-dimensional data model. In a star schema, there is a single fact table (which is at the centre of a star schema) and a single table for each dimension (dimension table) [3]. For convenience of discussion, we will use the star schema shown in Figure 6.1, which is slightly revised from the example which appeared in many recent publications, e.g. [3].

6.2.5 A materialised view for sales profit

Join operations in a star schema may be performed only between the fact table and any of its dimensions. Data mining has frequently been carried out on a relational view which is joined by the fact table with one or more dimension tables, followed by possible project and select

Table 6.1   Materialised view obtained by join operations on schema of Figure 6.1

RID	Product	P-colour	Store	S-size	Profit (1000$s)
0	jacket	blue	S1	small	− 20
1	jacket	blue	S2	medium	− 10
2	jacket	blue	S3	large	700
3	hat	green	S1	small	30
4	hat	green	S2	medium	− 100
5	hat	green	S3	large	− 10
6	glove	green	S1	small	200
7	glove	blue	S2	medium	− 30
8	glove	green	S3	large	20

operations. In addition, to facilitate data mining, such a view is usually materialised.

Table 6.1 is slightly revised from Parsaye [4], and can be considered as a materialised view obtained by join operations on the star schema shown in Figure 6.1. OrderID can be treated as TID in association rules. A row ID (RID) is used in the sense of bitmap indexing [2]. Both Figure 6.1 and Table 6.1 will be frequently cited in examples throughout the rest of this chapter.

6.3 Differences between OLAP and data mining

6.3.1 Basic concepts of data mining

The basic ideas and techniques in knowledge discovery in database (KDD) and data mining have been discussed by many researchers [14,15]. The particular aspect of data mining in which we are interested in this chapter is the fact that it can be carried out at different levels:

- *granularity level*: data at this level are individual elements and served as base data; various data-mining techniques have been developed and applied, including those discussions which can be found in other chapters of this volume;
- *aggregation level(s)*: data can be aggregated in many different ways; data at these levels are summary data; unique features of data-mining techniques at these levels have not been fully explored.

Although both OLAP and data mining deal with analysis of data, the focus and methodology are quite different. In this Section, we provide a discussion on this issue and use several examples to illustrate these differences. We point out the differences of data mining carried out at different levels, including different types of query which can be handled, different semantics of knowledge to be discovered at different levels, as well as different heuristics which may be used.

6.3.2 *Different types of query can be answered at different levels*

Different kinds of analysis can be carried out at different levels:

- *what are the features of products purchased along with promotional items?* The answer for this query could be association rule(s) at the granularity level, because we need to analyse actual purchase data for each transaction which is involved in promotional items (we assume information about promotional items can be found in product price).
- *what kinds of product are most profitable?* This query involves aggregation, and can be answered by OLAP alone.
- *what kinds of customers bought the most profitable products?* This query can be answered by different ways; one way is to analyse individual transactions and obtain association rules between products and customers at the granularity level; an alternative approach is to select all the most profitable products, project the whole set of customers who purchased these products, and then find out the characteristics of these customers; in this case we are trying to answer the query by discovering characteristic rules at an aggregation level (for example, customers can be characterised by their addresses).

6.3.3 *Aggregation semantics*

The above discussion further suggests that data mining at different levels may have different semantics. Since most people are familiar with semantics of knowledge discovered at the granularity level, here we will provide a discussion emphasising the kind of difference made by the semantics of knowledge discovered at aggregation levels (which will be referred to as aggregation semantics).

6.3.3.1 *Aggregation semantics for classification rules*

Recall the example in Table 6.1. In order to obtain rules to characterise the kinds of product which are profitable, we may first map the value of profit to a Boolean function yes or no. (Of course, we

Table 6.2   Summary data from aggregation operations as supported by data cube operator

Product	P-colour	Store	S-size	Profit (1000$s)
. . .	. . .	. . .	. . .	. . .
all	blue	all	all	640
. . .	. . .	. . .	. . .	. . .

may also use a more sophisticated multiple classification, e.g. profit 10 000 < profit < 20 000 will be classified as 'low' profit.) Classification rules can be discovered at the granularity level as usual. For example, we may have the following rule [4]:

Rule 6.1:
  if prodcolour = blue
  then profitable = no
  with confidence 0.75

Alternatively, we may apply aggregate functions on each particular kind of product; then, at aggregation level, there will be only one result (tuple) per each particular aggregation, so confidence will no longer make any sense. For example, if we apply the aggregation operations as supported by data cube operator [16], we will get the summary data shown in Table 6.2:

The following rule can be obtained:

Rule 6.2:
  if prodcolour = blue
  then profitable = yes

There is no need to specify confidence (because it is always 1).

Note that Rule 6.1 and Rule 6.2 are contradictory to each other. There is an inconsistency of knowledge discovered at the aggregation levels and at the granularity level. This is just an example of anomalies which may occur for data mining involving aggregation: knowledge discovered at the granularity level may not be (and usually is not) able to correctly derive results obtained at aggregation level. Since knowledge discovered at different levels has different semantics, there is no general answer to the question of 'which one is correct' when a kind of inconsistency exists.

Table 6.3   Summary table

Year	Month	sum(orderID)	sum(milk)	sum(bread)	sum(cigarette)	sum(beer)
1997	01	18 000	7000	8000	900	1000
1997	07	20 000	8000	9000	1600	5000

6.3.3.2 Aggregation semantics for association rules

Do association rules still make sense at aggregation levels? Maybe, but with different semantics. Consider the summary table in Table 6.3.

The primary key at the granularity level (orderID) has disappeared. We may be interested in how the sales data are related to the new primary key (year and month). Although at the granularity level TID serves only the purpose of the identifier (i.e., surrogate), the primary key in the summary table may bear more meaning, and may be used for explanation purpose. For example, the sale of beer is much higher in July than in January, because there were more outdoor social events in July than there are in January, owing to the weather.

The association between the sum of milk and the sum of bread is now examined in the orders involved in whole months, not in each individual order (namely, transaction). Therefore, in an extreme case, 7000 orders of milk may be from the same 8000 transactions which ordered bread, while in another extreme case, the purchase of milk and bread may be from 15 000 completely disjoint transactions.

But this is not to say that association rules will not make any sense at aggregation levels. The summary data obtained from different states may reveal some connections of attributes which can only be found at the aggregation level of the state. For example, we may have the following rule discovered:

Rule 6.3: states which have high sales in milk and eggs are likely to have high cheese sales in winter.

Note that what this rule said is different from saying that the same customer who purchased milk and eggs is likely to purchase cheese in winter. Therefore, association rules have different semantics between granularity and aggregation levels.

6.3.4 Sensitivity analysis

Related to the issue of inconsistency discussed above is the need for carrying out a kind of sensitivity analysis for knowledge discovered at aggregation levels. In fact, the change of a single value at the granularity level may significantly change the rules discovered at aggregation levels. Suppose we change the profit of RID 2 from 700 to ten, the overall evaluation for blue products will be changed significantly. Rule 6.1 remains true, if we can tolerate confidence at a lowered level (0.50). However, since the total profit as in Table 6.2 is now changed to -50, Rule 6.2 is no longer true. One well known lesson learned from this kind of example is to keep the numerical data as long as possible, namely, defer the mapping from numerical data to classifications [4]. However, the problem of how to determine the change of the numerical data which will affect the resulting classification is an issue yet to be studied.

6.3.5 Different assumptions or heuristics may be needed at different levels

Assumptions and heuristics are frequently needed to make the data-mining process more effective. For example, in order to discover rules characterising graduate students at the granularity level, the names of students can be dropped. Assumptions and heuristics are also important for data mining at aggregation levels, but they may be quite different from those at the granularity level.

Consider association rules at aggregation levels. We may compute the rate (percentage) of total orders for one product over some other products in each month. The following heuristic may be used: if for two products, the rate of orders is relatively stable over time, it may imply some kind of association between them; on the other hand, if the rate fluctuates highly, it may indicate little or no association between two products. For example, applying this heuristic to Table 6.3, we may find out that the total purchase of milk and total sale of bread is associated more closely than the total purchase of milk and total purchase of beer, because the total orders of milk changed very little from January to July (7000 to 8000), which is not proportional to the change of total orders for beer (from 1000 to 5000).

6.4 Combining OLAP and data mining: the feedback sandwich model

We have just examined the significant differences and intrinsic mismatch between OLAP and data mining; we have seen that there are a lot of tricky issues and pitfalls which need to be dealt with carefully. The purpose of the above discussion is to emphasise the challenges which must be faced in any effort to integrate them. In this Section we further examine two different ways of combining OLAP and data mining, and present the feedback sandwich model to capture both types of combination.

6.4.1 Two different ways of combining OLAP and data mining

6.4.1.1 Data-mining functions within the OLAP engine

We consider the following example from Parsaye [4]. We can verify that the following rules are valid based on Table 6.1:

- Rule 6.4: blue products are profitable overall, but much of the profit comes from jackets in large stores;
- Rule 6.5: green products are profitable too, but mostly in small stores.

An informal algorithm (or method) which is able to produce the above rules requires the following steps:

(i)   (pre)compute summary data grouped by product colour (using OLAP techniques);

(ii)   produce association/classification rule(s) associating product colour and profit (using data-mining techniques);

(iii) drill-down in the store dimension to produce revised association/ classification rules involving store size (using OLAP and data-mining techniques).

The last step is particularly interesting. How did we know that there is a need to drill-down in the store dimension, not any other dimensions? Or should we try to drill-down all dimensions and then discover the most important dimension? Useful methodologies and efficient algorithms should be developed, and even new operators for combined OLAP and data mining may be introduced.

This example illustrates the case which involves the interaction of OLAP and data mining on the same data (which may be a mix of historical and current data), and the need for incorporating data-mining functions within the OLAP engine. That is, an OLAP engine should be extended with certain data-mining facilities.

6.4.1.2 Data mining provides hindsight for online analysis of data

We now take a look at another way of combining OLAP and data mining. The need for premining in a data-warehousing environment has been well recognised [3]. The purpose of premining is to include useful data to construct the data warehouse and to provide some hindsight for the analysis of the data.

The idea of premining can be generalised to use the results obtained from data mining using previous (or historical) data. Such historical data can also shed light on the analysis of the current or future data. A unified way of treating previously discovered knowledge from historical data and knowledge obtained from premining has the advantage of providing some kind of impact on the warehouses where OLAP takes place. Note that the scenario described here is different from the scenario described in the previous subsection where OLAP and data-mining techniques are applied to the same data.

6.4.2 The feedback sandwich model

The discussion provided in the previous subsection can be summarised using a conceptual model, revised from an earlier model used by Parsaye [17] to capture the most important steps for data warehousing. The model consists of three elements: premining, warehouse the data, data mining. Since the warehouse sits in between the two steps of data mining, the model is referred to as the sandwich paradigm.

We now extend this paradigm in the following two ways. Note that the original sandwich model was used for data-warehouse design, but is now adopted and revised here for indicating a combination of OLAP and data mining:

1 First, the sandwich paradigm can be combined with Parsaye's other proposal [4] to reduce the gap between OLAP and data mining. According to this proposal, the task of data mining is to derive relationships among the dimensions; in other words, data mining is the analysis performed by rotating around the star schema. Therefore, the filling part of the sandwich is a rotating star schema, on which OLAP functionalities enriched by data-mining techniques can be performed.

2 Furthermore, we extend the sandwich paradigm by adding the feedback from the data-mining (bottom) layer to the filling layer. The intuition behind this feedback is that the taste of the 'meat and vegetable' (OLAP and its extended functions) in the filling part will be flavoured by the bottom-layer bread (data mining).

The result of these considerations is a feedback sandwich model, which puts emphasis on the overall process of combined OLAP and data mining. The model is depicted in Figure 6.2, where dark arrows denote connections among decision tables which are needed for data mining. Summary tables are not shown.

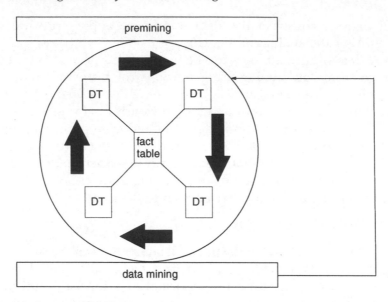

DT=dimension table

Figure 6.2   The feedback sandwich model

The top layer of this model indicates premining of data. The filling part of the sandwich is the combined OLAP/data-mining engine, which supports functionalities of both OLAP and data mining. The data-mining component can be embedded in the OLAP engine, can be maintained as a standalone component but closely interacting with the OLAP engine, or can be managed in some other form. The filling layer also takes care of multiple data-mining modules which may interact with each other for effective mining, as proposed in Han [9]. The bottom layer is the conventional data mining, the results of which can be used as a feedback to the filling part. Since tasks involved in data mining may be quite time consuming, the bottom layer also covers the case of some offline data-mining work which should be precomputed before its results can be used for OLAP and online data mining. Note that the bottom layer indicates discovered rules from the previous round of discovery which are to be 'carried' (or 'propagated') to the analysis in the future.

6.5 Towards integrated architecture for combined OLAP/data mining

To make use of the feedback sandwich model, an integrated architecture for combined OLAP/data mining is presented below; this

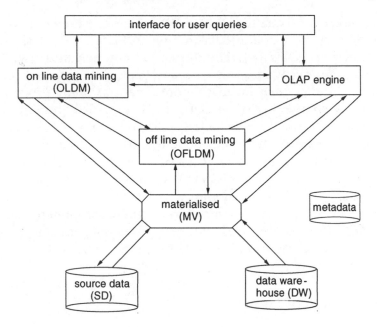

Figure 6.3   An integrated architecture for OLAP and data mining

architecture is proposed for data-warehousing environments. We focus on the different and complementary roles of OLAP and data mining in the overall process of intelligent data analysis in data-warehousing environments; that is, how to put together different aspects of OLAP and data mining.

Recall that the feedback sandwich model contains a loosely-coupled OLAP/data-mining engine, and sets emphasis on the feedback of previous data mining to current online analysis which involves both OLAP and DM. When this model is combined with the data-warehouse architecture as reviewed in Section 6.2, an integrated architecture for OLAP and data mining emerges, as shown in Figure 6.3.

It is interesting to point out that the architecture presented here can be considered as the result of adopting, revising and extending the integrated architecture of OLAP and data mining proposed by Han [9]. The major differences between our proposal and that of Han are the following:

(*a*) Our architecture is more general in that our discussion is concerned with materialised views (which are stored views) in general, rather than restricted to data cubes (which can be viewed as a restricted form of materialised views) as in the original diagram.

(*b*) As a direct consequence of the feedback sandwich model, we have considered both online data mining (OLDM) as well as offline data mining (OFLDM). The distinction between these two kinds of data mining is necessary, because the latter differs from the former in that it may involve a more time-consuming process, and it may also use historical data. Note that data mining in its traditional sense usually belongs to the latter. Also note the similarity between the results obtained from previous data mining on the one hand and materialised views on the other, because both are obtained from previous data and both are ready to be used for answering users' *ad hoc* queries.

(*c*) Since our focus is on the connection of these components (such as OLAP, MV, OLDM, OFLDM etc.), we will not include the application programs interface (API) in the current discussion.

6.6 Three specific issues

Using the feedback model and the integrated architecture as a guideline, we now discuss three specific issues related to combined OLAP/data mining. These three issues are: use and reuse of intensional historical data; how to benefit OLAP using data mining; how to enrich data mining using concepts related to OLAP.

6.6.1 On the use and reuse of intensional historical data

First, we provide some remarks on the use or reuse of discovered rules. In many cases, the rules (or other forms of knowledge) discovered from previous data are stored; they become intensional historical data and can be used or reused. Here the term intensional is used in the same sense as in intensional databases. Also note that the word historical refers to the knowledge discovered from previous data. The discovered knowledge (i.e., the intensional historical data) itself may or may not be time sensitive. This feature (or the absence of the feature) may affect how the intensional historical data may be used or reused.

To use a previously discovered rule is to apply that rule directly. The following are some examples to indicate how a previously discovered rule can be used in the case of nontime-sensitive data:

(i) *Provide predictions:* suppose that we have the following intensional historical data available:

Rule 6.6: in September 1997, the number of orders for blue products with prices which were marked x% down increased by $2x$% ($10 < x < 20$).

If a user wants to know in September 1998 when the price of blue jackets is to be marked down by 15 per cent, how the number of orders will be affected, then using the above rule a predicted increase of 30 per cent will be provided to the user as a quick response.

(ii) *Offer suggestions:* the above rule can also be used to guide users' decision making. For example, rule 6.6 can be used to suggest to users that they mark down the price for blue products if they want to have a significant increase in orders.

(iii) *Perform inference:* the above examples already indicate the use of inference (for example, *modus ponens* was used in prediction). Furthermore, the inference process can be carried out so that inference chains can be constructed. Suppose from the combined historical and current data, the following rule is discovered:

Rule 6.7: whatever the product, increasing the number of orders by 15 per cent or above will always bring significant profit.

From rules 6.6 and 6.7 the following can be inferred:

If we mark down the price for blue jackets in September 1998 by 12 per cent, then significant profit may be made.

In addition, time-sensitive intensional historical data can also be used for future data analysis and data mining, as exemplified in the following case:

(iv) *Perform second-order data mining:* generalisation or other forms of induction can be used to perform further data mining on intensional historical data. For example, consider the following summary table constructed from intensional historical data (i.e., each tuple is a rule discovered from previous sales):

On this summary table, we may perform further data mining in various directions, such as the impact of the colour or store size without considering years, or the general trend of colour or store size over years. Since this kind of analysis is to perform data mining on the intensional historical data, we call it second-order data mining. Second-order data mining provides an approach to deriving rules at aggregation levels.

Table 6.4

Year	ProdColour	StoreSize	Profitable
1994	blue	large	small
1994	yellow	small	large
. . .	. . .	. . .	. . .
1997	yellow	large	very large

Reuse of a previously discovered rule differs from direct use of a rule in that some adaptation or revision is needed before the discovered knowledge can be used. Just like when reusing a piece of previously developed software component, reuse of a rule requires necessary changes of some parameters. A kind of mapping may occur, which may take the form of analogical reasoning. The result of reusing a rule may be a derived candidate rule, the validity of which should be carefully checked. For example, consider the following intensional historical data rule 6.8, which is an association rule with certain support and confidence:

Rule 6.8: states that where there is a significant increase in the sale of sweet candies, there is also a moderate increase in the sale of iced tea.

An example of reusing this rule may result in the following somewhat speculative rule:

Rule 6.9: for states where there is a significant increase in the sale of salty peanuts, there may be a moderate increase in the sale of ginger ale.

Rule 6.9 is produced by using the following analogy:

sweet solid food : mild sweet liquid :: salt solid food : mild salt liquid

Of course, rules derived in this way should be validated carefully before they can actually be used (sometimes revision may be necessary). Since checking the validity of a candidate rule may incur less overhead than deriving a new rule, reuse may be an interesting technique deserving further exploration.

6.6.2 How data mining can benefit OLAP

In the following we describe several sample cases in which data mining may benefit OLAP.

6.6.2.1 Construction and maintenance of materialised views

Many data-mining techniques have already implicitly assumed the use of some basic functions of OLAP techniques; for example, the materialised view constructed from the star schema to be used for data mining. However, OLAP alone cannot decide which attributes should be used to form the schema of the view to be used for data mining. The feedback of data mining can be used to identify the most important attributes (that is, to determine the schema for constructing materialised views), as well as the most important conditions for selecting the data to be included in the materialised views.

Data mining may also provide help for handling indexing issues in evolving databases in a data-warehouse environment. The wave-index technique proposed by Shivakumar and Garcia-Molina [18] only considered the case where old data is deleted unconditionally. However, for various reasons, some old data should still be kept. Historical intensional data may provide useful hindsight for intelligently determining which old data should be kept, and for how long. Therefore, revised wave-indexing techniques can be developed.

6.6.2.2 Data-mining-guided aggregation for OLAP

In a previous section on the combined OLAP/data-mining engine, we mentioned that in order to determine which view should be materialised (precomputed), the common interests of *ad hoc* queries from existing and potential users should be studied.

Historical data mining may also provide a kind of guide for aggregation (namely, what and how to aggregate). For example, suppose from the historical data we have found that during weekends people tend to buy milk and bread together, but on weekdays they tend to buy milk and eggs together. After some promotional work based on the discovered knowledge (e.g., weekly special effective every Thursday or Friday), we may aggregate the sales involving transactions with milk and bread purchased together and the transactions involving milk and eggs together (rather than performing a new round of data mining) to see whether the promotion is effective. Note how data mining can guide the aggregation: previously we may not have known the need to precompute the sales of milk and bread together (although they were aggregated separately) from every Friday to the following Thursday (or from every Thursday to the following Wednesday). On the other hand, we will not precompute total sales involving eggs and bread together, because of a lack of significant association between these two items.

In a sense, the intensional historical data serves as a kind of knowledge base for data mining incorporating domain-related knowledge. Vendors of data-mining tools have already started providing products to support some kind of specialisation in data mining which can be customised for particular problems [6]. However, a theoretical examination is still needed.

6.6.2.3 Instructed construction of materialised views for data mining

We now further discuss how the need for data mining can instruct OLAP aggregation so that various materialised views can be constructed which can be used to discover rules at aggregation levels.

Yan and Larson [19] discussed a class of query transformation, called eager aggregation and lazy aggregation, which allows a query optimiser to move group-by operations up and down the query tree (eager group-by performs eager aggregation on all tables containing aggregation columns; lazy group-by is its reverse transformation). Their discussion was restricted to equivalent queries only; for example, they noted that group-by and join commutation cannot always be done. The issue of performing data mining at various aggregation levels is, of course, different from query rewriting involving aggregation functions (particularly, we are no longer worried about equivalence), but operations such as push-down and pull-up of group-bys can be adopted.

The following are some examples indicating different positions where aggregation may occur. We use the fairly standard syntax to indicate group-by and aggregation operations in relational algebra [20]. For convenience, the queries are expressed in formulae rather than as query trees. Also note that the following queries are not equivalent; rather, they indicate different rules which can be discovered corresponding to these aggregations. First, consider a materialised view constructed from the following query:

$$\Pi_{\text{storesize,prodcolour,profit}} \text{ store} \bowtie \text{fact} \bowtie \text{product}$$

There is no aggregation, and granularity-level rules may be discovered for storesize, prodcolour and profit. Now consider the following query:

$\Pi_{\text{storesize,prodcolour,profit}}\text{store} \bowtie \ _{\text{prodcolour}}G_{\text{sum profit}} \text{ fact} \bowtie \text{product}$

Using the materialised view constructed from this query, rules for granularity-level store size and grouped product colour and profit may be discovered.

By placing the group-by operator at different attributes, various materialised views can be constructed for data mining at aggregation levels or at mixed granularity-aggregation levels. In general, knowledge discovered earlier can always provide refined instructions for the construction of materialised views.

6.6.3 OLAP-enriched data mining

We now briefly describe another direction of connection between OLAP and data mining, namely, how OLAP can benefit data mining. Note that the data mining discussed in this subsection can be carried out at either the filling level (where data mining is intertwined with OLAP) or bottom level (where data mining is carried out as a separate task) of the feedback sandwich model.

6.6.3.1 Using OLAP to guide data mining

We use drill-down data mining as an example to illustrate how OLAP may provide useful guidelines for data mining. First, we note that summary data shows the general picture but lacks detail. For example, during a certain period, the sale of milk in Nebraska increased by ten per cent although, during the same period, the sale of milk dropped by five per cent in neighbouring Iowa. This could be caused by several factors. If we know that, during the same period, the sales of all kinds of goods dropped in Iowa but increased in Nebraska, then we may not need to pursue further analysis. On the other hand, if no convincing explanation exists, then we may have to perform some kind of data mining. In this case, the data-mining process is drill-down in nature, because we should examine several dimensions in more detail.

6.6.3.2 Discovery of influential association rules

Material presented so far in this chapter has largely consisted in discussions of proposed concepts for integrated OLAP/data mining. As an example of concrete results obtained from the research project guided by this author, in this subsection we sketch a recent study to illustrate how the OLAP-related concerns can enrich the study of data mining. In particular, we pay attention to a variation of association patterns. Given a transaction database, where each transaction is a set of items, an association rule is an expression of the form $X \Rightarrow Y$, where X and Y are sets of items. However, association patterns may be limited to basket data. For instance, in a sales database, the query 'how does product colour affect profits?' promotes 'colour' and 'profit' as the objects of analysis. The data domain of colour or profit is not the same as that of basket items, such as hat or glove. Moreover, the association between colour and profit (which is a numeric measure) suggests a new type of pattern—an influence pattern, which has not been covered by conventional association rules. The major purpose of influence patterns is to describe the influences of one set of objects called influencing factors on another set of objects called influence objects. Algorithms have been proposed for the discovery of influential association rules. Moreover, when conflicts exist for rules discovered at granularity and aggregation levels, a rule-refinement process is invoked to resolve the conflicts. This refinement process resembles the drill-down operation of OLAP. For example, when we consider the effect of product colour alone on the total sales, the rules obtained at the aggregation level may not agree with the rules obtained at the granularity level. The refined process may drill down to some other dimension (such as the time dimension), and resolve the difference by generating the following rule where two-dimensional attributes are involved:

<product colour, red> => <sales, high> with average value = 140, much of the sales come from <quarter, 4th> and <product, hat>.

A set of algorithms for the discovery and maintenance of influential association rules has been developed and a prototype system has been implemented. A very brief outline of the main algorithm for rule discovery is shown below. The terminology involved in the algorithm skeleton as well as a much more detailed discussion of this approach can be found in Chen [21].

Input: a relational view which contains a set of records and the questions for influence analysis;

Output: an influential association rule;

Method:
(i)   specify the dimension attribute and the measure attribute;
(ii) identify the dimension item sets and calculate support counts;
(iii) identify the measure item sets and calculate support counts;
(iv) construct sets of candidate rules, compute the confidence and aggregate value;

(v)   form a rule at the granularity level with greatest confidence, and form a rule at the aggregation level with largest abstract value of the measure attribute;

(vi)   compare the assertions at different levels, exit if comparable;

(vii)   for the case where the discovered rules are not comparable, derive the refined measure item set and the framework of the rule;

(viii)   if the value of the measure consists of both negative and positive values, form a rule indicating the summary value; otherwise, form a rule concerning average value;

(ix)   construct the final rule.

6.7 Conclusion

Data mining and online analysis processing (OLAP) are two complementary techniques for analysis of large amounts of data in data-warehouse environments to deal with decision-support queries. In this chapter we have examined the gap between these two techniques, and proposed a feedback sandwich model to combine OLAP and data mining. An integrated architecture has also been proposed. Our model and architecture differ from other proposals (e.g. [10]) in that they take care of the overall process of OLAP and data mining, offer flexibility for both loosely-coupled and tightly-coupled combinations of OLAP and data mining (because no particular structure of the extended OLAP/data-mining engine is specified) and allow the feedback of discovered knowledge to enhance future OLAP/data mining. We hope that the opinions presented in this chapter will stimulate more research efforts on the integration of OLAP and data mining.

6.8 References

1 WIDOM, J.: 'Research problems in data warehousing'. Proceedings of 4th *CIKM*. 1995

2 RAMAKRISHNAN, R.: 'Database management systems' (McGraw–Hill, 1998)

3 CHAUDHURI, S. and DAYAL, U.: 'An overview of data warehousing and OLAP technology', *SIGMOD Rec.*, 1997, **26**(1), pp. 65–74

4 PARSAYE, K.: 'OLAP & data mining: bridging the gap', *Database Program. Des.*, Feb. 1997, **10**(2), pp. 30–37

5 THOMSEN, E.: 'Mining your way to OLAP (decision support column)', *Database Program. Des.*. 1997, **10**(9), pp. 101–103

6 EDELSTEIN, H.: 'Where the data mining gold rush is headed (Decision support column)', *Database Program. Des..* 1997, **10**(12), pp. 78–79 and p. 85
7 HAN, J.: 'Mining knowledge at multiple concept levels'. Invited talk, Proceedings of *CIKM*, 1995
8 HAN, J. and FU, Y.: 'Discovery of multiple-level association rules from large databases'. Proceedings of 21st *VLDB*, 1995, pp. 420–431
9 HAN, J.: 'OLAP mining: an integration of OLAP with data mining'. Proceedings of 1997 IFIP conference on *Data semantics (DS–7)*, 1997, pp. 1–11
10 HAN, J.: 'Towards on–line analytical mining in large databases', *SIGMOD Rec.*, 1998
11 HAN, J., STEFANOVIC, N. and KOPERSKI, K.: 'Selective materialization: an efficient method for spatial data cube construction'. Proceedings of 1998 Pacific Asia Conference on *Knowledge discovery and data mining (PAKDD'98)*, 1998
12 INMON, W.H.: 'Building the data warehouse' (Wiley, 1996)
13 OLAP Council white paper, http://www.olapcouncil.org/research/whtpapco.htm, 1997
14 PIATETSKY-SHAPIRO, G. and FRAWLEY, W.J. (Eds.): 'Knowledge discovery in databases' (AAAI/MIT Press, Menlo Park, CA, 1991)
15 FAYYAD, U.M., PIATETSKY–SHAPIRO, G., SMYTH, P. and UTHUR-USAMY, R. (Eds.): 'Advances in knowledge discovery and data mining' (AAAI/MIT Press, Menlo Park, CA, 1996)
16 GRAY, J., BOSWORTH, A., LAYMAN, A. and PIRAHESH, H.: 'Data cube: a relational aggregation operator generalizing group-by, cross-tab, and sub-totals'. Proceedings of IEEE *Data Eng.*, 1996, pp. 152–159
17 PARSAYE, K.: 'The sandwich paradigm', *Database Program. Des.*, April 1995, **8**(4), pp. 50–55
18 SHIVAKUMAR, N. and GARCIA–MOLINA, H.: 'Wave–indices: indexing evolving databases'. *SIGMOD 1997*, pp. 381–393
19 YAN, W.P. and LARSON, P.-A.: 'Eager aggregation and lazy aggregation'. Proceedings of 21st *VLDB*, 1995, pp. 345–357
20 SILBERSCHATZ, A., KORTH, H.F. and SUDARSHAN, S.: 'Database system concepts' (McGraw–Hill, 1997, 3rd edn.)
21 CHEN, X.: 'Discovery of influential association rules'. Department of Computer Science, University of Nebraska at Omaha, 1998

Part II
Knowledge discovery and
data mining in practice

Chapter 7
Empirical studies of the knowledge discovery approach to health-information analysis

Michael Lloyd-Williams
University of Wales Institute Cardiff, UK

7.1 Introduction

Nowadays, digital information is relatively easy to capture and fairly inexpensive to store. The digital revolution has seen collections of data grow in size, and the complexity of the data therein increase. However, advances in technology have resulted in our ability to meaningfully analyse and understand the data which we gather lagging far behind our ability to capture and store this data [1]. A question commonly arising nowadays as a result of this state of affairs is, having gathered such quantities of data, what do we actually do with it [2]?

It is often the case that large collections of data, however well structured, conceal implicit patterns of information which cannot readily be detected by conventional analysis techniques [3]. Such information may often be usefully analysed using a set of techniques referred to as knowledge discovery or data mining. These techniques essentially seek to build a better understanding of data and, in building characterisations of data that can be used as a basis for further analysis [4], extract value from volume [5]. This Chapter describes a number of empirical studies in the use of the data-mining approach to the analysis of health information. The context is relatively unimportant, the examples described serving to highlight the factors perceived as influencing the success or otherwise of the data-mining approach in each case, and to illustrate the generic difficulties which may be encountered during the data-mining process, and how these difficulties may be overcome.

7.2 Knowledge discovery and data mining

It is generally accepted that the reason for capturing and storing large amounts of data is the belief that there is valuable information implicitly coded within it [2]. An important issue is, therefore, how is this hidden information (if it exists at all) to be revealed? Traditional methods of knowledge generation often rely largely upon manual analysis and interpretation [1]. However, as data collections continue to grow in size and complexity, there is a corresponding growing need for more sophisticated techniques of analysis [1]. One such innovative approach to the knowledge-discovery process is known as data mining.

Data mining is essentially the computer-assisted process of information analysis [4]. This can be performed using either a top-down or a bottom-up approach. Bottom-up data mining analyses raw data in an attempt to discover hidden trends and groups, whereas the aim of top-down data mining is to test a specific hypothesis [6]. Data mining may be performed using a variety of techniques, including intelligent agents, powerful database queries and multidimensional analysis tools [7]. Multidimensional analysis tools include the use of neural networks, such as described in the empirical studies presented in this chapter.

The data-mining approach expedites the initial stages of information analysis, thereby quickly providing initial feedback which may be further and more thoroughly investigated if appropriate. The results obtained are not (unless otherwise specified) influenced by pre-conceptions of the semantics of the data undergoing analysis. Patterns and trends may therefore be revealed that may otherwise remain undetected and/or not considered.

It should be clearly stated at this juncture that this chapter advocates the use of data-mining techniques in conjunction with traditional approaches to information analysis, and certainly not as a direct replacement.

7.2.1 The knowledge discovery process

According to Adriaans and Zantinge [8], there has been some confusion over the exact meanings of the terms data-mining and knowledge discovery. Indeed, some authors use the terms synony-mously and interchangeably. This chapter adopts the philosophy of those—including Adriaans and Zantinge [8] and Fayyad *et al.* [1]—who view data mining as being a key activity within the more elaborate process referred to as knowledge discovery. Therefore, from this point on, the term data-mining within this chapter is used to represent a specific activity within the knowledge-discovery process, namely, the analysis of data by means of data-mining software.

In its simplest form, knowledge discovery involves the capture of data and its manipulation to reflect the purpose of an investigation, the subjecting of this data to data-mining software and the interpretation of any results obtained. These results may, in turn, be subsequently used to direct the capture of further data which may also be fed into the knowledge-discovery process, thereby completing the virtual circle of Berry and Linoff [9]. A number of methodologies (which are essentially variations on this basic theme of data capture, data mining and interpretation of results) have been proposed which specify the steps involved in the knowledge-discovery process. These include those of Adriaans and Zantinge [8], Berry and Linoff [9] and Fayyad *et al.* [1]. The empirical studies presented within this chapter were performed using the approach proposed by Fayyad *et al.* [1], which asserts that the process of knowledge discovery *via* data mining can be divided into four basic activities as illustrated in Figure 7.1: selection, preprocessing, data mining and interpretation.

Selection involves creating the target dataset, i.e. the dataset about to undergo analysis. As discussed previously, modern datasets may be both large and complex. Large datasets which are not particularly complex may generally be subjected in their entirety to the analysis process (subject to technical constraints). Indeed, the larger the amount of available data, the greater the likelihood that an identifiable trend or pattern may be identified and statistically validated. However, if the dataset is relatively complex, it is often considered highly impractical to attempt to subject the complete set to analysis. It is a common misconception to assume that the complete dataset may be submitted to the data mining software, which in turn will resolve any problems and make sense of any inconsistencies which may be present. This is not, in fact, the case, partly because the data may well represent a number of different aspects of the domain which are not directly related. Subjecting such data to automated analysis may indeed result in the identification of patterns or trends, which in turn may be found to be statistically significant. However, these patterns are likely to be trivial or meaningless within the context of the main purpose of the investigation, and will therefore represent a waste of time and effort. Careful thought should therefore be given as to the

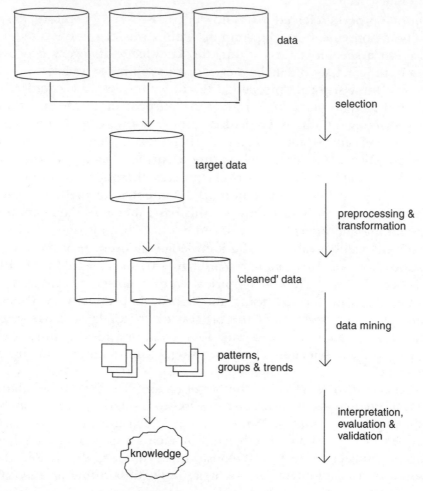

Figure 7.1   The knowledge-discovery process

purpose of the analysis exercise, and a target dataset created which contains data that reflects this purpose.

Preprocessing involves preparing a dataset for analysis by the data mining software to be used. The preprocessing activities may in fact result in the generation of a number of (potentially overlapping) subsets of the original target dataset, rather than a single dataset. Depending on the original source of the data and the storage format employed, preprocessing may also involve converting the data into a format acceptable to the data mining software being used. The manipulation of data during the preprocessing stage is sometimes referred to as cleaning [6].

Preprocessing may also involve activities such as resolving undesirable data characteristics, including missing data (noncomplete fields), irrelevant fields, nonvariant fields, skewed fields and outlying data points. This is not an exhaustive list of the potentially problematic forms of data; nevertheless it does provide an indication of the types of undesirable data characteristic which may be encountered. All of these characteristics have the potential to adversely impact upon any results obtained, sometimes in an extremely subtle manner. Such characteristics should therefore be either resolved or, at a minimum, recognised and documented prior to any further activities. Although sometimes time consuming, this will generally prove to be an extremely useful investment of effort. A brief description of undesirable data characteristics follows.

Noncomplete data fields are (as would be expected) those for which a proportion of records within a given dataset do not hold any information. There has been some discussion surrounding the proportion of records which may not hold information before the field should be considered incomplete (and therefore not included in the cleaned dataset). It has been suggested that data fields may generally be viewed as being complete if 70 per cent or more of the records contain values [10]. However, it is the opinion of the author that it is rather unwise to unilaterally accept such prescriptions, as the prevailing circumstances are likely to vary widely between projects. It is also felt that the 70 per cent threshold proposed is too low, and that a higher figure would be more appropriate. In cases where the field is considered theoretically complete, but in fact is less than 100 per cent complete, various techniques, such as estimation or assigning the category mode, are available for producing synthetic data. The generation of accurate values to represent missing data is currently one of the main research areas occupying the data mining community [11].

The experience of the author in conducting studies including those described later in this chapter suggests that the approach of making use of up to 30 per cent synthetic data is over simplistic, and that factors such as the dimensionality of the data undergoing analysis should also be taken into account when deciding whether a data field is sufficiently complete to warrant inclusion in the cleaned data. For instance, a dataset consisting of records made up of relatively few fields is likely to be far more sensitive to the effects of introducing synthetic data than would be a dataset consisting of records made up of a relatively large number of fields. Careful consideration should also be

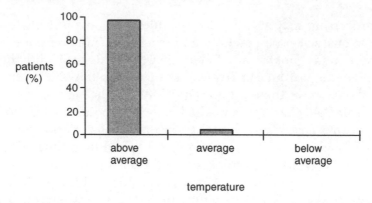

Figure 7.2   Nonvariant temperature field

given as to whether the proportion of synthetic data within a dataset is becoming too great. For instance, if a dataset consists of records made up of five fields, and if three of these fields require the generation of synthetic data, then it may be the case (if the 70 per cent threshold is being used) that 18 per cent of the cleaned data is in fact synthetic. Obviously, if the proportion of synthetic data does become too great, then any results obtained will be questionable.

Irrelevant fields are those that contain values which may be considered unimportant within the context of the purpose of the analysis exercise. For instance, a dataset containing information on patients admitted to hospital suffering from a particular medical condition may include personal information such as name, telephone number, next of kin, etc. This type of information would obviously be irrelevant within the context of the patient's condition, and should therefore be removed from the cleaned dataset prior to processing. However, care should be taken in deciding whether a field is irrelevant or not. For instance, the address field within the dataset (although apparently of a similar nature to the personal information) should not be considered irrelevant within this context, as the geographical location of each of the patients may indeed be a contributing factor to the medical condition.

Nonvariant fields are those for which there is little or no variation in value across all of the records within the dataset, and which therefore are unable to provide discriminatory information. For this reason, it is recommended that they should generally be removed from the cleaned dataset. For example, Figure 7.2 illustrates the temperatures of patients being admitted to hospital for treatment for a particular medical condition. It can be seen that 97 per cent of the patients had

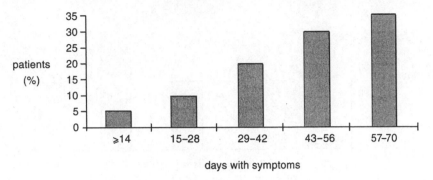

Figure 7.3   Skewed distribution of field values

an above average temperature upon admission, and that the field is therefore nonvariant in nature. We are unlikely to gain any meaningful insights by including this field in the processing, as we can see that temperature associated with this medical condition is generally always above average.

Skewed fields are those for which values are not normally distributed within a dataset. For instance, if we consider once more the example of hospital admissions, Figure 7.3 illustrates the number of days for which the patients experienced symptoms of the medical condition prior to admission to hospital. It can be seen that the distribution of values is skewed towards the right, with the largest number of patients (35 per cent) experiencing symptoms for between 57 and 70 days prior to admission.

A normal distribution would see the largest percentages towards the middle of the available range (in this case, between 29 and 42 days), and a uniform distribution would see roughly equal percentages of each of the available range of values. In a data mining exercise, either of these distributions would be preferable to a skewed distribution, with a uniform distribution being preferred (thereby providing equal numbers of records possessing each available value). If a variable is discovered to present a skewed distribution of values, then that variable should either be omitted from the cleaned dataset, or the skew should be corrected by the application of an appropriate mathematical function (as provided by numerous data-analysis software tools) to provide a more uniform distribution.

Outlying data points are those that fall outside the normal range of values for that particular data field. For instance, Figure 7.4 illustrates the distribution of ages of the patients in the hospital admissions example. It can be seen in Figure 7.4 that the age variable follows a

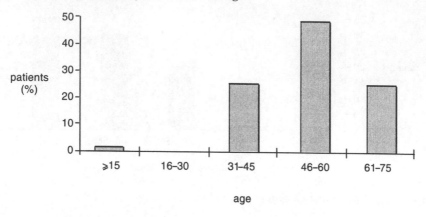

Figure 7.4   Outlying data point

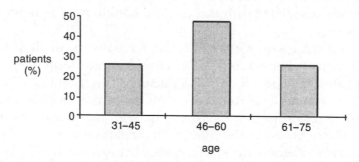

Figure 7.5   Normal distribution achieved

normal distribution, apart from an outlying data point (owing to two per cent of patients being within the age range ≥15). Such outlying data points would have the potential to distort any results obtained. It is therefore recommended that records representing outlying data points for any given field be removed from the dataset in order to produce a more normal distribution of values for that field (see Figure 7.5). In this example, the removal of the outlying data point (or clipping of the tail) only involves the loss of two per cent of the total data. Obviously, consideration should be given as to whether the amount of data to be removed constitutes too large a proportion of the available total. It may be argued that the removed data may hold some potentially interesting information (for instance, in this example, relating to why such young patients experienced the particular medical condition) and so should warrant further investigation. This may indeed be the case; however it is recommended that this data is examined by traditional means, and not as part of the automated (data-mining) process.

Data mining, as previously described, involves subjecting the cleaned data to analysis by data-mining software in an attempt to identify hidden trends or patterns, or to test specific hypotheses. The empirical studies presented in this chapter make use of a neural-network approach. However, it is important to recognise that many other techniques (such as data visualisation, genetic algorithms and decision trees) are also available. It is strongly recommended that any (apparently) significant results obtained during data mining are validated using traditional statistical techniques at this stage (i.e. prior to being presented to subject experts for further analysis).

Interpretation involves the analysis and interpretation of the results produced. Obviously, this stage will be driven primarily by input from experts in the domain under investigation. Results obtained during this activity may well instigate returning to previous stages to carry out additional activities in order to provide further information if necessary. Therefore, although the knowledge-discovery process may be viewed as comprising distinct stages, it is in practice highly iterative in nature.

7.2.2 *Artificial neural networks*

One of the techniques commonly associated with data mining is that of artificial neural networks. Neural networks are defined as information-processing systems inspired by the structure or architecture of the brain [12]. They are constructed from interconnecting processing elements which are analogous to neurones. The two main techniques employed by neural networks are known as supervised learning and unsupervised learning.

Supervised learning is essentially a two-stage process; first, training the neural network to recognise different classes of data by exposing it to a series of examples and, secondly, testing how well it has learned from these examples by supplying it with a previously unseen set of data.

Unsupervised learning is so called as the neural network requires no initial information regarding the correct classification of the data with which it is presented. The neural network employing unsupervised learning is able to analyse a multidimensional dataset in order to discover the natural clusters and subclusters which exist within that data. Neural networks using this technique are able to identify their

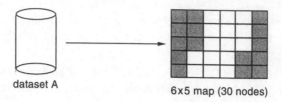

dataset A   6×5 map (30 nodes)

Figure 7.6   Data mapped onto a Kohonen self-organising map

own classification schemes based upon the structure of the data provided, thus reducing its dimensionality. Unsupervised pattern recognition is therefore sometimes referred to as cluster analysis [13].

The empirical studies presented in this chapter were carried out primarily using the unsupervised learning technique based upon the Kohonen self-organising map. The principles underpinning the Kohonen map have been described in some detail in works such as those by Kohonen [14] and Zupan and Gasteiger [15], and therefore only a brief description is provided here. The Kohonen map is essentially constructed as a two-dimensional grid of nodes. To each node within the grid is attributed a number of parameters corresponding to the number of fields making up the records within the incoming dataset. For instance, if the records within the dataset each consist of ten fields, then to each node within the Kohonen map are attributed ten parameters. The values of these parameters are initially randomly assigned.

Each record within the dataset is then presented sequentially to the grid. The nodes within the grid compete in order to represent the data pattern currently being presented. One node will win this competition (the node with the parameter values most closely resembling the values of the fields within the incoming record), and will have its parameters altered so that if this same data pattern were to appear again, the same node would have the best chance of winning. The overall effect is a two-dimensional grid of nodes which each respond to some subset or cluster of the incoming multidimensional data. Differing patterns are represented by nodes which are separated on the grid by varying distances, according to the level of difference. Similar clusters of data will therefore appear in close proximity on the output map, and differing clusters will be clearly separated, the distance between them varying according to the level of difference.

The overall principle is illustrated in Figure 7.6. The content of dataset A has been mapped onto a 6×5 map, the shaded areas of the map representing the locations of the nodes which represent the data. It can be clearly seen that the content of dataset A can in fact be viewed as comprising two distinct clusters of data. If dataset A contained details of patients experiencing a particular medical condition, then Figure 7.6 clearly suggests that although all the patients are experiencing the same condition, they may in fact be divided into two distinct categories or types, a situation which may warrant further investigation.

In summary, the Kohonen map maps the high-dimensional continuous space occupied by the input data patterns into a lower-dimensional discrete space formed by an organised lattice of nodes [16]. Given its ability to organise data in terms of the natural relationships which exist within that data [17], the Kohonen self-organising map was viewed by those conducting the empirical studies described in this chapter as being a particularly useful tool. The Kohonen-map approach has been widely and successfully used in multivariate data analysis, and being closely related to other methods (such as the *k*-means type), is often seen as the best choice of analysis method from an interpretational point of view [18].

7.3 Empirical studies

This Section presents details of three empirical studies of the application of the knowledge-discovery approach to the analysis of health information. The information analysed during these studies was extracted from the World Health Organisation's 'Health for all' database, the 'Babies at risk of intrapartum asphyxia' database and a series of databases containing infertility information. These studies serve to highlight the factors perceived as influencing the success or otherwise of the projects concerned, to illustrate the generic difficulties which may be encountered during the data-mining process and to examine how these difficulties might have been overcome.

7.3.1 The 'Health for all' database

The World Health Organisation's (WHO) 'Health for all' (HFA) database was created to make health-related data collected by the WHO available to outside users. The database contains statistical indicators for the WHO HFA targets relating to 'Health for all' in Europe by the year 2000. These include: better health, mortality/ morbidity, lifestyles conducive to health, healthy environment, health services and health policies. Other statistical indicators relate to demographics, socioeconomics and other supplementary health-related information. Data are present for all European countries and include those countries in existence before and after the recent political changes in central and eastern Europe as well as the former Soviet Republics. Data are included from 1970 to 1993 inclusive, although it is important to note that there are gaps in the data that are available.

The approach taken to analysing the HFA database generally corresponded with that illustrated in Figure 7.1. During the selection process, mortality data relating to the following conditions were extracted from the database: life expectancy at birth; probability of dying before five years of age; infant mortality; postneonatal mortality; standardised death rates (SDR) for circulatory diseases; SDR for malignant neoplasms; SDR for external causes of injury and poisoning; SDR for suicide and self-inflicted injury.

Data were extracted for 39 European countries. Although a far higher number of countries are represented on the database, the data could only be considered complete for 39 of them. The data were then converted into a format acceptable to the software being used. An underlying aim of the study was to track any changes in the data that may have occurred over the years for the same samples of countries in order to examine whether any patterns identified remained consistent over time. This necessitated the selection of data that were separated by intervals of three to four years (where possible) since it was expected that changes, if any, would be more apparent on this time scale. Three years was the chosen interval, giving three subsets of data (1982, 1986 and 1989). The extracted data were then analysed by custom-written Kohonen self-organising map software in order to identify possible groupings. Finally, standard statistical techniques were used to evaluate the validity of the groupings. This investigation therefore made use of the bottom-up data-mining approach described previously.

Preliminary work resulted in two distinct groups or clusters of countries in each year being apparent [19]. The health profiles of the two groups identified during the preliminary analysis are as follows.

Group 1:
• Relatively low mean life expectancy in comparison with group 2, coupled with relatively high probability of dying before five years of age and infant mortality rate; the range of life expectancies in this group is between 65.1 and 72.3 years; the mean probability of dying

before five and the mean infant mortality rate are more than twice those of group 2;
- relatively high SDRs for diseases of the circulatory system and for external causes of injury and poisoning;
- mean SDR for suicide and self-inflicted injury is only marginally higher than in group 2;
- although the mean SDR for malignant neoplasms is lower than that of group 2, this has been increasing over the years.

Group 2:
- relatively high mean life expectancy in comparison with group 1, coupled with relatively low probability of dying before five, and infant mortality rate; the lowest mean life expectancy in this group is 74.4 years, and the highest is 77.8 years (in 1989); the probability of dying before five and infant mortality rate have declined over the years, and mean life expectancy has increased over the period under consideration; a similar trend is also observed in group 1;
- relatively low mean SDR for diseases of the circulatory system, and declining; the mean SDR for external causes of injury and poisoning is just over half the mean value for group 1 in 1989;
- the mean SDR for malignant neoplasms declined slightly 1982–86 (in contrast to the trend in group 1).

It was observed that all countries in the first of the groups were from central and eastern Europe or from the former Soviet Republics, and all countries in the second group were from northern (i.e. the Nordic countries), western or southern Europe. A two-sample *t*-test was used to validate the groupings identified. The results obtained confirmed that the identified groups were significantly different or separated from each other.

In addition to the geographical division, the classification also appeared to reflect differences in wealth. Countries in the first of the groups were relatively poor; all countries (excluding the former Soviet Union) had GNP *per capita* of less than US$5000 in 1989 (the latest year for which GNP figures were available). Countries in the second of the groups were relatively wealthy; all countries had GNP per capita exceeding US$5000 (except Portugal, for which the 1989 GNP *per capita* was just under US$4300). A *t*-test was performed, and the result indicated a significant difference between the two groups in terms of GNP per capita. The observation that the classification appeared to reflect two different GNP groups suggested that GNP could be interrelated with the health indicators. In order to further explore this possibility, the coefficient of correlation was calculated between GNP and all seven HFA indicators used in the initial analysis. Results obtained indicated that GNP is strongly and positively correlated with life expectancy, and strongly but negatively correlated with the SDR for diseases of the circulatory system. A small and positive correlation was found to exist between GNP and the SDR for malignant neoplasms, with fairly large negative correlations between GNP and all the other indicators, except the SDR for suicide and self-inflicted injury. Overall, the available data indicated that death rates for malignant neoplasms tended to rise with increasing affluence, and death rates for other diseases tended to fall.

Further work was then performed in order to obtain a finer classification. This work resulted in the identification of six groups, which were essentially subdivisions of the two groups produced by the preliminary work [20]. Characteristics of the groups ranged from the lowest life expectancy, coupled with the highest probability of dying before five and infant mortality rate (group 1), to the highest mean life expectancy, coupled with the lowest probability of dying before five and infant mortality rate (group 6). Over time, mean life expectancy increased, and the probability of dying before five and infant mortality rate both decreased for all groups. Detailed summary statistics of each group may be found elsewhere [21].

Group membership of all six groups remained relatively stable over the period under consideration. Eight of the 39 countries did experience movement between groups over the years; however, in all such cases cumulative movement was limited to an adjacent group.

In order to validate the groupings identified, Euclidean distances were calculated, and the generalised *t*-test used to find out if the underlying means of each group pair were significantly different from each other. Results obtained confirmed that the identified groups were significantly different or separated from each other. The classifications obtained can therefore be said to be valid, based upon the available data.

The success of the application of the data-mining approach to the analysis of the HFA database may be attributed to a number of factors, as follows. Careful initial selection and associated preprocessing ensured that the target dataset was largely complete, containing only highly relevant data appropriate to the investigation. No nonvariant or skewed fields were included. Similarly, no fields in the available data contained outlying data points.

7.3.2 The 'Babies at risk of intrapartum asphyxia' database

The 'Babies at risk of intrapartum asphyxia' database was analysed in conjunction with staff at the Sheffield Children's Hospital. This database contains data collected from a wider study on the relationship between intrapartum asphyxia and neonatal encephalopathy (NE). Neonatal encephalopathy is a condition characterised by impairment of consciousness, and abnormalities of muscle tone and of feeding. There is also frequent evidence of injury to other organs such as the heart, kidney and gastrointestinal system. Neonatal encephalopathy is thought to arise when there is significant intrapartum asphyxia, that is, the foetus is deprived of oxygen during labour.

The 'Babies at risk of intrapartum asphyxia' database contains detailed obstetric data, including cardiotocogram[1] (CTG) traces taken during labour. Both the foetal heart rate (FHR) and the uterine contractions are represented on the trace produced. Also present on the database are prelabour assessments of maternal and antenatal risk factors which might influence the outcome of the labour. Factors relating to the quality of intrapartum obstetric care are also recorded.

In order to construct the database, the paper CTG traces were manually analysed by dividing each trace into 30-minute epochs, and then examining each epoch for abnormal FHR patterns. A severity score was then applied to each abnormality detected. Each of the 128 patients represented on the database is therefore associated with a number of epochs, the average being 14 (the minimum being one, and the maximum being 40, indicating periods of labour of 30 minutes and 20 hours, respectively). Each epoch in turn is further described using a number of parameters representing various aspects of the associated FHR.

All activities relating to data capture, analysis and initial database construction were carried out by medical staff involved in the wider study on the relationship between intrapartum asphyxia and neonatal encephalopathy.

Owing to the purpose of the main study, much of the data represented on the database is encoded, rather than being specifically represented. For instance, the baseline FHR in beats per minute (bpm) recorded on the database varies from 100–109 at the lowest level to >180 at its highest. The baseline FHR is recorded on a scale of − 2 (representing 100–109 bpm) to +3 (representing >180 bpm). These figures represent whether or not the baseline FHR is slower or

---

[1] Monitoring both foetal heart rate (*cardio*) and uterine contractions (*toco*).

faster than would be expected. The bradycardia parameter is used to indicate a slow FHR (<100 bpm). In the absence of bradycardia, this parameter is set to zero (normal). A period of greater than three minutes with recovery is represented by a value of +3, and a value of +4 if there is no recovery. This use of a zero value to indicate a normal reading is employed in a large proportion of the parameters of the database.

The Kohonen self-organising-map software employed to analyse the dataset expects the data therein to be presented on an interval or ordinal scale, that is, that the range of parameter values stand in some relationship to each other. The software also expects values which lie adjacent to each other within a parameter range to be similar to each other. However, some parameters on the database occupy a nominal scale where parameter values do not relate at all to each other. For instance, the uterine contractions parameter is represented as zero (normal), +3 (over contracting) or +1 (the recording of the contraction on the trace is technically poor). This parameter was therefore considered to be inappropriate for use in its existing form, and removed from the target dataset.

Initial work was not without its difficulties, owing to the nature of the data involved. At one stage of processing, 52 per cent of the available dataset presented parameters which were all set to zero (indicating a normal response), apart from the baseline FHR. This extremely high level of nonvariant data resulted in no discernible patterns being present at the early stage of work.

After performing further selection and preprocessing activities (including the removal of the majority of nonvariant data), some success was achieved. Two distinct groups were identified within the database, and their existence statistically validated using a two-sample *t*-test. Further work involved the training of a neural network employing the radial-basis-function (RBF) approach to recognise the two groups, and to differentiate between members of these groups. During this period, an overall probability of correct recognition of 85 per cent was achieved, providing further evidence that the groups identified did exist within the database.

Further work on the database resulted in a refinement of the original two groups being achieved. The resulting four groups were again found to be statistically different from each other, each exhibiting specific combinations of FHR patterns. The use of the RBF software again resulted in successful identification of the groups, with 100 per cent of records within the first group, 97 per cent of records within the second group and 99 per cent of records within the third and fourth groups being correctly identified.

Although the identification of statistically valid groups may indicate that this data-mining exercise was successful, it should be noted that the data used to obtain these groups represented only a proportion of that available. The high proportion of nonvariant data present precluded much of the database from being used in the analysis process. Further limiting factors in this case included the use of a nominal scale to represent certain parameters. The fact that the data provided had already undergone precoding by a subject expert also placed clear restrictions on the ability to perform any subsequent meaningful data manipulation, as the original data values were in many instances unknown, and the subject expert who had performed the coding unavailable.

7.3.3 Infertility databases

Despite recent improvements in infertility diagnosis and the increase in sophistication and variety of treatment techniques, there still appears to be great difficulty in successfully predicting how a particular patient will respond to a specific treatment. Although many types of data can be collected which in theory are relevant to the likelihood of successful treatment, in reality the complexity of the interactions between these parameters appears to be beyond the current capabilities of conventional methods of analysis. The primary aim of this investigation was therefore to investigate the use of the data-mining approach to assist in predicting whether a specific patient would be successfully treated using a particular treatment pathway. Against this background, three databases holding data relating to three different aspects of infertility diagnosis and treatment were provided for analysis using the data-mining approach.

The first of these databases contained details of patients who had undergone ovulation-induction with gonadotrophins. This database was analysed in conjunction with staff at the Jessop Hospital, Sheffield. Ovulation induction with gonadotrophins is one of the first treatment options available to infertility specialists, and is aimed at patients who are not ovulating normally. The principle of the treatment is to stimulate the ovaries to produce a single mature follicle, and for fertilisation to occur subsequently by natural means. The ovulation induction database holds 17 parameters for each of the 122 patients represented. Information held within the database relates to such factors as age, duration of infertility, the number of live births, pregnancies and miscarriages in the past, whether the patient is a smoker, the menstrual pattern (in terms of days), ovulatory status, tubal status and details of any past treatments. The database also includes information relating to the treatment outcome for each patient, i.e. whether the patient became pregnant or not. The main objective of this study was to attempt to identify the combination of patient characteristics which appeared to indicate a successful (or otherwise) treatment outcome. Such information would be of benefit to both patient and clinician in providing an indication of whether a particular treatment pathway is likely to be successful, prior to embarking upon that pathway.

A second database containing details of patients who had undergone stimulated cycles of *in vitro* fertilisation (IVF) treatment was analysed in conjunction with staff at St. Michael's Hospital, Bristol. IVF involves fertilisation of the female eggs outside the body, and subsequently transferring the resulting embryos to the female's womb. Each of the 403 patients represented by the IVF database had had three fertilised eggs implanted (perceived as being the optimal number required to achieve one successful pregnancy while avoiding multiple pregnancies). For each patient represented on the database, there were therefore four possible outcomes (0–3 pregnancies). Information held on the database includes details of the treatment outcome, the number of children the couple have previously had together, the number of children the female and male have previously had (together and otherwise), the diagnosis of the case, details of mobile sperm density, details of donor insemination (if applicable), the number of eggs collected, the number of mature eggs collected, the number of embryos formed, and the age of the patient receiving the eggs. The main aim of this study was to identify the characteristics of patients who are most likely to achieve a single successful pregnancy, the clinicians wishing to avoid the potential for multiple (and hence potentially complicated) pregnancies.

A third database containing details of 65 patients who had undergone natural-cycle IVF treatment was also analysed in conjunction with staff at St. Michael's Hospital, Bristol. Each patient is represented on the database by 12 parameters and a corresponding diagnostic category (endometriosis, tubal damage or unexplained infertility). Information held on the database includes details of the treatment outcome, the follicle diameter from two days before treatment to the day of treatment, and corresponding measurements (from two days before treatment to one day after treatment) of serum oestradiol and luteinising hormone. The aim of this study was slightly different from the previous two described in attempting to determine whether the specific combination of 12 parameter values could be associated with the diagnostic category of the patient.

All three databases were analysed by making use of the custom-written Kohonen self-organising-map software and, where appropriate, a neural network employing the RBF approach was also used. However, the knowledge discovery *via* data-mining approach failed to provide the information which was specifically required in all three of the cases described. During the initial stages of investigation, all three datasets provided appeared to be highly suitable for analysis using the knowledge discovery approach. Despite the fact that some parameters represented data values using a nominal scale, the original databases exhibited little missing data, few irrelevant fields, no nonvariant fields, few skewed fields and few outlying data points. Any limited undesirable characteristics that were originally present were subsequently removed during the selection and preprocessing activities.

The main problem encountered during this investigation appears to be fundamental in that the patterns representing the information required appeared not to be present within the available datasets. It was therefore concluded that the knowledge discovery *via* data-mining approach was unable to assist in the analysis of the data provided. This appeared to be primarily due to the fact that the range of factors which fully determine a couple's ability to conceive is not known. It is therefore reasonable to assume that, in this case, the pattern (or a recognisable proportion of that pattern) formed by these factors was not present in the data provided.

7.4 Conclusions

This chapter has provided an introduction to the concepts of knowledge discovery and data mining. The empirical studies presented are intended to highlight the factors perceived as contributing to the success or otherwise of the knowledge discovery *via* data-mining approach in each of the cases presented.

It should be evident from the studies described that the potential for the success of a knowledge-discovery exercise is determined to a large extent prior to the actual data-mining activity, i.e. during the activities performed leading up to the production of the cleaned data. Extreme care should therefore be taken during selection and preprocessing activities in order to ensure wherever possible that the target dataset actually contains relevant and usable data. Actions performed during the early stages of the data-mining process can clearly determine the success (or otherwise) of the project. This point was evidenced by the analysis of the 'Babies at risk of intrapartum asphyxia' database, where coding activities performed as a result of a wider study precluded much of the data from analysis by data mining. Given that the likelihood of success or otherwise of a knowledge discovery *via* data-mining project is highly dependent upon the quality and format of the data made available, the amount of time and effort required to prepare suitable data will be a very useful investment, even if at times the required effort might appear excessive when measured against the time available for the project as a whole.

It is also apparent from the studies described (and in particular, the analysis of the infertility databases) that if the data provided does not contain useful information within the context of the focus of the investigation, then any amount of data mining cannot generate such information any more than traditional analysis techniques can. However, it may well be the case that the use of neural networks for data mining does allow this conclusion to be reached more quickly than might ordinarily be the case.

Finally, it should be stated once more that this chapter advocates the use of data mining as an approach which can be used to expedite the initial stages of information analysis in order that the results obtained may be more thoroughly investigated. It should be used in conjunction with traditional approaches, not in direct competition.

7.5 References

1 FAYYAD, U., PIATETSKY-SHAPIRO, G. and SMYTH, P.: 'The KDD process for extracting useful knowledge from volumes of data', *Commun. ACM*, 1996, **39**(11), pp. 27–34
2 FAYYAD, U. and UTHURASAMY, R.: 'Data mining and knowledge discovery in databases', *Commun. ACM*, 1996, **39**(11), pp. 24–26
3 LLOYD-WILLIAMS, M., JENKINS, J., HOWDEN-LEACH, H., MATHUR, M., MORRIS, C. and COOKE, I.: 'Knowledge discovery in an infertility database using artificial neural networks'. IEE colloquium on *Knowledge discovery in databases*, IEE Digest 1995/021(B)
4 LIMB, P.R. and MEGGS, G.J.: 'Data mining—tools and techniques', *Br. Telecom Technol. J.*, 1995, **12**(4), pp. 32–41
5 SCARFE, R. and SHORTLAND, R.J.: 'Data mining applications in BT'. IEE Colloquium on *Knowledge discovery in databases*, IEE Digest 1995/021(B)
6 HEDBERG, S.R.: 'The data gold rush', *Byte*, 1995, **20**(10), pp. 83–88
7 WATTERSON, K.: 'A data miner's tools', *Byte*, 1995, **20**(10), pp. 91–96, 4

8 ADRIAANS, P. and ZANTINGE, D.: 'Data mining' (Addison-Wesley, Harlow, 1996)

9 BERRY, M.J.A. and LINOFF, G.: 'Data mining techniques' (Wiley, New York, 1997)

10 SPSS Inc.: 'Neural connection applications guide' (SPSS Inc., Chicago, 1995)

11 FAYYAD, U., PIATETSKY-SHAPIRO, G., SMYTH, P. and UTHURASAMY, R.: 'Advances in knowledge discovery and data mining' (AAAI/MIT Press, Cambridge, 1996)

12 CAUDILL, M. and BUTLER, C.: 'Naturally intelligent systems' (MIT Press, Cambridge, 1990)

13 BACKER, E.: 'Cluster analysis by optimal decomposition of induced fuzzy sets'. Delftse Universitaire Pers. Thesis, Delft University, 1978

14 KOHONEN, T.: 'Self-organisation and associative memory' (Springer-Verlag, New York, 1988)

15 ZUPAN, J. and GASTEIGER, J.: 'Neural networks for chemists' (VCH, Weinheim, 1993)

16 WILKINS, M.F., BODDY, L. and MORRIS, C.W.: 'Kohonen maps and learning vector quantization: neural networks for analysis of multivariate biological data', *Binary*, 1993, **6**, pp. 64–72

17 DAYHOFF, J.E.: 'Neural networks architecture: an introduction' (Van Nostrand Reinhol, New York, 1990)

18 MURTAGH, F. and HERNÁNDEZ-PAJARES, M.: 'The Kohonen self-organizing map method: an assessment', *J. Classification*, 1995, **12**, pp. 165–190

19 LLOYD-WILLIAMS, M., WILLIAMS, S., BATH, P. and MORRIS, C.: 'Knowledge discovery in the WHO Health for all database: developing a taxonomy of mortality patterns for european countries', *in* RICHARDS, B. and De GLANVILLE, H. (Eds): 'Current perspectives in healthcare computing. Proceedings of HC96, 1996, Weybridge; BJHC, pp. 551–556

20 LLOYD-WILLIAMS, M. and WILLIAMS, S.: 'A neural network approach to analysing healthcare information', *Topics in Health Information Management*, 1996, **17**(2), pp. 26–33

21 WILLIAMS, T.S.: 'Knowledge discovery in the WHO health for all database: developing a taxonomy of mortality patterns for European countries'. MSc thesis, University of Sheffield, Sheffield, England, 1995

Chapter 8

Direct knowledge discovery and interpretation from a multilayer perceptron network which performs low-back-pain classification

M. L. Vaughn and S. J. Cavill
Cranfield University (RMCS), UK

S. J. Taylor, M. A. Foy and A. J. B. Fogg
Princess Margaret Hospital, UK

8.1 Introduction

At some time in their lives 60–80 per cent of the population will experience one episode of low-back pain (LBP), of whom 90 per cent will get better within six to eight weeks without need for treatment or investigation [1,2]. The remaining ten per cent incur 70–90 per cent of the medical costs arising from low-back pain and represent a challenge to health practitioners in providing an accurate diagnosis and successful management [3]. The number of patients who receive a specific diagnosis is small and several authors have highlighted the difficulty of diagnosing LBP [3,4]. Low-back pain is a multifactorial problem that includes physical, psychological and social aspects of illness [2].

The costs of back pain to society are very high and continue to rise. UK government statistics [1] for 1993–94 estimate 106 million working days lost in the UK due to back-pain incapacity, £480 million annual National Health Service costs for back-pain treatment, £3.5 billion costs to industry in lost production and £1.4 billion in social security benefits.

In previous research Bounds *et al.* [5,6] evaluated the performance of artificial neural networks (NNs) for the classification of low-back-pain patients. It was found that the mean diagnostic accuracy of the NN predictions was higher than the mean accuracy produced by the clinicians. Neural networks are being increasingly used as decision-support tools [7,8] and are well suited to classification problems of this type since they are robust, fault tolerant and generalise to similar input cases. However, neural networks are currently undermined by their inability to explain or justify their output classifications [9].

Using a new method published by the first author [10], the multilayer perceptron (MLP) network can be 'opened' and directly interpreted on a case-by-case basis to provide user explanation facilities and discover previously unknown data relationships. The method enables the knowledge learned by the MLP network from an input training case to be expressed as a data relationship from which a valid rule can be directly induced [11], avoiding the need for a combinatorial search-based approach [9]. The validation of all the training-data relationships, with the assistance of domain experts, then provides a method for validating the MLP network.

The aim of this chapter is to discover the key inputs which a low-back-pain MLP network uses to classify selected training-case examples using Vaughn's knowledge-discovery method and to show how a rule can then be directly induced from each training example. Preliminary results are presented of the top-ranked key inputs which the LBP MLP uses to classify all training cases for each diagnostic class. It is shown how the validation of the top-ranked key inputs by the domain experts can lead to the validation of the LBP MLP network during both training and testing.

8.2 The MLP network

The MLP network is one of the most widely used neural networks in the field of neural computing [7,8] and came into use in the mid 1980s with the development of the backpropagation learning algorithm [12]. The example MLP network shown in Figure 8.1 is a fully connected, feedforward network with three layers of processing neurons—an input layer, a hidden layer and an output layer. The connections between each layer of neurons have an associated synaptic weight which can be positive or negative.

Input data to the MLP network can be encoded as binary $(0,1)$, bipolar $(-1,+1)$ or continuously valued within these ranges. Other encodings are possible such as normalising the input data for each attribute according to zero mean and unit variance [13].

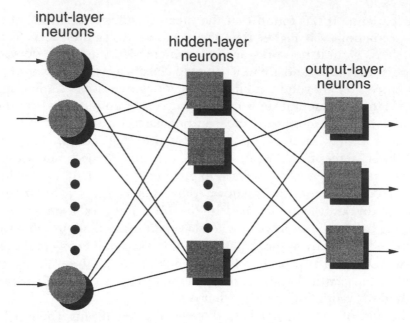

Figure 8.1 A multilayer perceptron network

Inputs to the MLP network are passed from the input layer to each hidden-layer neuron, which calculates the weighted linear combination of the input values. The combined sum is transformed using an activation function which determines the hidden-layer neuron's activation. A widely used activation function is the sigmoidal (or squashing) function which produces a neuron activation level between 0.0 and 1.0, depending on the neuron's threshold value. Activations from the hidden-layer neurons are passed to the output-layer neurons and processed in a similar way to produce the network outputs.

The network learns to perform a classification task by supervised training when the network is presented with examples of training inputs with associated output values. The MLP network weights are initially assigned low random values. At each subsequent presentation of a training example (a cycle) the network weights are modified using the generalised delta (backpropagation) rule so as to decrease the network's output error.

The MLP network is considered trained when the output error is acceptably low. It has been found empirically that the network with the best generalisation ability occurs when an independent test dataset has the lowest error during the training process. The aim of network training is to find the optimal network architecture which exhibits the best overall generalisation performance [14].

8.3 The low-back-pain MLP network

For this study, LBP is classified into three diagnostic classes: simple low-back-pain (SLBP) — mechanical low-back pain, minor scoliosis and old spinal fractures; root pain (ROOTP) — nerve root compression owing to either disc, bony entrapment or adhesions; abnormal illness behaviour (AIB) — mechanical low-back pain, degenerative disc or bony changes with signs and symptoms magnified as a sign of distress in response to chronic pain.

A dataset of 198 actual cases was collected from patient questionnaires, physical findings and clinical findings. In this study, the MLP network is a fully connected, feedforward network with 92 binary-encoded input neurons corresponding to 39 patient attributes. For example, the attribute 'age' is divided into three groups, <20, 20–55, >55, where a patient 34 years old would be encoded as '010'. Similarly, three output–layer neurons were selected to represent a diagnostic class, with output–layer activation '100' representing class SLBP, '010' representing class ROOTP and '001' representing class AIB.

Using the sigmoidal activation function and generalised delta learning rule the network was trained with 99 randomly selected patient cases. The MLP network architecture with the lowest test-set error was found with ten hidden layer neurons at 1100 cycles when the training set had a 96 per cent classification accuracy and a test set, with 99 patient cases, had a 65 per cent classification accuracy.

8.4 The interpretation and knowledge-discovery method

The interpretation and knowledge-discovery method first finds the hidden-layer neurons which positively activate the output-classifying neuron. This leads to the discovery of the key positive inputs in each MLP input case which positively drive the output classification, as follows.

8.4.1 Discovery of the feature-detector neurons

For an MLP input case, Vaughn's method defines the feature-detector neurons as the hidden neurons which positively activate the classifying output neuron. For sigmoidal activations the hidden-layer neuron activation is always positive and, hence, the feature detectors are hidden neurons connected to the classifying neuron with positive weights. The hidden-layer bias (which replaces the output neuron's threshold) also makes a positive contribution when the bias connection weight is positive.

In performing a classification task, the first author has shown [15] that the MLP network finds sufficiently many hidden-layer feature-detector neurons with activation ≥ 0.5 which positively activate the classifying output neurons and negatively activate the nonclassifying output neurons. The relative contribution of the feature detectors to the MLP output classification can be found by ranking the detectors in order of decrease in classifying output activation when selectively removed from the hidden layer.

8.4.2 Discovery of the significant inputs

The knowledge-discovery method defines the significant inputs as the inputs in an MLP input case which positively activate the classifying output neuron. Thus, the significant inputs positively activate the feature-detector neurons and, for binary encoded inputs, are positive inputs connected to the feature detectors with positive weights.

This is shown schematically in Figure 8.2 for an MLP network which classifies an input case 01011010 as class A. The two hidden-layer feature detectors are the hidden-layer neurons connected with a positive weight to the class A output neuron. Three inputs with value +1 are significant inputs—these are the nonzero inputs connected with a positive weight to one or more feature detectors. These inputs positively activate the feature detectors which, in turn, positively activate the class A neuron. It can be noted that one nonzero input is not a significant input.

The relative contribution of the significant inputs to the MLP output classification can be found by ranking the significant inputs in order of decrease in activation at the classifying neuron when each is removed (switched off) at the MLP input layer. There is evidence [11,15] that the most significant inputs are the MLP inputs which most uniquely discriminate the input case.

8.4.3 Discovery of the negated significant inputs

The knowledge-discovery method defines the negated significant inputs in an MLP input case as the significant inputs for another class which deactivate the feature detectors for that class when not active at the MLP input layer. For binary inputs these are zero-valued inputs

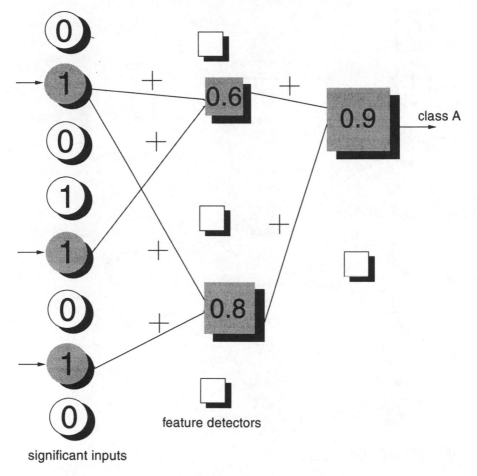

Figure 8.2 Significant inputs for an input case

connected to hidden neurons which are not feature detectors with positive weights.

This is shown schematically in Figure 8.3 for the MLP input case 01011010 where two of the inputs are negated significant inputs. These are the zero-valued inputs connected with a positive weight to one or more of the three hidden-layer neurons which are not feature detectors. The negated inputs have the effect of reducing the activation of these hidden-layer neurons.

The relative contribution of the negated significant inputs to the MLP output classification can be found by ranking the negated significant inputs in order of decrease in activation at the classifying neuron when each is included (switched on) at the MLP input layer.

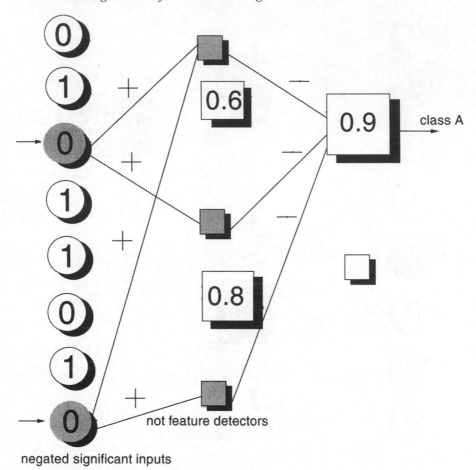

Figure 8.3   Negated significant inputs for an input case

8.4.4 Knowledge learned by the MLP from the training data

Using Vaughn's method, the knowledge learned by the MLP from the training data can be expressed as a nonlinear data relationship and as an induced rule which is valid for the training set, as follows.

8.4.4.1 Data relationships

The knowledge learned by the network from an input training case is embodied in the data relationship between the significant (and negated significant) inputs and the associated network outputs, as follows:

significant (and negated significant) => associated network
training inputs   outputs

The data relationship is nonlinear owing to the effect of the activation functions at each processing layer of neurons. The most important inputs in the relationship can be ranked in order of decrease in classifying neuron activation, as discussed above. The ranked data relationship embodies the graceful degradation properties of the MLP network.

8.4.4.2 Induced rules

A rule which is valid for the MLP training set can be directly induced from the data relationship, as discovered in Section 8.4.4.1, for an input training example in order of significant (and negated significant) input rankings [11,15]. The most general rule induced from each training example represents the key knowledge that the MLP network has learned from the training case.

From the most general rule for each training example a general set of rules can be induced which represents the key knowledge which the MLP network has learned from the training set. However, rules do not embody the fault-tolerant and graceful-degradation properties of the MLP network and are not a substitute for the network. The rules, however, define the network knowledge and can be used to validate the network.

8.4.5 MLP network validation and verification

The validation of the trained MLP network can be undertaken, with the assistance of the domain experts, by validating the data relationships and induced rules which the network has learned from all the training examples.

In MLP network testing the test-data relationships can be used to verify that the network is correctly generalising the knowledge learned by the network from the training process. Testing is not expected to reveal new significant input data relationships since network generalisation is inferred from the network knowledge acquired during training.

The validation process can lead to the discovery of previously unknown data relationships and the analysis leading to this discovery provides a method for data mining.

8.5 Knowledge discovery from LBP example training cases

The knowledge-discovery method is demonstrated for three example cases: a class SLBP training case, a class ROOTP training case and a class AIB training case, which have classifying output-neuron activations of 0.96, 0.93 and 0.91, respectively.

8.5.1 Discovery of the feature detectors for example training cases

Using Vaughn's method, as presented in Section 8.4, the feature detectors for each class are discovered to be the hidden-layer neurons H_3, H_4, H_6 and H_8 for the SLBP case, the hidden-layer neurons H_1, H_3, H_7 and H_{10} for the ROOTP case and the hidden-layer neurons H_1, H_2, H_5 and H_8 for the AIB case. The feature detectors are ranked in order of contribution to the classifying output neuron when the detector is removed from the hidden layer. These contributions are shown in Tables 8.1*a*, 8.1*b* and 8.1*c*.

8.5.2 Discovery of the significant inputs for example training cases

The LBP MLP inputs are binary encoded and thus the significant inputs have value $+1$ and a positive connection weight to the feature detectors. The significant negated inputs have value $+0$ and a positive connection weight to hidden neurons not feature detectors.

For the SLBP training case, there are 24 significant inputs, of which 16, including the input bias, show a decrease in the output activation when selectively removed from the input layer. Similarly, the ROOTP training case has 26 significant inputs, of which 15 show negative changes at the output neuron when selectively removed from the input layer. Finally, the AIB training case has 33 significant inputs, with 17 showing a decrease in the output activation when selectively removed from the input layer.

8.5.3 Data relationships and explanations for example training cases

For the SLBP and ROOTP example cases the top ten combined ranked significant and negated inputs account for a total decrease in the classifying output activation of more than 95 and 96 per cent, respectively, when removed together from the MLP input layer, as shown in Tables 8.2*a* and 8.2*b*. For the AIB case the top four combined

Table 8.1a Hidden-layer feature detectors — SLBP training case

Hidden-layer feature detector	Activation of feature detector	Connection weight to classifying neuron	Contribution to output activation	Feature-detector rank
H_3	+1.0000	+0.5797	+0.5797	3 (−3.2%)
H_4	+0.9998	+1.5108	+1.5104	1 (−12.8%)
H_6	+0.9999	+0.8979	+0.8979	2 (−5.7%)
H_8	+0.9552	+0.5704	+0.5448	4 (−2.9%)
		Positive input	+3.5327	
		Negative input	−0.3984	
		Total input	+3.1344	
		Sigmoid output	+0.9583	

Table 8.1b Hidden-layer feature detectors — ROOTP training case

Hidden-layer feature detector	Activation of feature detector	Connection weight to classifying neuron	Contribution to output activation	Feature-detector rank
H_1	+0.9999	+1.4073	+1.4072	2 (−17.7%)
H_3	+1.0000	+0.3424	+0.3424	3 (−2.8%)
H_7	+1.0000	+1.8821	+1.8821	1 (−27.9%)
H_{10}	+0.7355	+0.4446	+0.3270	4 (−2.6%)
		Positive input	+3.9587	
		Negative input	−1.3657	
		Total input	+2.5930	
		Sigmoid output	+0.9304	

Table 8.1c Hidden-layer feature detectors — AIB training case

Hidden-layer feature detector	Activation of feature detector	Connection weight to classifying neuron	Contribution to output activation	Feature-detector rank
H_1	+0.8475	+0.0393	+0.0333	3 (−0.3%)
H_2	+0.9967	+1.7291	+1.7234	1 (−29.1%)
H_5	+0.9901	+1.7100	+1.6932	2 (−28.3%)
H_8	+0.1648	+0.1861	+0.0307	4 (−0.3%)
		Positive input	+3.4805	
		Negative input	−1.1554	
		Total input	+2.3250	
		Sigmoid output	+0.9109	

ranked inputs account for a total decrease of more than 97 per cent in the classifying activation, as shown in Table 8.2c.

The ranked inputs represent a nonlinear data relationship and it can be seen from Tables 8.2 that the data relationship for each example case is exponentially decreasing with respect to the classifying output activation. The ranked inputs in Tables 8.2 provide a direct explanation for the clinicians about how the low-back-pain MLP classifies the example cases. In a similar way, explanations can be provided automatically on a case-by-case basis for any input case presented to the MLP network.

8.5.4 Discussion of the training-example data relationships

From Table 8.2a it can be seen that, in the SLBP case, the patient presents back-pain symptoms as worse than leg pain (rank 2) which supports no leg-pain symptoms (rank 5) and not leg pain worse than back pain (rank 6). Also, a straight-leg raise (SLR) $\geqslant 70°$ (rank 7) is substantiated by no limitation on the SLR test (rank 10). This particular patient case indicates possibly a not normal psychological profile (rank 3,4).

From Table 8.2b it can be seen that, in the ROOTP case, high-ranked inputs are negated SLBP key inputs indicating leg-pain symptoms: not back pain worse than leg pain (rank 1), not no leg-pain symptoms (rank 4) and not SLR $\geqslant 70°$ (rank 5). From Table 8.2c it can be seen that, in the AIB case, three key inputs are associated with the left leg (rank 1,2,4) and the other key input is claiming invalidity/disability benefit (rank 3).

8.5.5 Induced rules from training-example cases

As discussed in Section 8.4.4.2, using Vaughn's method, a rule which is valid for the MLP training set can be directly induced from the data relationship for an input training example in order of significant and negated significant input rankings. This is demonstrated for each of the example training cases.

8.5.5.1 SLBP example training case

Using the knowledge-discovery method the following rule, which is valid for the MLP training set, is induced in order of the highest-ranked significant and negated significant inputs in the data relationship for the SLBP example training case, as shown in Table 8.2a:

Table 8.2a   SLBP case training-data relationship

Rank	SLBP training case (− 95%)	Accumulated classifying activation	Accumulated decrease
1	pain brought on by bending over	0.94	− 1.6%
2	back pain worse than leg pain	0.67	− 29.6%
3	not low Zung depression score	0.33	− 65.9%
4	not normal DRAM	0.13	− 86.0%
5	no leg-pain symptoms	0.07	− 92.8%
6	not leg-pain worse than back pain	0.06	− 93.6%
7	straight right-leg raise ⩾70°	0.05	− 94.5%
8	back pain aggravated by sitting	0.05	− 94.6%
9	back pain aggravated by standing	0.05	− 94.6%
10	straight right-leg raise not limited	0.04	− 95.2%

Table 8.2b   ROOTP case training-data relationship

Rank	ROOTP training case (− 96%)	Accumulated classifying activation	Accumulated decrease
1	not back pain worse than leg pain	0.91	− 1.6%
2	not lumbar extension <5°	0.90	− 3.3%
3	not pain brought on by bending over	0.75	− 19.8%
4	not no leg-pain symptoms	0.42	− 54.4%
5	not straight right-leg raise ⩾70°	0.34	− 63.3%
6	back pain aggravated by coughing	0.27	− 70.9%
7	loss of reflexes	0.23	− 74.9%
8	lumbar extension (5 to 14°)	0.15	− 84.2%
9	not straight right-leg raise not limited	0.07	− 92.6%
10	not high MSPQ score	0.04	− 96.4%

Table 8.2c   AIB case training-data relationship

Rank	AIB training case (− 97%)	Accumulated classifying activation	Accumulated decrease
1	not straight left-leg raise limited by leg pain	0.87	− 4.7%
2	straight left-leg raise ⩽45°	0.41	− 54.8%
3	claiming invalidity/disability benefit	0.06	− 93.1%
4	not straight left-leg raise (46 to 69°)	0.02	− 97.6%

IF pain brought on by bending over AND back pain worse than leg pain
   AND NOT low Zung depression score AND NOT normal DRAM
   AND no leg-pain symptoms
THEN class SLBP

This rule represents the key knowledge that the MLP network has learned from this training case. The most general rule for the example case that can be found (from the above rule) which is valid for the MLP training set is given by:

IF no leg-pain symptoms THEN class SLBP

8.5.5.2 ROOTP example training case

Using the knowledge-discovery method the following rule, which is valid for the MLP training set, is induced in order of the highest-ranked significant and negated significant inputs in the data relationship for the ROOTP example training case, as shown in Table 8.2*b*:

IF NOT back pain worse than leg pain AND NOT lumbar extension <5°
   AND NOT pain brought on by bending over
AND NOT no leg pain symptoms AND NOT straight right-leg raise ≥70°
   AND back pain aggravated by coughing
THEN class ROOTP

This is the most general rule that can be found for this example case which is valid for the MLP training set.

8.5.5.3 AIB example training case

Using the knowledge-discovery method the following rule, which is valid for the MLP training set, is induced in order of the highest-ranked significant and negated significant inputs in the data relationship for the AIB example training case, as shown in Table 8.2*c*:

IF NOT straight left-leg raise limited by leg pain
   AND straight left-leg raise ≤45° AND claiming invalidity/disability benefit
   AND NOT straight left-leg raise (46 to 69°) AND smoker
THEN class AIB

This is the most general rule that can be found for this example case which is valid for the MLP training set.

8.6 Knowledge discovery from all LBP MLP training cases

Using the knowledge-discovery method, the ranking of the significant inputs and the negated significant inputs can be discovered for all cases in the MLP training set. The average highest-ranked significant inputs in each of the three diagnostic classes are shown in Table 8.3 and the average highest-ranked negated inputs for each class are shown in Table 8.4.

8.6.1 Discussion of the class key input rankings

The key positive inputs in Table 8.3 indicate that a typical SLBP patient presents with back pain worse than leg pain (rank 1), good range of lumbar flexion (rank 2), no limitation of straight-leg raise (SLR) (rank 3, 9, 10) and minimal disability when performing everyday activities (rank 6). The ROOTP rankings in Table 8.3 indicate that a typical ROOTP patient presents with leg pain greater than back pain (rank 2), limited lumbar movements (rank 3, 4), pain aggravated by coughing (rank 1, 9), a normal psychological profile (rank 5, 6, 7) and some walking aids owing to pain (rank 8).

The key negated inputs in Table 8.4 indicate that a typical SLBP patient does not present with many of the key positive inputs of class ROOTP patients and *vice versa*. There is an indication that some SLBP patients may not have a normal psychological profile (rank 6, 8), possibly because patients with chronic back pain have the potential to develop signs of AIB.

The rankings in Table 8.3 indicate that a typical AIB patient is one claiming invalidity/disability benefit (rank 1), limited SLR (rank 2) but not limited by tension signs (rank 6), high Waddell's inappropriate signs (rank 3), psychological profile indicating distress (rank 4, 9) and back pain a predominant symptom (rank 10). It can be noted that some attributes are key inputs to both the SLBP and AIB classes. This is to be expected since AIB patients are SLBP patients who go on to develop signs of illness behaviour manifested by distress. It can be noted from Table 8.4 that many of the key negated AIB inputs support the key positive inputs of class AIB patients.

Table 8.3   Top ten averaged ranked positive inputs for all training cases in each diagnostic class

Rank	All SLBP training cases	All ROOTP training cases	All AIB training cases
1	back pain worse than leg pain	back pain aggravated by coughing	claiming invalidity/ disability benefit
2	lumbar flexion ⩾45°	leg pain worse than back pain	straight left-leg raise ⩽45°
3	straight right-leg raise ⩾70°	lumbar flexion <30°	high Waddell's inappropriate signs
4	no leg-pain symptoms	lumbar extension (5 to 14°)	distressed depressive
5	pain brought on by bending over	normal DRAM	pain brought on by bending over
6	minimal ODI score	low MSPQ score	straight left-leg raise limited by hamstrings
7	lumbar extension <5°	low Zung depression score	pain brought on by falling over
8	no back-pain symptoms	use of walking aids	back pain aggravated by standing
9	straight left-leg raise (46 to 69°)	leg pain aggravated by coughing	high Zung depression score
10	straight right-leg raise not limited	pain brought on by lifting	back pain worse than leg pain

Table 8.4   Top ten averaged ranked negated inputs for all training cases in each diagnostic class

Rank	All SLBP training cases	All ROOTP training cases	All AIB training cases
1	back pain aggravated by coughing	back pain worse than leg pain	straight left-leg raise limited by leg pain
2	lumbar flexion <30°	lumbar flexion ≥45°	low Waddell's inappropriate signs
3	lumbar extension (5 to 14°)	pain brought on by bending over	normal DRAM
4	equal back and leg pains	no leg-pain symptoms	low Zung depression score
5	smoker	minimal ODI score	leg pain worse than back pain
6	normal DRAM	straight right-leg raise ≥70°	leg pain aggravated by walking
7	loss of reflexes	lumbar extension <5°	chronic back pain
8	low Zung depression score	acute back pain	straight left-leg raise (46° to 69°)
9	recurring back pain	high Zung depression score	back pain aggravated by coughing
10	leg pain worse than back pain	high MSPQ score	straight right-leg raise limited by back pain

8.7 Validation of the LBP MLP network

As discussed in Section 8.4.5, validation of the trained MLP network can be undertaken by validating the data relationships and induced rules which the network has learned from all the training cases. However, the discovery of the average key input rankings for each diagnostic class can also be used to validate the LBP MLP network. This is demonstrated as follows.

8.7.1 Validation of the training cases

Preliminary results of the average highest-ranked positive and negated inputs for all training cases in each of the diagnostic classes, as shown in Tables 8.3 and 8.4, indicate to the domain experts that the LBP MLP network has largely determined relevant attributes as typical character-istics of patients belonging to the three diagnostic classes. However, for the SLBP class, the eighth-ranked attribute 'no back pain' is contradictory to the top-ranked attribute 'worse back pain'. Further investigation revealed that (the only) two SLBP training cases with attribute 'no back pain' had been incorrectly included in the training set. This reveals the sensitivity of both the MLP network and the knowledge-discovery method.

As a result of the two incorrect training cases the training performance of the LBP MLP network was reassessed at 98 per cent classification accuracy.

8.7.2 Validation of the test cases

Of the 99 test cases, 35 were apparently misclassified by the LBP MLP network. By directly interpreting each of the misclassified test cases using the knowledge-discovery method it was possible to compare the top-ranked significant and negated inputs of each case with the average class rankings shown in Table 8.3 and Table 8.4. Many of the misclassified case test rankings indicated a high correlation with the average class rankings.

On further investigation it was agreed by the domain experts that 16 of the apparently misclassified cases were likely to have been correctly classified by the LBP MLP and incorrectly classified by the clinicians, based on the evidence of the average class rankings. Of these, 13 cases (out of 19) were correctly classified by the network as class AIB, 2 (out of 11) were correctly classified by the network as class ROOTP and 1 (out of 5) was correctly classified by the network as class SLBP. The difficulty in diagnosing AIB patients by clinicians has been observed in other studies [16].

As a result of the 16 test cases correctly classified by the MLP network, the test performance of the LBP MLP network was reassessed at 81 per cent classification accuracy which is similar to the results of Bounds *et al.* [5].

8.8 Conclusions

Using the interpretation and knowledge-discovery method this chapter discovers the key inputs which a low-back-pain MLP network uses to classify selected training-case examples and presents this knowledge in the form of data relationships and induced rules. The chapter also presents the average top-ranked key positive inputs and key negated inputs that the LBP MLP uses to classify all training cases for each diagnostic class.

Preliminary results indicate that the MLP network has determined potentially valid attributes as typical characteristics of each diagnostic class of low-back-pain patients. One evidently invalid SLBP attribute, however, revealed that two training cases had been incorrectly included in the training set. This demonstrates the sensitivity of both the MLP network and the knowledge-discovery method.

By directly interpreting 35 misclassified test cases it was agreed by the domain experts that 16 cases were likely to have been correctly classified by the LBP MLP based on the evidence of the average class rankings for the training set. This revealed the greater consistency achieved by the MLP network in classifying the AIB patients when compared with that achieved by the clinicians.

It is concluded that the low-back-pain MLP has high potential value in classifying LBP patients for medical decision support. It is also concluded that the interpretation and knowledge-discovery method has high potential value in validating any MLP network and for providing user explanation facilities directly on an input case-by-case basis.

8.9 Future work

Future research work will seek to evaluate clinically the class rankings and to automatically induce a valid rule for each training input case to further enhance the MLP network-validation process. Studies will also be made to discover whether the knowledge learned by the network is invariant with respect to parameters in the learning environment such as network architecture, input/output data encoding, activation function, selection of initial weights and learning rules. The results of this research will be presented subsequently.

8.10 Acknowledgments

The financial support for this research was provided by the Ridgeway Hospital and Compass Health Care.

8.11 References

1 Clinical Standards Advisory Group: 'Report on Back Pain'. HMSO, London, 1994

2 WADDELL, G.: 'Biophysical analysis of low back pain', *Baillieres Clin. Rheu.*, 1992, **6**, (3), pp. 523–557

3 NACHEMSON, A.: 'Newest knowledge of low back pain – a critical look', *Clin. Orth. Rel. Res.*, 1992, **279**, pp. 8–19

4 BIGOS, S., BOWYER, O., BRAEN, G. *et al.*: 'Acute low back problems in adults'. Clinical Practice Guideline 14, 1994, AHCPR Publication 95-0642, U.S. DHHS

5 BOUNDS, D.G., LLOYD, P.J., MATHEW, B.G. and WADDELL, G.: 'A multi layer perceptron network for the diagnosis of low back pain'. Proceedings of IEEE international conference on *Neural networks*, San Diego, California, 1988, pp. 481–489

6 BOUNDS, D.G., LLOYD, P.J. and MATHEW, B.: 'A comparison of neural network and other pattern recognition approaches to the diagnosis of low back disorders', *Neural Netw.*, 1990, **3**, pp. 583–591

7 PATTERSON, D.: 'Artificial neural networks theory and applications' (Prentice Hall, Singapore, 1996)

8 LOONEY, C.G.: 'Pattern recognition using neural networks' (Oxford University Press, New York, 1997)

9 ANDREWS, R., DIEDERICH, J. and TICKLE, A.B.: 'Survey and critique of techniques for extracting rules from trained artificial neural networks', *Knowl.-Based Syst.*, 1995, **8**, (6), pp. 373–389

10 VAUGHN, M.L.: 'Interpretation and knowledge discovery from the multilayer perceptron network: opening the black box', *Neural Computing & Applications*, 1996, **4**, (2), pp. 72–82

11 VAUGHN, M.L., ONG, E. and CAVILL, S.J.: 'Interpretation and knowledge discovery from the multilayer perceptron network that performs whole life assurance risk assessment', *Neural Computing & Applications*, 1997, **6**, (4), pp. 203–213

12 RUMELHART, D.E., HINTON, G.E. and WILLIAMS, R.J.: 'Learning internal representations by error propagation', *in* RUMELHART, D.E.,

MCCLELLAND, J.L., and PDP Research Group (Eds): 'Parallel distributed processing: explorations in the microstructure of cognition, vol. 1: foundations' (MIT Press, Cambridge, MA, 1986)

13 BISHOP, C.M.: 'Neural networks for pattern recognition' (Clarendon Press, Oxford, 1995)

14 TARASSENKO, L.: 'A guide to neural computing applications' (Arnold, London, 1998)

15 VAUGHN, M.L.: 'Derivation of the multilayer perceptron weight constraints for network interpretation and knowledge discovery'. Submitted to *Neural Networks*

16 WADDELL, G., BIRCHER, M., FINLAYSON, D. and MAIN, C.: 'Symptoms and signs: physical disease or illness behaviour', *BMJ*, 1984, **289**, pp. 739–741

Chapter 9

Discovering knowledge from low-quality meteorological databases

C. M. Howard and V. J. Rayward-Smith

University of East Anglia, UK

9.1 Introduction

Knowledge discovery in databases (KDD) is a multistage process that, given data describing a number of past experiences of a situation, can be used to find useful knowledge in the form of patterns which may be hidden therein; this knowledge may be used to make future predictions. There is strong commercial interest in data mining because of the potential for companies to gain an advantage over their competitors. The seven key stages of KDD [1] are:

- define problem and goals;
- data collection and warehousing;
- data preprocessing;
- data mining;
- rule analysis;
- trial;
- implementation.

A more detailed description of the knowledge-discovery process and, in particular, of data mining can be found in Fayyad *et al.* [2] and Holsheimer and Siebes [3].

9.1.1 The meteorological domain

Meteorological societies and universities worldwide frequently collect vast amounts of data from satellites and weather stations. Given a collection of datasets, we were asked to examine a sample of such data and look for patterns which may exist between certain geographical locations over time. Similar work has been carried out for some time using standard statistical techniques [4] and occasionally neural networks [5]; part of the aim of the work was to determine whether an approach to data mining based on rule induction using simulated annealing could be used to accomplish the same task. The datasets used throughout the work include sea and land surface temperatures [6], sea-level pressures, geomagnetic data and global indicators such as El Niño; recently solar activity has also been suggested as having strong links to long term forecasting [7]. Very little consistency existed between the datasets in terms of their format and grid resolution making extensive pre-processing necessary. Because of the methods used to collect these datasets during the first half of the 20th century, a large number of values are missing in approximately half of the databases. We find that even where data is available in the earlier years, there is a degree of unreliability which accompanies it [8]. If such a degree of reliability for different periods can be provided by the domain experts, this uncertainty [9,10] could be built into the data-mining' algorithm using fuzzy or rough sets [11,12]. The reliability factor may take the form of a step function where, for example, readings for years prior to 1940 may have one level of reliability, readings from 1940 to 1960 may have another level and readings from 1960 onwards may be totally reliable.

In comparison to some modern databases which occupy terabytes of storage, the database described in this chapter may seem relatively small. However, it is the shape of the meteorological database which differs most from other databases found in data-mining activities. A typical commercial database may have millions of records with a comparatively small number of fields. In contrast, the meteorological database initially has over 12 000 fields but with less than 100 records; one record for each year this century. This transposed shape of the data causes problems for many techniques because of the resources required and the complexity. Although the shape of this database may seem strange to people working in the area of data mining, it is common among meteorological problems. The data must be for-matted in this way to accommodate the concept of time into the problem.

The overall aim of the work is to generate a set of rules which can be used to predict certain grid squares a number of months in advance; these predictions can be used by meteorologists to make mid-long-term forecasts. For example, if we were looking for a September prediction, we may choose to use data for March through June as the input fields. Using this method, only data up to and including June of the current year may be required to make a prediction for September.[1]

9.2 The preprocessing stage

The data-mining stage of the KDD process has received most attention in terms of research and development. However, the importance of the preprocessing stage should not be underestimated. If the quality of the data is low [13] or formalisation of the problem incorrect, the algorithms used in later stages will either behave inefficiently or produce erroneous results, possibly none at all.

A number of vital areas that should be addressed in the preprocessing stage are considered below. These areas focus on the problems of data quality, volume and format and suggest methods which can be applied to overcome these.

9.2.1 Visualisation

Through the entirety of the KDD process it is important to have sufficient understanding of the data. One of the simplest methods of understanding the data seems to be visualisation; a number of packages exist for visualisation in a data-mining environment, e.g. [14–16]. The plotting of simple two- and three-dimensional graphs can occasionally indicate patterns between fields with very little extra work, although most of the time it is not that simple. The graphing of fields may show erroneous values which exist, possibly owing to errors at the time of data input, or it could show that certain large constant values may have been used to represent missing values. This visualisation aspect is of particular interest from a meteorological perspective as data (and the location of missing data) can be overlaid with relative ease onto coastline maps.

9.2.2 Missing values

The database examined in this chapter has a significant amount of missing data which not only causes problems when evaluating rules but also to many of the techniques used in the preprocessing stage. Figure 9.1 shows how much of the data is missing from each field; for

---

[1] Data for a particular month is usually available sometime during the following month, after it has been collected from all stations and combined to form the gridded database. For this reason it is not possible, for example, to use August and normally July, to make a September prediction.

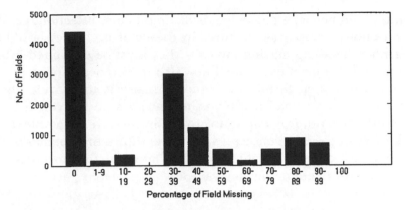

Figure 9.1   Frequency of missing values in initial database

example, 36.76 per cent of the fields in the database are complete, i.e. contain no missing values. We also note that 25 per cent (3000) of the fields in the database have between 30 and 39 per cent of data missing; the explanation for this figure relates to the datasets which only exist from 1945–1950 onwards, i.e. collection of data started just after the Second World War.

Another method of visually examining missing values is to plot the locations on a coastline map. Figure 9.2 clearly shows where large amounts of data are missing around the polar and desert regions.

Many packages usually require explicit instructions from the user on how to handle missing values and how these are represented. The more naive packages have no facility at all to deal with missing values and those represented by a constant value, usually a large negative number, are taken to be valid data. One of the first places where

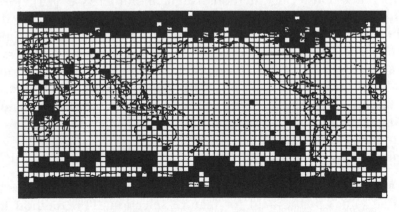

Figure 9.2   Location of missing values for land and sea temperature data

missing values becomes a problem is during feature selection, i.e. the identification of important features in the database. Care should be taken when handling missing values as they must be examined in the context of the domain of the field in which they appear. For example, a common question format in a questionnaire is to provide check boxes where placing a tick in the box indicates yes, and leaving the box empty indicates no. It is important to realise that in this context the blank entry in the box denotes a valid value within the domain of the field and not a missing value. We shall now discuss a number of approaches for handling missing values.

9.2.2.1 Discarding data

The simplest way of dealing with records or fields which contain missing values is to discard them from the database. However, if there are only a small number of fields or a relatively small number of records, discarding those which contain missing values may leave very little of the database to work with. This approach may also remove vital information contained within those records or fields; in fact, it may be the position of the missing values that is important.

9.2.2.2 Estimating the missing data

A variety of techniques can be used to approximate the values missing from each field [17,18]. The simplest and quickest method of completing missing values is using the arithmetic mean of the field values although, in meteorological work, climatic averages are favoured which are normally taken over a period of 30 years. Unsupervised clustering methods, such as autoclass–c [19], group similar records according to the input fields; records with missing data can be compared to complete records in the same cluster to estimate missing values. Neural networks can also be used to complete missing values [20]. Using means to complete the missing values is often considered unwise, although for the problem at hand, there are too few records in the database for the more involved methods to work sufficiently well.

9.2.2.3 Deferring the problem

Another approach to handling missing values is to use only the available values in the field for feature selection. This method may have the disadvantage of making each field a different length but the feature score will be determined only by the correct values in the field and not distorted by placeholders for missing data. When missing values are ignored in this way, the feature score is adjusted to reflect the use of an incomplete field. The approach of working with missing values rather than completing them so that feature selection can take place means that the problem can be deferred until the data-mining stage. In this later phase it will become easier to handle the missing data more accurately since there will be fewer fields as a result of the feature selection. However, not all techniques for feature selection and data mining are suitable if the missing values are not completed.

9.2.2.4 Hybrid method

A fourth approach to dealing with missing data involves combining the above two methods. The database is temporarily completed, possibly using one of the methods previously described, and feature selection is then applied to reduce the number of fields. Once feature selection is complete, the filled-in values are removed in order to return the database to its original state. The missing values are then handled during the data-mining stage.

We recall from Rayward-Smith *et al.* [21] that for a database, D, the number of records is defined as $d = |D|$. Then, for any field, f, we define d_f to be the number of records in the database for which that field is defined so $1 \leqslant d_f \leqslant d$. If $d_f = d$ the field is said to be complete. The records for which field f is defined form a subset of records, D_f, from the database, D. If f is complete, $D_f = D$. If $D_f = D$ for all fields, the database itself is complete.

9.2.3 Unreliable data

In addition to working with databases containing missing values, there is also the question of the reliability and quality of some of the data. For example, methods for collecting marine temperature data were far more unreliable at the beginning of the 20th century than they are now. We might therefore favour rules constructed using records in the latter half of the century over those constructed using records from the earlier half.

If r is a record and f is a field, $f(r)$ will denote the entry in the field f of r. With uncertain data, each entry, $v \in Dom_f$, in the database has an associated reliability, $rel(v)$: if $rel(v) = 1$ we are 100 per cent certain that the entry is v; if $rel(v) = 0$ we are 100 per cent certain that the entry is not v. Reliabilities lying in $]0,1[$ represent some degree of doubt about the entry. We can extend this to define the reliability of a set of possible values, V, for a particular entry in the database as:

$$rel(V) = \sum_{v \in V} rel(v)$$

and state the following axioms:

- $0 \leqslant rel(V) \leqslant 1$;
- $rel(\phi) = 0$, $rel(Dom_f) = 1$;
- $rel(V \cup W) = rel(V) + rel(W) - rel(V \cap W)$;

and hence the reliability of the complementary set, $rel(V') = 1 - rel(V)$. The reliability of the complementary set, V', can be referred to as the unreliability of V, denoted $unrel(V)$. When reliability or unreliability is applied to a singleton set, $\{v\}$, we will write simply $rel(v)$ or $unrel(v)$.

For the problem at hand we can now say that a reliability of 1 indicates total reliability in a value and, where data is missing, we can equate this with an allocation of ϕ to an entry with the associated reliability of 0. If we limit our focus to missing values alone, we find we are dealing with the case where reliability is 0/1 for all entries, i.e. a value is either missing or it is available with total reliability.

Throughout the following work it is assumed that the reliability of a value in the database is independent of other values in the same field, or in the same record. Although this is quite a substantial assumption it does, for now, simplify the problem to allow initial work to be done.

9.2.4 Discretisation

Discretisation and clustering [22–24] have many uses in the knowledge-discovery process; they can be used to reduce the resource requirements of the data and, more importantly, to simplify the data-mining problem. Clustering is the process of grouping together similar values and representing that grouping by a discrete value. Most data-mining tools, particularly those used for classification, require the output field to be a discrete value rather than a range of values such as temperature. The Fisher algorithm [25,26] can be used to discretise the range of values into a specified number of clusters. Using temperature as an example, two clusters may represent high and low, three may represent average with low and high extremes, and so on. Any rules generated in the data-mining stage would therefore describe a range of values represented by a discrete value and the applicability of the rule is controlled by the number of classes in the target field.

9.2.5 Feature selection

For most databases with a large number of fields, the feature-selection task is possibly the most critical in the data preprocessing stage. The identification of highly predictive fields can prove beneficial in many ways. It allows particular fields to be identified and examined in greater detail; some of these fields may also contain similar information thus making one or more fields redundant. If the acquisition of certain datasets is financially expensive, fields can be sampled and tested to determine whether the purchase of additional data is beneficial. Storage and processing costs can also be reduced by eliminating poorly predictive fields from the database. One of the main advantages of selecting strong fields in terms of knowledge discovery is the simplification of the problem for the data-mining stage. During feature selection, each field is assigned a quality factor determined by a particular algorithm. This score can be used to rank the fields in order of importance and to compare the information provided by one field relative to another.

Feature selection is of particular interest from a meteorological perspective as each field in the database corresponds to a geographical location. By examining the location and time of the high-scoring fields, it is possible to construct feature maps. These maps highlight areas of particular interest and show how the relevant fields may shift location with time.

Techniques commonly used for feature selection are described in Debuse and Rayward-Smith and Howard and Rayward-Smith [27,28].

For this particular work we have found information gain to be a good indicator of important features; the standard algorithm has been modified as shown below to cope with missing values in the database. Information gain is probably seen most frequently as the test used in partitioning the database in the ID3 tree induction algorithm [29], although its origins are from information theory [30]. For a particular decision, the current dataset is split into one or more subsets and a measure of how much information has been gained in performing the split is calculated. The information gain is calculated using the entropy function as a measure of randomness (impurity) within the data. The algorithm is adjusted when missing values exist in the database [31] by scaling the information-gain score according to the percentage of data available in the field.

For a field, f, the subset of the database for which the records are defined has been denoted by D_f; clearly $|D_f| = d_f$. The information-gain algorithm is applied to this subset and adjusted such that:

$$\text{infogain}(f) = \frac{d_f}{d} \times \text{infogain}(D_f)$$

The simulated-annealing approach (described later) can also perform feature selection during the search for rules by means of a selection operator. Other techniques which do not handle missing values could be modified in the same way, although this is difficult with most commercial packages.

9.2.6 Feature construction

Although in the previous section we try to reduce the number of fields, the complementary action is also advantageous. Constructing a new field from two or more of the original fields can sometimes convey more information than can using the fields in isolation.

A particularly useful approach with meteorological data is to calculate differences between fields. The El Niño [32] phenomenon and the North Atlantic oscillation index [33], which is based on the pressure difference between Iceland and the Azores, have been shown to have strong effects on weather conditions worldwide; features such as these could be found using feature construction.

9.3 The data-mining stage

Our approach to the data-mining stage is to search for rules of the form $\alpha \Rightarrow \beta$, where α is the precondition of the rule in disjunctive normal form and β is the target postcondition. We then use $\alpha(r)$ to denote that α is true for record r.

In Rayward-Smith *et al.* [21] three subsets of the database, D, were defined:

$$A = \{r \mid \alpha(r)\}, \ B = \{r \mid \beta(r)\} \text{ and } C = \{r \mid \alpha(r) \wedge \beta(r)\} = A \cap B$$

The values a, b and c were then defined as:

$$a = |A|, \ b = |B| \text{ and } \ c = |C|$$

and used in the following ratios to measure properties of rules

$$\text{accuracy}(\alpha \Rightarrow \beta) = \frac{c}{a}$$

$$\text{coverage}(\alpha \Rightarrow \beta) = \frac{c}{b}$$

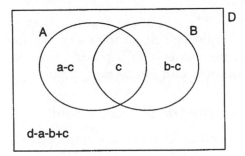

Figure 9.3   Venn diagram showing the database subsets A, B and C

9.3.1 Simulated annealing

Simulated annealing (SA) is a heuristic search algorithm, used for optimisation problems, that is analogous to physical annealing, i.e. the controlled cooling of a material. From an arbitrary starting solution, a subset of feasible solutions is generated using neighbourhood operators and scored using an evaluation (fitness) function. Unlike a standard hill-climbing algorithm which accepts only new solutions that are an improvement on previous ones, SA allows some poorer solutions to be accepted under controlled conditions. The acceptance of a downhill (poorer) move is governed by a temperature generated from a selected cooling schedule. A feasible solution in the data-mining problem domain is represented by any valid rule which can be evaluated against the database. The precondition of the rule consists of one or more inequalities which select and describe tests on certain fields. The postcondition is usually fixed by the problem instance to search for rules describing records in one particular class. Proposed neighbouring solutions are generated by operators which modify the components of an inequality in some way or toggle the inclusion of the field in the rule. Throughout the search, fields are switched on and off repeatedly to produce new solutions which maximise the coverage and accuracy of the rule. It is this field selection operator that allows SA to select subsets of fields during the construction of the rule. This type of feature selection is referred to as wrapper selection as opposed to filter-selection methods described in previous Sections which take place prior to the data-mining stage.

Previous work [21] has shown SA to be a powerful search tool which can be applied to data-mining problems. The SA experiments detailed in this work have been carried out using the toolkit described in a later Section. The evaluation function used to score rules produced in this way is $\lambda c - a$, where λ is a coefficient which controls the accuracy and coverage of the rule. The aim of the simulated-annealing experiments is to maximise $\lambda c - a$ thus giving strong rules. A good starting value of λ is typically d/b; afterwards reducing λ increases the accuracy but at the expense of coverage, and *vice versa*.

9.3.2 SA with missing and unreliable data

When a rule generated by SA is evaluated for a particular record, each inequality in the rule is tested against the corresponding entry in the record. If all inequalities hold, the precondition of the rule scores 1 (the corresponding a is incremented by 1). If the postcondition of the rule holds when tested on the record, the postcondition scores 1 (the corresponding b is incremented by 1). If both the precondition and the postcondition hold, the entire rule scores 1 (the corresponding c is incremented by 1); otherwise it scores 0. If the entry being tested is missing, i.e. has the value ϕ, the inequality cannot be directly evaluated and one of the following choices could be made:

- assume that the inequality holds and let the entry count towards the precondition score;
- assume that the inequality fails which in turn fails the precondition and hence the entire rule;
- adjust the scoring system so that a record is penalised if the corresponding field values in the rule are missing without failing the precondition and hence entire rule.

Consider a condition, α, defined on k fields. A record, r, is said to totally satisfy that condition if the k fields used in α are all defined in r and the corresponding field values satisfy the condition defined by α. Consider a predicate α defined on k fields $f_1, \ldots, f_k$ of the form:

$$\alpha = \bigwedge_{i=1}^{k} f_i R_i x_i$$

where $R_i \in \{=, \neq, >, \leq\}$ and $x_i \in \Re$. If the field, f_i, is missing for a record, r, then $f_i(r) R_i x_i$ will be undefined. Defining *true* $\wedge$ *undefined* = *undefined* $\wedge$ *true* = *undefined* and *false* $\wedge$ *undefined* = *undefined* $\wedge$ *false* = *false*, we say a record, r, partially satisfies α iff:

$$\bigwedge_{i=1}^{k} f_i(r) R_i x_i \text{ is undefined}$$

totally satisfies α iff the result is true otherwise α is not satisfied. If r satisifes α (either partially or totally) the strength with which it satisfies α is defined by:

$$s(r, \alpha) = \prod_{i=1}^{k} rel(f_i(r))$$

Hence, $s(r, \alpha) = 1$ if r totally satisfies α. We also define $s(r, \alpha) = 0$ if r does not satisfy α. In the absence of further information, we can make the assumption that all fields in a rule contribute equally towards the strength when applied to a particular record. In practice this may not always be the case and there is scope here for further research. We can now extend the definitions of a, b and c to allow for incomplete and inaccurate data by defining:

$$a = \sum_{r \in D} s(r, \alpha)$$

$$b = \sum_{r \in D} s(r, \beta)$$

$$c = \sum_{r \in D} s(r, \alpha) \cdot s(r, \beta)$$

The definitions of accuracy and coverage can then use the new values of a, b and c.

One possible strategy to adopt is a conservative strategy where only data occurring in the database can contribute to the value of a, b and c. We will also consider the adoption of a more comprehensive strategy where we more fully exploit the potential of reliability.

As an example, consider the three-field-rule precondition:

$$(f_1 > 5) \wedge (f_2 > 5) \wedge (f_3 > 5)$$

which could be the result of some data-mining experiment.

The finite domains of f_1, f_2 and f_3 are Dom_1, Dom_2 and Dom_3, respectively. The precondition can now be evaluated with the following example values of v_1, v_2 and v_3 where $v_1 \in Dom_1$, $v_2 \in Dom_2$ and $v_3 \in Dom_3$:

	v_1	v_2	v_3	a
example 1	6	6	6	1
example 2	2	6	6	0

Example 1 shows the simple case where all inequalities are satisfied and each contributes equally towards a maximum score of 1; example 2 illustrates how the entire example (record) would score 0 if one or more inequalities were to fail. Now, suppose the value of v_1 in example 1 has a reliability of 50 per cent. Taking the naive approach we could multiply through by $\frac{1}{2}$ to reflect this.

	v_1	v_2	v_3	a
example 3	6 (rel(6) $=\frac{1}{2}$)	6	6	
	$\frac{1}{2}$	1	1	$\frac{1}{2}$

The introduction of the reliability factor has a decremental effect on scoring; the score for example 3 has been reduced to $\frac{1}{2}$ from 1 to reflect the 50 per cent of unreliability associated with the value of v_1. In example 2 we notice that because the value of v_1 (2) did not satisfy the inequality, the entire example scores 0, but what if this value was unreliable? The example will have failed because of a single unreliable value where all other inequalities were satisfied with totally reliable values. We now consider this example again, but this time the offending value has a reliability of 50 per cent.

	v_1	v_2	v_3	a
example 4	2 (*rel*(2) $=\frac{1}{2}$)	6	6	
	?	1	1	?

The value of v_1 has a reliability of 50 per cent which means there is a further 50 per cent associated with the other possible values within the domain of f_1. It is possible that one or more of these other values could satisfy the inequality for f_1; this would make a positive contribution towards the total score and the example would not fail with a score of 0. In the absence of any further information, suppose that the remaining 50 per cent of reliability (the unreliability of the value 2) is distributed equally among the remaining values in the domain of f_1.

From the definitions, it follows that:

$$rel(v_f) = unrel(Dom_f - \{v_f\})$$

and

$$rel(Dom_f - \{v_f\}) = unrel(v_f)$$

If the entry in the record is missing we have a special case where the entry is the empty set, ϕ, and we recall that $rel(\phi) = 0$ which implies $unrel(\phi) = rel(Dom_f - \phi) = 1$.

Let E be the subset $Dom_f - \{v_f\}$ where we are concerned with the satisfaction of an inequality of the form fRx:

$$E_1 = \{y \mid (y \in E) \wedge (yRx_1)\}$$

We can now define:

$$e = |E| \text{ and } e_1 = |E_1|$$

The reliability associated with the remaining values in the domain of f which also satisfy the inequality for f can now be calculated as:

$$rel(E_1) = rel(E) \times \frac{e_1}{e}$$

9.3.2.1 Unreliability example 1

Considering example 4 again, suppose that the domain of f_1, Dom_1, is the set of positive integers from 1 to 10 inclusive. We can now say that:

$$E = Dom_1 - \{2\} = \{1, 3, 4, 5, 6, 7, 8, 9, 10\}$$

and given that

$$E_1 = \{y \mid (y \in E) \wedge (y > 5)\} = \{6, 7, 8, 9, 10\}$$

we calculate

$$e = 9 \text{ and } e_1 = 5$$

and

$$rel(E_1) = \frac{1}{2} \times \frac{5}{9} = \frac{5}{18}$$

Example 4 then becomes:

		v_1	v_2	v_3	a
example 4a	2 (rel=50%)	6	6	
	$\frac{5}{18}$	1	1	$\frac{5}{18}$

Part of the unreliability of v_1 has made a positive contribution, albeit only 5/54, towards the total score of this example. More importantly, this contribution is based on the unreliability of v_1 which would satisfy the inequality involving f_1. As v_1 does not satisfy the inequality there is no contribution from $rel(v_1)$. Since the example no longer fails we have not lost the dominating contributions of v_2 and v_3.

9.3.2.2 Unreliability example 2

This second example shows what happens if the unreliable value satisfies the corresponding inequality; we will use the values from example 3 to illustrate this. The domain of f_1 is the same as the previous example:

$$E = Dom_1 - \{6\} = \{1, 2, 3, 4, 5, 7, 8, 9, 10\}$$

and given that

$$E_1 = \{y \mid (y \in E) \wedge (y > 5)\} = \{7, 8, 9, 10\}$$

we calculate

$$e = 9 \text{ and } e_1 = 4$$

and

$$rel(E_1) = \frac{1}{2} \times \frac{4}{9} = \frac{4}{18}$$

We then have:

	v_1	v_2	v_3	a
example 3a	6 (rel=50%)	6	6	
	$(\frac{1}{2}+\frac{4}{18}) = \frac{13}{18}$	1	1	$\frac{13}{18}$

Adopting the more comprehensive strategy we see that the reliability of the entry, v_1, is the sum of the reliability of v_1 (1/2) and part of the unreliability of v_1 (4/18).

9.3.2.3 Example with missing values

Finally, we consider the following example where the entry for v_1 is missing; once again the domain of f_1 is as before:

	v_1	v_2	v_3	a
example 5	*missing*	6	6	
	?	1	1	?

$$E = Dom_1 - \phi = \{1, 2, 3, 4, 5, 6, 7, 8, 9, 10\}$$

and given that

$$E_1 = \{y \mid (y \in E) \wedge (y > 5)\} = \{6, 7, 8, 9, 10\}$$

we calculate

$$e = 10 \text{ and } e_1 = 5$$

and

$$rel(E_1) = 1 \times \frac{5}{10} = \frac{1}{2}$$

Example 5 then becomes:

	v_1	v_2	v_3	a
example 5a	*missing*	6	6	
	$\frac{1}{2}$	1	1	$\frac{1}{2}$

When the value of a is compared in examples 3a, 4 and 5 we find that the case where v_1 is unreliable but satisfies the inequality $(a=\frac{13}{18})$ is more favourable to the case where v_1 is missing $(a=\frac{1}{2})$ which in turn is more favourable to the case where the entry is unreliable but does not satisfy the inequality $(a=\frac{5}{18})$, as one would expect.

9.4 A toolkit for knowledge discovery

Finding good solutions to a data-mining problem requires many repeated experiments at each stage with different samples of data, different feature subsets and modification of the search parameters. In order to maintain a level of usability of these methods and make the KDD process efficient, a toolkit has been developed which packages the methods described in this chapter with standard database functionality and visualisation tools all controlled *via* a simple user interface.

Current features of the toolkit include:

(i)   *Database functionality*: standard data-manipulation techniques such as sorting, searching, replace, viewing, appending records, appending fields, record sampling, field selection, importing and exporting of data.

(ii) *Data preprocessing*: simple visualisation by way of 2D graphs, histograms and tabular views. Three methods of discretisation using equal-width clustering, equal-frequency clustering or Fisher clustering. Feature selection is available using information gain or gain ratio. Other features include missing-data summary, database summary and field construction.

(iii) *Data mining*: rule extraction is available by means of controlled rule induction using embedded simulated annealing or hill-climber search engines from the Templar framework [34]. Tree induction algorithms are also available *via* external links.

(iv) *Analysis*: the rule editor allows visual editing of the extracted rules to experiment with the properties of the rules and how each field contributes towards the total score. The rules may be evaluated individually or the disjunction taken.

In addition to the standard features described above, a number of specialised items are also available for this meteorological application. A number of data-conversion routines have been provided along with co-ordinate plots and coastline overlays for enhanced visualisation; the importance of plotting data onto this type of map has previously been discussed.

9.5 Results and analysis

The meteorological database described in Section 9.1.1 has been used to find patterns describing average temperatures in northern France during September (NFTS). The database underwent a series of pre-processing and formatting stages before feature selection took place. The output field, NFTS, was discretised into classes 0 and 1; this

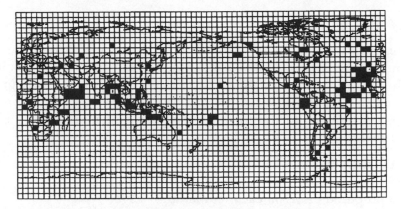

Figure 9.4   Important temperature fields with respect to NFTS

roughly equates to above and below average temperatures, respectively. The modified information gain algorithm was applied to the 12 000 fields in the initial database and the fields ranked in descending order with respect to NFTS. The best 100 fields were plotted onto the coastline diagram in Figure 9.4; this highlighted features of geographical areas which were found to have relationships with our selected target area. These findings have been passed on to domain experts for further investigation.

These 100 fields were then used in the data-mining stage, giving us a size problem which could be processed in a reasonable amount of time. The database was randomly split into training and testing sets with approximately a 2:1 ratio. The resulting databases have the following properties:

	training set	testing set	total
records in class 0	30	19	49
records in class 1	35	11	46
total	65	30	95

Experiments have been carried out using the simulated-annealing engine in our toolkit and the C5.0 algorithm found in the Clementine package [35]. C5.0 was used in these experiments as it also directly supports rule induction when values are missing from the database. Many of the other standard techniques that we would normally apply cannot be used without completing the values, which would not be a fair comparison.

9.5.1 Results from simulated annealing

Simulated annealing was used to find rules describing each of the two output classes. The conservative approach to handling missing values has been used throughout the SA experiments. Since reliability figures are not directly available for the database, the more comprehensive strategy is reserved for future work. The parameters used for the SA experiments were:

- initial temperature of 1.0;
- a geometric cooling schedule with a factor of 0.99;
- 250 proposed moves at each temperature stage;
- 200 temperature stages per experiment;
- λ value of 1.9 for class 0 and 2.0 for class 1.

The best rules found during the experiments on the training set were applied to the testing set to evaluate the performance.

	training set					testing set				
	a	*b*	*c*	acc	cov	*a*	*b*	*c*	acc	cov
rule for class 0	25	30	21	84.0	70.0	18	19	15	83.3	78.9
rule for class 1	40	35	30	75.0	85.7	12.5	11	7.5	60.0	68.2

9.5.2 Results from C5.0

The C5.0 algorithm was used to produce a ruleset describing the output field; the default settings were used for these experiments. The resulting ruleset contained six rules: two describing class 0, four describing class 1. Of these six rules, three could be considered as fairly strong rules but of these three rules, only two performed reasonably when applied to the testing set; performance from the other four rules was poor. Selecting the best rule for each of the classes gave the following results:

	training set					testing set				
	a	*b*	*c*	acc	cov	*a*	*b*	*c*	acc	cov
best rule for class 0	54	30	30	55.6	100.0	26	19	16	61.5	84.2
best rule for class 1	20	35	16	80.0	45.7	13	11	6	46.2	54.5

9.5.3 Comparison and evaluation of results

The following results, comparing the performance of C5.0 and SA, show the misclassifications for training and testing sets. Each pair of class values denotes the expected class and the predicted class.

	training set						testing set					
	0–0	0–1	1–0	1–1	correct	wrong	0–0	0–1	1–0	1–1	correct	wrong
C5.0	30	24	4	16	46	28	16	10	7	6	22	17
SA	21	4	10	30	51	14	15	3	4	7.5	22.5	7

The three tables above show that both techniques found rules describing each of the output classes. The rules found using SA were generally of higher accuracy and coverage than those found using C5.0. It is noticeable from both sets of results that it was simpler to describe class 0 than class 1; however, with only two outcomes we may be able to make the assumption that anything not classified as class 0 by the first rule can be classified as class 1. Although the accuracy of the SA rule for class 1 is relatively low at 60 per cent this may be significant in the meteorological domain. It is quite common for any improvement over selecting a class at random, however small, to be advantageous in the eyes of the data owner.

When the rules generated by SA are evaluated using data from March–June 1997, we find that the rule describing class 0 does not fire (evaluates to false) and that the rule describing class 1 fires (evaluates to true). The prediction for NFTS, based on the SA approach, is therefore class 1.

9.6 Summary

Using the techniques described in this chapter, meteorological datasets have been collected and formatted. Information gain, modified to handle missing values, has been used to identify and extract important features to form a single working database. Decision-tree induction and a version of simulated annealing, modified for missing values as detailed above, have been applied to this subset of the database; rules describing the classes of records in the database were generated. The ruleset has been analysed by experts from the meteorological community and possible justification for the results has been given. It has generally been found that preconditions of the extracted rules have indirect, rather than direct, relevance to the postcondition in terms of climatic features. We note that rules constructed using simulated annealing were generally more accurate and have greater coverage than those produced by decision trees. The toolkit, feature subsets and rules produced from this work have been of commercial interest.

When the prediction made in the previous section was later tested against the actual station data for NFTS in September 1997, we found that the value did indeed belong to class 1, hence the prediction was correct. A more significant factor associated with this finding is that this is the first year since 1991 that has belonged to class 1; the previous six years have been class 0. This would suggest that the patterns found in the rules have identified some change between 1991–6 and 1997.

9.7 Discussion and further work

Work on unreliable values in the databases is still in the infant stage. Two assumptions were made that greatly simplified this initial problem. The first was that the reliability of a value is independent of all other values in the field and the record; the second that the unreliability of a value is distributed evenly among the remaining values in the field domain. In real-world problems this is unlikely to be true for most instances. In the meteorological domain, particularly with gridded datasets, the unreliability of a reading can be confirmed to a degree by examining surrounding readings. Similarly, the records represent readings which have been taken over time; it may be possible to examine readings either side of an unreliable reading to improve its reliability. Nevertheless, there could still be unreliability introduced by the equipment used in taking the readings in the first place. The second assumption was necessary because the unreliability of a value is unlikely to be evenly distributed among the entire domain of a field; the more likely case is some form of normal distribution centred around the unreliable value. However, it may not be possible to assign this type of unreliability to each unreliable value in the database; this problem somewhat lies with the domain experts. If it were possible to have a reliability function or range associated with every unreliable value, another question would be how to store this information. To represent an entry in the database as a set of values, each with a reliability measure, would be difficult in standard relational databases where each entry is of a simple data type; one method would be to place a foreign key as the entry in the field and use this with a lookup table to get the values in the set. Modern object databases are more suitable for storing information of this form. Each entry in a field could be a complex data structure (object) which holds a set of values and their reliabilities. Although this is one possible solution to this problem, relational databases are currently the more common system and the newer object database architecture would still have to interface with the data-mining systems.

Both of these problems raise interesting questions and have great potential for further research. It is the authors' intention to continue this work and discuss some of these questions further and to implement the reliability properties into our current toolkit.

9.8 References

1 FAYYAD, U.M., PIATETSKY-SHAPIRO, G., SMYTH, P. and UTHUR-USAMY, R. (eds): 'Advances in knowledge discovery in databases' (AAAI Press/The MIT Press, 1995), chapter 1
2 FAYYAD, U., PIATETSKY-SHAPIRO, G. and SMYTH, P.: 'Knowledge discovery and data mining: towards a unifying framework'. Proceedings of second international conference on *Knowledge discovery and data mining (KDD-96)* (AAAI Press, 1996)
3 HOLSHEIMER, M. and SIEBES, A.: 'Data mining: the search for knowledge in databases'. Technical Report CS-R9406, CWI, Amsterdam, 1994
4 COLMAN, A. and DAVEY, M.: 'Linear regression forecast of Central England temperature for July–August 1996'. Technical report, Hadley Centre for Climate Prediction and Research, July 1996
5 MIYANO, T. and GIROSI, F.: 'Forecasting global temperature variations by neural networks'. Technical report, Massachusetts Institute of Technology, August 1994
6 JONES, P.D.: 'Hemispheric surface air temperature variations: a reanalysis and an update to 1993', *J. Clim.*, 1994, **7**, (11)
7 CORBYN, P.: 'Breakthroughs in long range forecasting' (Weather Action Ltd., 1995)
8 CHENOWETH, M.: 'Nineteenth-century marine temperature data: comments on observing practices and potential biases in marine datasets', *Weather,* 1996, **51**, (8), pp. 280–284
9 HUNTER, A.: 'Uncertainty in information systems' (McGraw-Hill, 1996)
10 McLEAN, S. and SCOTNEY, B.: 'Role of uncertainty in data mining'. Proceedings of *Methods and tools for data mining,* UNICOM, 1997
11 ZADEH, L.A.: 'From circuit theory to system theory', *Proc. Institute of Radio Engineers,* 1962, **50**, pp. 856–865
12 ZADEH, L.A.: 'Fuzzy sets', *Inf. Control,* 1962
13 TAYI, G.K. and BALLOU, D.P.: 'Examining data quality', *Commun. ACM,* 1998, **41**(2)

14 ROBERTS, H. and TOTTEN, K.: 'Data mining in BT'. *Data mining 96*, UNICOM, April 1996

15 SGI, 'MineSet'. Silicon Graphics Inc., 1995

16 TATTERSALL, G.D. and LIMB, P.R.: 'Visualisation techniques for data mining', *BT Tech. J.*, 1994, **12**, (4), pp. 23–31

17 WALTON, T.L. JR: 'Fill-in of missing values in univariate coastal data', *J. Applied Statistics*, 1996, **23**, (1), pp. 31–39

18 SHARPE, P.K. and SOLLY, R.J.: 'Dealing with missing values in neural network-based diagnostic systems', *Neural Computing and Applications*, 1995, **3**, pp. 73–77

19 LAKSHMINARAYAN, K., HARP, S.A., GOLDMAN, R. and SAMAD, T.: 'Imputation of missing data using machine learning techniques'. Proceedings of second international conference on *Knowledge discovery and data mining*, AAAI Press, 1996

20 GUPTA, A. and LAM, M.S.: 'Estimating missing values using neural networks', *J. Operational Research Society*, 1996, **47**, pp. 229–238

21 RAYWARD-SMITH, V.J., DEBUSE, J.C.W. and DE LA IGLESIA, B.: 'Discovering knowledge in commercial databases using modern heuristic techniques'. Proceedings of the *KDD '96* conference, AAAI, 1996

22 HO, K.M. and SCOTT, P.D.: 'Zeta: a global method for discretisation of continuous variables'. Proceedings of the *KDD '97* conference (AAAI, 1997).

23 KERBER, R.: 'ChiMerge: discretization of numeric attributes'. Proceedings of ninth national conference on *Artificial intelligence*, AAAI 1992, pp. 123–128

24 LIU, H. and SETIONO, R.: 'Chi2: feature selection and discretization of numeric attributes'. 7th IEEE international conference on *Tools with artificial intelligence*, 1995, pp. 388–391

25 DEBUSE, J.C.W. and RAYWARD-SMITH, V.J.: 'One and a half dimensional clustering'. Proceedings of the conference on *Applied decision technology 95*, UNICOM, 1995, pp. 377–389

26 HARTIGAN, J.A.: 'Clustering algorithms' (John Wiley & Sons, Inc., 1975, 1st edn.)

27 DEBUSE, J.C.W. and RAYWARD-SMITH, V.J.: 'Feature subset selection within a simulated annealing data mining algorithm', *J. Intell. Inf. Syst.*, 1997, **9**, pp. 57–81

28 HOWARD, C.M. and RAYWARD-SMITH, V.J.: 'Streamlining a meteorological database for knowledge discovery'. IEE digest 97/340, 1997, colloquium on *IT strategies for information overload*

29 QUINLAN, J.R.: 'Decision trees and decisionmaking', *IEEE Trans. Syst. Man. Cybern.*, March/April 1990, **20**, (2)

30 SHANNON, C.E. and WEAVER, W.: 'The mathematical theory of communication' (Illini Books, 1964)

31 QUINLAN, J.R.: 'Unknown attribute values in induction'. Proceedings of the 6th international *Machine learning workshop*, San Mateo, CA, Morgan Kaufmann, 1989, pp. 164–168

32 Britannica Online, El Niño (oceanic phenomenon), http://www.eb.com, March 1998

33 HURRELL, J.W.: 'Decadal trends in the North Atlantic oscillation: regional temperatures and precipitation', *Science*, 1995, **269**, pp. 676–679
34 JONES, M.S.: 'The Templar framework'. Technical report SYS-C9801, University of East Anglia, 1998
35 'Clementine v2.0 user guide'. Integral Systems Ltd., 1995

Chapter 10

A meteorological knowledge-discovery environment

Alex G. Büchner
University of Ulster, UK

J.C.L. Chan
City University of Hong Kong, China

S.L. Hung
City University of Hong Kong, China

John G. Hughes
University of Ulster, UK

10.1 Introduction

Geophysical data is the most important material that meteorologists use to model the behaviour of the earth's atmospheres and oceans. Although most research dedicated to explanation and prediction has been based on the application of a specific statistical or artificial intelligence technique, only a few endeavours have tackled the holistic nature of the subject. One possible way of approaching this target is the application of knowledge-discovery techniques or, as P. Stolorz *et al.* have put it: 'The important scientific challenge of understanding global climate change is one that clearly requires the application of knowledge discovery and data mining techniques on a massive scale' z[1].

Owing to the highly heterogeneous nature of the data and the vast amount of available domain expertise, traditional data-mining techniques by themselves have proven infeasible. Additionally, owing to the large quantity of available historical data, discovery of knowledge from a virtual data view as created in distributed and heterogeneous databases and presented in Büchner *et al.* and Chan and Stolfo [2–4] supersedes the capacity of up-to-date algorithms and hardware. An alternative approach, which has proven successful in other disciplines such as finance, retail and manufacturing, is the discovery of knowledge from a materialised view, represented in a data warehouse.

We have followed that approach and designed the meteorology and data-mining environment (MADAME), which resulted in a promising platform for further research being carried out in this area. The work was motivated by a project in which the authors were involved, and which had the objective of establishing the feasibility of forecasting high-intensity rainfall over different areas of the territory of Hong Kong using data-mining techniques with a view of improving the existing landslide warning system [5]. The material of this project is used to show the applicability of the designed and developed environment.

10.2 Some meteorological background

The intention of this Section is to give some fundamental meteorological background for better understanding of this naturally complex subject. Most of the examples used stem from the project mentioned above. Although this might seem to limit the generic applicability, almost all artefacts have their equivalents in related activities.

Different geographical areas are influenced by different meteorological conditions, which influence local weather scenarios. Depending on the location, weather predictions for a certain region can be of different complexity. Various parts of the entire Asian continent, for example, are influenced by a monsoon climate, which can result in very heavy rainfall (>100 mm per hour) during the summer period. The prediction of that type of condition is of a much shorter timescale (hence, nowcasting) than are long-term predictions during the winter or in more continental regions (hence, forecasting). Both techniques can be tackled with various approaches, for example human expertise, formal models, simulation, persistence (also known as null adaptation), or hybrids thereof.

Currently most weather forecasting centres use a mixture of human observation of recorded data, based on previous experience, and IT-supported decision-support tools. These two components—data and existing support mechanisms—are described in the following two subsections.

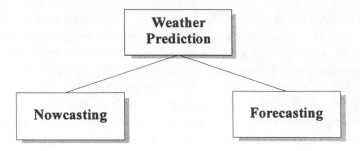

Figure 10.1   Taxonomy of weather predictions

10.2.1 Available data sources

The data usually available for predicting weather conditions on whatever timescale are highly diverse and consist of five main sources, which can be subdivided into textual and graphical data.

Amounts of rainfall are measured at rainfall stations, the density of which can vary quite enormously over the different countries or other observed areas. Automatic weather stations record information on the ground about air and wind-related measures, such as wind direction, wind speed, gusts, temperature, wet-bulb temperature, dew point, relative humidity, rainfall and the mean sea-level pressure. The upper air data provides information about pressure, geopotential height, wind direction, wind speed, temperature, dew point and relative humidity. The measures, telemetered by radiosondes which are used worldwide to create synoptic weather maps, are provided every six hours for the wind-related data and every 12 hours for all other measures.

In addition to these conventional data, every six minutes a 256 km range 3 km CAPPI radar reflectivity picture is taken and stored as a bitmap file (256 by 256 pixels). Two example radar pictures—one showing little, one showing heavy overcast—are given in Figure 10.2.

The most useful information that is implicitly stored in radar pictures is the total amount of rainfall and the location(s) of heavy rainfall. The acquisition of that knowledge will be described in more detail at the information extraction stage in Section 10.4.2.

Additionally, satellite imagery at the horizontal resolution (infrared as well as visible as shown in Figure 10.3) is being taken every six hours. These pictures contain information about water vapour and implications about the type of cloud structure. The World Meteorological Organization classifies clouds, according to their appearance, into ten genera based on their main characteristic forms (cirrus, cirrocumulus,

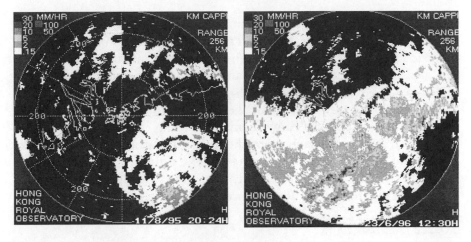

Figure 10.2 CAPPI radar reflectivity pictures

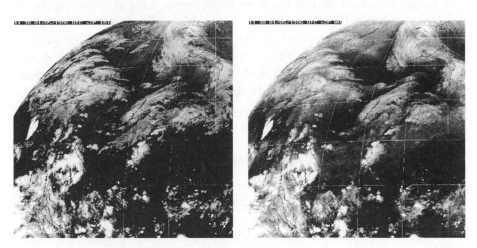

Figure 10.3 Infrared satellite pictures

cirrostratus, etc.). Each of the genera comes in one or more of 14 species, depending on peculiarities in the shapes or internal structures of the clouds [6].

The five available data sources contain a wide range of schematic and semantic heterogeneities, which have to be resolved before the data can be used as input for any data-mining exercise. The main types of heterogeneity are incompatible units (measures and timezones) as well as spatial inconsistencies. The latter does not only affect x and y coordinates, but adds a third dimension, *viz.* geopotential height. The second crucial aspect of the data is that of temporal granularity. Although some measures are taken in five-minute intervals, others are recorded only twice a day. Finally, the number of missing values within the data needs special attention, and noise rarely exists in meteorological data (see also Section 10.4.3).

A summary of the diversity of the available data from Hong Kong Observatory—after resolving schematic naming conflicts—is given in Table 10.1. As can be seen from the Table, the graphical data in the project was partly incomplete because of extraction problems from the raw data at the Observatory. Only data from disastrous events was made available for feasibility purposes.

10.2.2 Related work

Analytical weather forecasting is based on solving extremely complex dynamical mathematical models, which demand substantial computing power, detailed atmospheric measurements, and accurate updates of various boundary conditions [7]. Although very few weather forecasting centres actually facilitate artificial intelligence approaches to performing forecasting, there has been some substantial work done in that area. A representative set of approaches is described, which has tackled meteorological problems in the past.[1] The endeavours are subdivided into neural networks, case-based reasoning and numerical models.

10.2.2.1 Neural-network approaches

Atlas *et al.* [8] have used meteorological data to test their sophisticated artificial neural networks to forecast weather scenarios. In their study, the neural network(s) also performs nonlinear regression among load and weather patterns. When compared with classification methods such as classification and autoregression trees, the network shows a superior performance in terms of accuracy. McCann [9] has used a similar technique to forecast thunderstorms.

The Tampere University of Technology has carried out a study in which it endeavoured to model short-term district heat-load forecasting by applying multilayer perceptron networks [10]. The objective was to create a system which can be built with a reasonable amount of example data. The different factors affecting the structure and

---

[1] In addition to the briefly described systems here, there are various commercial systems available (for instance Merlin or Storm) which promise the predictability of weather-related scenarios and which are supposedly based on some artificial intelligence techniques. Since these are commercial systems, no detailed information is available of their exact techniques.

Table 10.1   *Available data sources*

Type	Source	From	To	Interval (mins)	Total number of records	Field name	Field unit
Textual	rainfall	04/84	09/96	5	4 110 912	date time	HKT
						station	1..75
						value	1/10 mm
	AWS	04/87	09/96	60	263 544	date time	HKT
						station	1..24
						wind direction	10° steps
						wind speed	1/10 m/s
						gust	1/10 m/s
						temperature	1/10 °C
						wet bulb temp	1/10 °C
						dew point	1/10 °C
						relative humidity	%
						rainfall	1/10 mm
						mean sea level pressure	1/10 hPa
	sonde	04/87	09/96	720	21 962	date time	GMT
						pressure	hPa
						geopotential height	m
						temperature	1/10 °C
						dew point	1/10 °C
						relative humidity	%
	wind	04/87	09/96	360	43 924	date time	GMT
						pressure	hPa
						wind direction	10° steps
						wind speed	1/10 m/s
Graphical	radar			6		amount of rainfall	mm
						entropy	0..1
						direction	10° steps
	satellite			360		cloud type	<set of cloud types>
						water vapour	g/kg

construction of the model are discussed, and the model proves to be working well when tested with independent test data.

Chow and Cho [7] have used a recurrent sigma-pi neural network to build a prototypical nowcasting system. The input nodes represented 28 values derived from radar images (see also Section 10.4.2) as well as three averaged rain-gauge values. The network is based on back-propagation learning and achieved reasonably good results.

The Hong Kong Polytechnic University is currently carrying out a study into possible applications of multiple-strategy machine learning and discovery methods including:

(i)   methods of knowledge-based approximation and automatic function construction under the control of domain expert knowledge and heuristic rules;

(ii) ideas of variable generation and variable reduction with the aid of an exploration matrix and instance tensor to facilitate discovery of new forecasting rules;

(iii) performance improvement approaches which include self-error-correction algorithms and rule-improvement algorithms for the refinement of discovered rules;

(iv) hybrid approaches of existing algorithms and exploring methods, such as integrating the approaches of the inductive paradigm and the connectionist paradigm.

The approach uses mainly advanced statistical techniques and the connectionist paradigm [11].

10.2.2.2 Case-based reasoning approaches

Jones and Roydhouse [12] have built a workbench which serves as an intelligent assistant for meteorologists: 'a kind of memory amplifier that allows meteorologists to locate and analyse historical situations'. The system is fully based on case-based reasoning techniques and has handled 2500 cases over three and a half years; another 10 000 cases are currently being incorporated. The workbench provides facilities to run (manual or automatic) queries against the case base and to return the scenario(s) with the closest match(es).

10.2.2.3 Numerical approaches

The vast majority of built prediction models that are used in weather forecasting centres are based on numerical models, for example Yeung and Chang's simulation model [13] is used in Hong Kong. Collier *et al.*

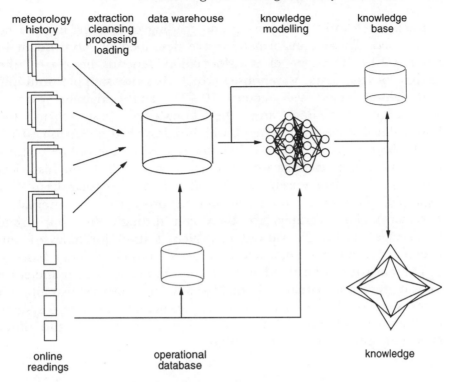

Figure 10.4 A meteorological knowledge-discovery architecture

have built a complex numerical prediction model using satellite images and radar information [14]; Lam has used radar pictures only [15] and Rodriguez and Eagleson have used their model to describe characteristics of rain storms using temporal and altitudinal data as input [16].

10.3 MADAME's architecture

To incorporate available temporal, spatial and altitudinal data as described in Section 10.2.1 and support machine-learning algorithms as outlined in Section 10.2.2 a meteorological knowledge-discovery architecture has been designed, which is depicted in Figure 10.4.

The top part of the architecture deals with historical meteorological information, which consists of a battery of data sources as described above. Owing to their extreme heterogeneity and complexity, various extraction, cleansing, processing and loading operations have to be performed. These transformations are described in more detail in Section 10.4. The type of transformation depends heavily on the design of the data warehouse, which has to support multiple materialised views (see Section 10.4.1). The remaining parts— knowledge modelling and the knowledge base—form the knowledge-discovery component, which is described in Section 10.5.

The bottom part of the architecture represents the online component. The online readings are transformed identically to the historical data, and the data warehouse is updated on a regular basis (for example, after every monsoon season or a shorter interval if necessary). The readings are then run through the appropriate knowledge model, the output of which is used for analyses and predictions, and which is, if relevant, stored in the knowledge base.

This environment can either be connected to any existing meteorological prediction system and provide complementary information on forecasting or can be used as an experimental standalone system. Further parts of this architecture are visualisation tools and other reporting and/or analysing techniques.

10.4 Building a meteorological data warehouse

In this Section, individual parts and transformation operations of the data-warehousing components are described. For illustration purposes, examples from the project carried out in Hong Kong are used as mentioned in the introduction. The arsenal of preprocessing tools has proved sufficient to perform standard meteorological exercises; for more specialised tasks, enhancements might be necessary and these can easily be integrated.

10.4.1 The design

Although the design of a meteorological data warehouse depends crucially on the purpose of the environment, most parts are of a rather generic nature. The most typical dimensions of geophysical data are time, spatiality and pressure.[2] An extensible hypercube which shows these three dimensions is depicted in Figure 10.5. Each dimension

---

[2] Meteorologists measure altitude at a certain pressure and not *vice versa*. Exceptions are measures taken at ground stations.

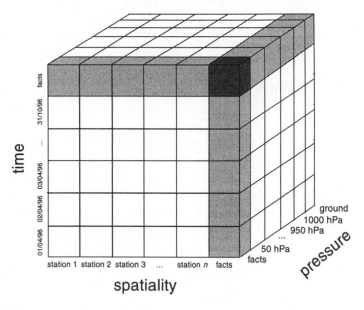

Figure 10.5   A meteorological hypercube

contains a number of attributes, as well as factual summarisation information.

Internally, each dimension is represented as a relation, which is connected to a fact table. This star schema is sufficient for one given set of scenarios, which uses data input of the same granularity [17]. For more advanced operations, as necessary in the meteorological context, a snowflake schema is required, which supports multiple granularities. Snowflake schemas provide a refinement of star schemas where the dimensional hierarchy is explicitly represented by normalising dimension tables [18]. For instance, in the case of the Hong Kong data, stations can be located in various spatial schemes [7] or in a Cartesian coordinate system and time can be grouped into hourly intervals, six-hour ranges or days, among others. As the modelling of the schema itself is a database-related problem, further details are omitted here.

10.4.2 Information extraction

The purpose of information extraction is the derivation of new values from existing data [19]. An example is the calculation of the adiabatic lapse rate derived from two temperatures t_1 and t_2 at two heights h_1 and h_2 as:

$$alr = -\frac{t_1 - t_2}{h_2 - h_1}$$

which indicates temperature inversion. More interesting, however, is the information which it is possible to extract from graphical material.

As mentioned at the data-prospecting stage in Section 10.2.1, the most important meteorological information that it is possible to extract from radar pictures is the amount of rainfall, the position of the rainfall area with the strongest impact and the cohesion of rainfall areas. After converting the radar information into Cartesian coordinates, the amount of rainfall is calculated as the sum of all rainfall pixels, in mm per hour. Cluster detection [20,21] can then be used to find all rainfall areas. The order of their impact (represented as the weight w_i) is computed as the ratio of intensity and size. The direction is the relative position of the centre of gravity of the observed area to the centre of attention, m. The cohesion of one radar scenario is calculated as follows:

$$c(x, m) = \frac{1}{n}\sum_{i=1}^{n}\frac{\Delta(x_i, m)}{w_i}$$

where n represents the number of rainfall areas and $\Delta(x_i, m)$ the distance from the centre of gravity of each rainfall area to the centre of attention, m, which was in the project's case Hong Kong.

Chow and Cho [7] have applied a similar technique, which has been adapted from Lam [15]. It converts the radar echoes into rainfall rates with greater density in the immediate vicinity of the centre of attention m, with less dense blocks further away from m. In the case of the Hong Kong data, this led to 28 new values which were used as input for a neural network, as described in Section 10.2.2.1.

Similarly, water-vapour measures can be extracted from satellite pictures. Also, a supervised artificial neural network can be applied to classify cloud genera. This particular extractor has not been implemented yet, but is part of further work (see Section 10.7).

10.4.3 Data cleansing

Data cleansing is concerned with the treatment of incorrect and irrelevant measures. Outliers (for example, negative temperatures in a subtropical climate) and errors (for instance, wind directions greater than 360° or relative humidity greater than 100 per cent) are the most often found faulty values.

Irrelevant measures are more dependent on the geographical area which the meteorological knowledge-discovery environment facilitates than on errors. For instance, as major rainfall-related catastrophes in south east Asia happen between April and September, only those months have been chosen for further evaluation. Further, before April 1987 only rainfall data was available, which is rather fruitless for data-mining purposes, and thus has been ignored. This has resulted in a reduction of the original data of more than 50 per cent.

Another type of incorrect measurement is noise. Although more feasible in other domains in which equipment with less accuracy (including human beings!) is used, it can have some impact in the field of meteorology. For example, weather radar detects rain in the atmosphere and determines the amount and distance from the time delay and signal strength of microwave echoes. The radar system has to be manually recalibrated every two to three years, which incorporates some mismatch in the data when compared with previous measures. This type of modification has to be considered in the data-cleansing module.

Null values have to be dealt with; for example, the rain-gauge data as well as other measures may often be missing for one or two time slots, especially in bad weather conditions. These values can either be replaced with default values, considered in the decision-making mechanism, or filled in with a calculated value. The latter is usually based on statistical methods such as interpolation, which is described in more detail in Section 10.4.4.

10.4.4 Data processing

The two main objectives of data processing are resolving semantic and schematic heterogeneities in the data and mapping the data onto different materialised views.

Semantic interoperability among different data sources is guaranteed by applying standard conversion functions. For instance, for all date and time values the chosen canonical form is usually the local time zone (radar information is stored in GMT), all pressures are given in hPa, all temperatures in degree Celsius, and so forth.

To resolve the spatial heterogeneity between the different weather-station types (rainfall stations and automatic weather stations), a lookup table has been created which is based on the coordinate system of the area of observation and divides the covered area into an appropriate number of quadrants. For this project the Hong Kong territory was organised into a seven by five matrix. Chaudhuri and Dayal [18] suggested three further schemes based on more meteorological grounds using two, three and ten areas, respectively. These different schemes are then modelled and stored in the built data warehouse.

Altitudinal data, that is tuples distributed over different heights (pressures), have to be stored as such. But, depending on the knowledge model built, different ranges are of interest. For example, the involved domain expert in Hong Kong was particularly interested in the data at a pressure of 850 hPa, which gives a representational height for rainfall characteristics. Cheng and Wallace [22] have carried out a study which concentrated on the 500 hPa height field.

To overcome the temporal heterogeneity across data sources, various interpolation and summarisation steps need to be performed. Depending on the interval length, time-related data have to be either summarised or interpolated. To perform the discovery of general characteristics (associations and classifications) of heavy rainfall, a 24-hour interval has been used, which requires summarising and aggregating of data. To perform the discovery of sequential patterns, an hourly interval has been used which, of course, can be extended or shrunk. Data with a granularity of less than 60 minutes were summarised and aggregated to be analogous to the 24-hour interval; data with a greater interval had to be interpolated. For all nonradial measures standard interpolation has been used; for radial data (wind directions) the value was distributed over missing values to be filled in. Again these are temporal intervals used for the project carried out; every other combination of granularity which is needed as data-mining-algorithm input is supported by the data warehouse.

10.4.5 Data loading and refreshing

Finally, after extracting, cleansing and transforming, data must be loaded into the data warehouse. Additional processing, such as checking integrity constraints, sorting, indexing, etc. may be required. The mainly databases-related details are omitted and can be found in Chaudhuri and Dayal [18].

The refreshing of the data warehouse has to be performed at regular intervals to retrain the built knowledge model(s). Typical intervals are daily, weekly, monthly or after every weather season. An alternative approach, which is feasible in meteorological contexts, is refreshing after every important event, for example landslides caused by heavy rainfall or a high-scale storm warning.

The loaded data warehouse forms a smooth interface to the knowledge-discovery components, which are described in the following Section.

10.5 The knowledge-discovery components

10.5.1 Knowledge modelling

Owing to the openness of the architecture there is no limit to the type and number of supported knowledge-modelling techniques. The only prerequisite is the acceptance of data input from the materialised view and output which is actionable in meteorological prediction terms. A further optional requirement is the incorporation of domain knowledge as described in Section 10.5.2. A set of data-mining algorithms used in the Hong Kong project is described below.

Two general data-mining exercises have been performed; the first was looking for patterns at 24-hour intervals. This discovered knowledge is useful for forecasting purposes; it gave a first impression of the data being mined, and also gave some insights into general characteristics of heavy rainfall. The second exercise dealt with the more interesting one-hour intervals which also considered the temporal dimension of the data, which is relevant for nowcasting. Both data-mining runs considered data of the 850 hPa height field. In order to validate the discovered patterns (see Section 10.6) the data has been split up into two parts: the training data encompasses the years 1990 to 1996, the testing data encompasses 1987–1989. The reason for this particular division is based on the reverse chronological way in which the data was provided by the observatory.

10.5.1.1 Modelling forecasting knowledge

The preprocessed data has been clustered into the three groups, low (less than 20 mm for the entire observed region per day), moderate (between 20 and 100 mm), and heavy (more than 100 mm) rainfall. Owing to the fact that the number of heavy rainfall cases exceeds the number of the other cases, these cases were artificially balanced to a quasiequal level.

To discover associations across the preprocessed data, the general rule-induction algorithm GRI [23] has been applied. For the purpose of this data-mining exercise the declared rainfall groups have been chosen as the antecedent. An example rule is:

raingroup==**heavy**
   sonde_temperature>11,35°C and
   AWS_relativehumidity>88,369% and
   AWS_meansealevelpressure<1009,55 hPa
   (support:15,85% confidence:76.0%)

The preunderscore part of each attribute indicates the source (sonde, AWS, wind and rainfall), and the postunderscore part is the field itself. The support value represents the ratio of the number of the records in the database for which the rule is true to the total number of records in the database. Confidence expresses the belief in the consequent being true for a record once the antecedent is known to be true. With a minimal support threshold of one per cent and a confidence threshold of 50 per cent, 47 rules were found by GRI.

To discover classifications in the data, three different techniques were applied, all being based on the C5.0 classification algorithm [24]. First, classification trees were used and a set of rules derived. The strongest rule being discovered is shown below. The notation of accuracy values and field names is identical to that described for associations:

Rule #4 for **heavy**
   if   AWS_wetbulbtemp<=26,115%
   and AWS_relativehumidity>85,514%
   and sonde_temperature>17,95°C
   and wind_windspeed>0,54 m/sec
   then->**heavy**
   (support:28,96% confidence:89,1%)

The second approach was to apply a backpropagation neural network [25], which led to a model with an input layer with 25 neurons, a hidden layer with seven nodes and an output layer with three neurons. Each input node represents one field in the materialised data view with a certain weight allotted to it; each output node represents a value of the classification label (heavy, moderate or low). The training of the artificial neural network was stopped after the lowest error was found in the training set and the network had not improved for persistent cycles.

The last approach used the discovered neural network as input for the classifier which slightly improved the accuracy of the C5.0 model.

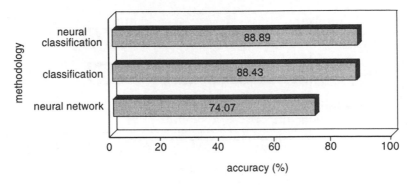

Figure 10.6   Accuracy comparison of different forecasting models

Comparing the accuracies of the three approaches on the forecasting training data gives the following result, which shows a clear advantage of the rule-based approaches over the neural network (see Figure 10.6). Owing to the fact that the output field of all three models is symbolic, the accuracy represents the total number of correct cases expressed as a percentage of the total number of cases.

10.5.1.2 Modelling nowcasting knowledge

The main differences between mining the one-hour data and the 24-hour data are the increase in input tuples by a factor of 24 and its temporal nature. An additional hour field represents this time component. To exploit this time field for predicting purposes a history operation has been performed, which puts previous values of one or more fields into the current record and adds new fields to each record which passes through it. To find patterns that consider information about up to four hours before heavy rainfall occurs the offset (which indicated the latest record prior to the current record from which field values should be extracted) of four and span (which indicates the number of records from which to extract values) of one have been used.

Again, three types of data-mining exercise to discover sequential patterns which were then used to classify the data into low, moderate and heavy rainfall have been performed. A backpropagation neural network, the C5.0 classifier, and the synergy of both approaches, that is, the output of the neural network, have been used as input for the classifier. Similarly to the artificial neural network used above, the network used all data-source input fields (considering the temporal

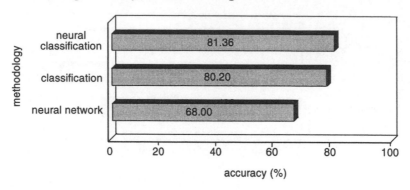

Figure 10.7   Accuracy comparison of different nowcasting models

nature this led to 78 input neurons), 37 neurons in the hidden layer and three output nodes.[3]

The discovered patterns have the same format as those in the previous Section, the only amendment being the format of temporal components. Every variable without an extension belongs to the current time window; every variable with an extension of the format <variable>_x ($1 \leqslant x \leqslant 4$) belongs to the time window x hours ago. An example rule is as follows:

Rule #17 for **heavy**:
    if   AWS_dewpoint<=25.025°C
    and AWS_meansealevelpressure<=10106.5 hPa
    and wind_winddirection==southeast
    and AWS_windspeed_2<=6 m/sec
    and AWS_relativehumidity_1<=85.571%
    and AWS_rainfall_3<=11.833mm
    and rainfall_2>2mm
    and rainfall_2<=139mm
  then->**heavy**
  (support:10,38% confidence:95,2%)

Depending on the support and confidence thresholds used, the number of discovered rules varied, but did not exceed the number of rules discovered in the forecasting scenario. The comparison of the accuracies of the three models on the nowcasting training data is shown in Figure 10.7, which indicates a clear advantage of the classification approach over the neural network. It also shows that it is

---

[3] The system used, which is based on an expert system containing rules for dynamic configuration, generates the topology of the artificial neural network automatically.

winddirection user_interval
start
   gt   0.0 le   22.5 N
   gt 22.5 le   67.5 NE
   gt 67.5 le 112.5 E
   gt 112.5 le 157.5 SE
   gt 157.5 le 202.5 S
   gt 202.5 le 247.5 SW
   gt 247.5 le 292.5 W
   gt 292.5 le 337.5 NW
   gt 337.5 le 360.0 N
end

Figure 10.8   Extrinsic-domain-knowledge example

possible to improve the quality of the accuracy of the classifier using the generated artificial neural network.

10.5.2 Domain knowledge

Domain-knowledge elicitation and incorporation is an essential step in every data-mining process. The major objectives of this phase are reducing the dimensionality of the search space and constraining the rule space, and thus improving the knowledge quantity and quality. The collected domain knowledge is then stored in the knowledge base.

In general, available domain knowledge can be divided into extrinsic (subjective) and intrinsic (objective) knowledge [26]. In the domain of meteorology, the first is relatively easy to capture and harness, whereas the latter needs some more attention. Various samples of explicit knowledge have been used implicitly at the data preprocessing stage as described in Section 10.4. Examples are often well known facts (for the involved experts), such as that there is no heavy rainfall between October and March in subtropical areas in the northern hemisphere, that some weather stations are only used for testing purposes etc. An example of extrinsic domain knowledge is given in Figure 10.8, in which numeric wind directions are clustered into eight wind-direction groups using the MKS domain-knowledge format.[4]

Much harder is the incorporation of intrinsic knowledge, that is knowledge which a meteorologist uses on a day-to-day basis, because it

---

[4] MKS is the mining kernel system, developed at the authors' laboratory [27].

Table 10.2   Accuracy of testing dataset

Methodology	Accuracy training data (%)	Accuracy test data (%)	Accuracy test data (high only) (%)
Neural network	68.00	66.53	68.75
Classification	80.20	50.00	74.71
Neural classification	81.36	54.44	53.57

has to be put down in a formalised way. There are various different mutually inclusive possibilities concerning how to elicit a domain expert's knowledge in the data-mining process, for example attribute constraints, hierarchies or thresholds [28]. For the purpose of this study, which aims to show the feasibility of the application of data mining in the meteorology domain, only extrinsic knowledge has been incorporated. Further intrinsic knowledge will be elicited at the refinement stage.

10.6 Prediction trial runs

To show the applicability of the built models, we concentrated on the one-hour interval nowcasting data, since that provides the most helpful information to improve the prediction of heavy rainfall in monsoon areas like Hong Kong. In order to perform this trial, two different approaches were run. First, we used the data of 1987 to 1989 to test the built models, which have been built with the training data from 1990 to 1996. Second, we picked a set of days when landslides occurred and matched the values against the discovered rules.

10.6.1 Nowcasting of heavy rainfall

To test the built nowcasting models the 1987 to 1989 data was preprocessed in exactly the same way as was the training data. This preprocessed data was then used as input for the knowledge models developed during the data-mining exercise and accuracies on the testing data compared to those of the training data. The outcomes of the models are listed in Table 10.2.

These results can be interpreted as follows. The neural network performs better when applied to the entire dataset, whereas the classifier outperforms the net when only looking for high rainfall,

Table 10.3 *Nowcasting trial-run results*

Day/time	Neural network	Classifier	Neural classifier
11/04 17:00	high	low	low
11/04 18:00	low	low	low
11/04 19:00	low	low	low
11/04 20:00	low	low	low
11/04 21:00	low	low	low
11/04 22:00	low	low	low
11/04 23:00	low	low	low
12/04 00:00	missing	missing	missing
12/04 01:00	low	moderate	moderate
12/04 02:00	high	high	high
12/04 03:00	high	high	high
12/04 04:00	high	high	high
12/04 05:00	high	high	high

which was the objective of the study. The full list of analyses of the testing of the three models is given in the final project report [5].

10.6.2 Landslide nowcasting

To simulate a trial forecast, the data from 12 August 1995 has been used, when 60 landslides occurred, two of which were most disastrous. The three models were run for data of every single hour and the outcome has been monitored in Table 10.3. The official flooding warning was raised on 12 August at 04:45.

The outcome of the test run can be interpreted as follows. All three models triggered the alarm at the same time, which is not surprising, since one of the most destructive catastrophes during summer 1995 has been chosen. The official alarm was raised shortly after the first landslides occurred; hence all three models triggered the alarm too early, which can be caused by the following not mutually exclusive factors:

- the models being built are over sensitive and triggered at a threshold which is too low;
- more than one consecutive trigger is required to call a serious alarm;
- the missing values at midnight are highly likely to have disrupted the findings of sequences.

No matter what the exact cause of the behaviour, a major fact can be drawn from the observation: the outcomes clearly show the feasibility of the applicability of the designed and developed meteorological knowledge-discovery environment.

For the given time, the three weather stations at which the heaviest rainfall occurred between 01:00 and 02:00 were identified; the amount of rainfall is listed in Table 10.4. In fact, one of the landslides occurred in the area of the New Territories in which the stations N12 and N14 are based.

10.7 Conclusions and further work

A meteorological knowledge-discovery environment has been developed, which includes both a data-warehousing and a data-mining component. Both parts have been described in detail and the applicability of the system has been shown. The architecture has been designed in such a way that it is highly extensible in order to allow the performing of as many meteorological experiments as possible. This holds for the data warehousing side as well as the machine-learning algorithms and the knowledge base. The case study has also shown some advantages of hybrid data mining, which combines various artificial intelligence techniques at different levels.

Further work will be based on the existing architecture. Work in progress includes the information extraction from satellite images to detect cloud genera as outlined in Section 10.4.2. Also, the domain-knowledge incorporation has to be improved and this will be performed in collaboration with involved meteorologists. In addition to the two performed case studies a third study needs to be carried out to show the applicability of the environment. Seasonal prediction involves the discovery of general patterns for a certain time of the year in a certain area.

Table 10.4   Location of heavy rainfall

Station	Rainfall 01:00–02:00 (mm)
N14	115
R42	100
N12	100

10.8 Acknowledgments

We would like to thank the Geotechnical Engineering Office at Hong Kong SAR Government for funding the work carried out. We would like to acknowledge the support from the Royal Observatory Hong Kong for providing us with large quantities of meteorological data. We would also like to thank Hughs Man from Global Systems Company, Hong Kong for his support in preprocessing some of the vast amounts of that data.

10.9 References

1 STOLORZ, P., MESROBIAN, E., MUNTZ, R.R., SHEK, E.C., SANTOS, J.R., YI, J., NG, K., CHIEN, S.-Y., NAKAMURA, H., MECHOSO, C.R. and FARRARA, J.D.: 'Fast spatio-temporal data mining of large geophysical datasets'. Proceedings of first international conference on *Knowledge discovery and data mining*, 1995, pp. 300–305

2 BÜCHNER, A.G., ANAND, S.S., BELL, D.A. and HUGHES, J.G.: 'A framework for discovering knowledge from distributed and heterogeneous databases'. Proceedings of IEE colloquium on knowledge discovery and data mining, London, 1996, pp. 8/1–8/4

3 BÜCHNER, A.G., YANG, B., RAM, S., BELL, D.A. and HUGHES, J.G.: 'A holistic architecture for knowledge discovery in multi-database environments'. Proceedings of ACM SIGMOD workshop on *Research issues on data mining and knowledge discovery (DMKD'97)*, Tucson, AZ, 1997, p. 87

4 CHAN, P. and STOLFO, S.: 'Learning arbiter and combiner trees from partitioned data for scaling machine learning'. Proceedings of first international conference on *Knowledge discovery and data mining*, 1995, pp. 39–44

5 CHAN, J.C.L., HUNG, S.L. and BÜCHNER, A.G.: 'Feasibility study on improved forecasting of high intensity rainfall for landslip warning'. Final project report, City University of Hong Kong, 1998

6 BATTAN, L.J.: 'Fundamentals of meteorology' (Prentice-Hall International, 1984, 2nd edn.)

7 CHOW, T.W.S. and CHO, S.Y.: 'A novel neural based rainfall nowcasting system in Hong Kong', *J. Intell. Syst.*, 1997, 7, (3–4), pp. 245–264

8 ATLAS, L.E., COLE, R., MUTHUSAMY, Y., LIPPMAN, A., CONNOR, G., PARK, D.C., EL-SHARKAWI, M. and MARKS, R.J. II: 'A performance comparison of trained multi-layer perceptrons and classification trees', *Proc. IEEE*, 1990, **78**, pp. 1614–1619

9 McCANN, D.W.: 'Forecasting techniques, a neural network short-term forecast of significant thunderstorms', *Weather & Forecasting*, 1992, 7, (3)

10 LEHTORANTA, O., SEPPALA, J., KOIVISTO, H. and KOIVO, H.: 'Neural network based district heat load forecasting'. Technical report, Tampere University of Technology, 1994

11 LIU, J. and WONG, L.: 'A case study for Hong Kong weather forecasting'. Proceedings of international conference on *Neural information processing*, September 24–27, 1996, pp. 787–792

12 JONES, E.K. and ROYDHOUSE, A.: 'Intelligent retrieval of archived meteorological data', *IEEE Expert*, 1995, **10**, (6), pp. 50–57

13 YEUNG, K.K. and CHANG, W.L.: 'Numerical simulation of mesoscale meteorological phenomena in Hong Kong'. Proceedings of international conference on *East Asia and Western Pacific meteorology and climate*, 1989, pp. 451–460

14 COLLIER, C.G., GODDARD, D.M. and CONWAY, B.J.: 'Real-time analysis of prediction using satellite imagery, ground-based radars conventional observations and numerical model output', *Meteorology Magazine*, 1989, **118**, (1398), pp. 1–8

15 LAM, C.Y.: 'Digital radar data as an aid in nowcasting in Hong Kong'. Proceedings of *Nowcasting-II* symposium, Norrköping, Sweden, 1984

16 RODRIGUEZ, I. and EAGLESON, P.S.: 'Mathematical models of rain storm events in space and time', *Water Resource*, 1987, **23**, (1), pp. 181–190

17 BERSON, A. and SMITH, S.J.: 'Data warehousing, data mining and OLAP' (McGraw-Hill, 1997)

18 CHAUDHURI, S. and DAYAL, U.: 'An overview of data warehousing and OLAP technology'. Technical report MSR-TR-97-14, Microsoft Research, 1997

19 ANAND, S.S. and BÜCHNER, A.G.: 'Decision support through data mining' (Financial Times Pitman Publisher, 1998)

20 MIYAMOTO, S.: 'Fuzzy sets in information retrieval and cluster analysis' (Kluwer Academic Publications, Dordrecht, Boston, London, 1990)

21 MESROBIAN, E., MUNTZ, R.R., SANTOS, J.R., SHEK, E.C., MECHOSO, C.R., FARRARA, J.D. and STOLORZ, P.: 'Extracting spatio-temporal patterns from geoscience datasets'. IEEE workshop on visualization and machine vision, 1994

22 CHENG, X. and WALLACE, J.M.: 'Cluster analysis of the northern hemisphere wintertime 500-hpa height field: spatial patterns', *J. Atmos. Sci.*, 1993, **50**, pp. 2674–2696

23 DOMINGOS, P.: 'Using partitioning to speed up specific-to-general rule induction', Proceedings of AAAI workshop on *Integrating multiple learned models for improving and scaling machine learning algorithms*, 1996, pp. 29–34

24 Rulequest. http://www.rulequest.com, 1998

25 BIGUS, J.P.: 'Data mining with neural networks' (McGraw-Hill, 1996)

26 SILVERSCHATZ, A. and TUZHILIN, A.: 'What makes patterns interesting in knowledge discovery systems', *IEEE Trans. Know. Data Eng.*, 1996, **8**, (6), pp. 970–974

27 ANAND, S.S., SCOTNEY, B.W., TAN, M.G., McCLEAN, S.I., BELL, D.A., HUGHES, J.G. and MAGILL, I.C.: 'Designing a kernel for data mining', *IEEE Expert*, 1997, **12**, (2), pp. 65–74

28 ANAND, S.S., BELL, D.A. and HUGHES, J.G.: 'The role of domain knowledge in data mining'. Proceedings of the fourth international ACM Conference on *Information and knowledge management*, 1995, pp. 37–43

Chapter 11

Mining the organic compound jungle – a functional programming approach

K. E. Burn-Thornton
Plymouth University, UK

J. Bradshaw
Glaxo Wellcome Research & Development, UK

11.1 Introduction

The main aim of this work was to conduct a feasibility trial to determine whether data mining had the potential to provide an enabling technology for the pharmaceutical industry, to provide researchers with the capability of determining the common key characteristics of compounds that determine their functionality, irrespective of compound size. A secondary aim of this work was to investigate whether the powerful lazy evaluation of the functional programming language, Gofer, could be applied to this task, to which it would appear to be ideally suited.

11.2 Decision-support requirements in the pharmaceutical industry

Pharmaceutical companies are continually striving to determine the common key characteristics that determine the functionality of compounds (e.g. relief of asthma) so that they may continue to provide safe and effective medicines. This process is usually conducted in two phases [1]. During phase 1 compounds which possess the same functionality are identified; phase 2 consists of determining the common key characteristics of these compounds. This section describes the historical methods used for the task of determination of the common characteristics of compounds possessing the same functionality, as well as recent advances.

11.2.1 *Graphical comparison*

Historically, the task of determining common key characteristics was carried out by visually comparing graphical representations of the structures of compounds (often stored in large databases) in order to determine key substructures [2]. This was often very time consuming but could be improved by comparison of the structures with key substructures (of known functionality — pharmacophores). However, this approach still required repeated examination of a large number of molecules for comparison with each key substructure of known functionality. With the advent of high throughput screening techniques providing data on enormous numbers of compounds, this technique became inappropriate since a human operator can only accurately compare a limited number of complex compounds in a day before fatigue sets in. The failure of the ability of human operators to screen such high throughputs of data led to structural keys being employed for high-speed screening of chemical databases [3].

11.2.2 *Structural keys*

A structural key is a bitmap representation showing whether or not a specific structural feature (pattern) is present. In order to create the structural key, the structural features (patterns) of importance must be determined. Structural keys have a large variance in size since the size depends upon the special feature of interest. The size of the structural keys may be of the order of tens of bits, if an electronic configuration is the feature of interest (sp3 carbon), and of the order of thousands of bits if a ring or ring system is of interest (napthalene). Once the structural key is generated it is compared with bitmap representations of all compounds in a given database.

One problem which arises when using structural keys is that the choice of feature of interest determines the search speed. For instance, a good choice of key will screen out all structures which are not of interest and will lead to fast searching. However, a bad choice of key will cause many false hits and slow the search down. In addition, all keys must be compared with all compounds in the database being searched. Furthermore, the choice of pattern also depends on the nature of the queries to be made. A structural key of use to pharmaceutical researchers may not be as useful to petrochemical researchers. There was a requirement for a more generic version of the key to be developed – this generic version of the key was called the fingerprint [4].

11.2.3 Fingerprints

Fingerprints attempt to solve the problem of the lack of genericity found in structural keys by eliminating the requirement for specified patterns of interest. A fingerprint is a bitmap, but each bit does not have a specific meaning. The overall pattern is characteristic of the compound but a definite meaning cannot be given to a specific bit as with a structural key. In the fingerprint there is no assigned meaning to each bit; in the same way, features in human fingerprints do not specifically identify the individual but a combination of the features does.

Fingerprint algorithms are used to generate the fingerprint by examination of the molecule. In essence, the algorithm generates a pattern to represent each atom, each atom and its nearest neighbours (plus the bonds which join them), each group of atoms and bonds connected by paths up to two bonds long, atoms and bonds connected by paths up to three bonds long and paths up to four, five, six and seven bonds long. For instance, Daylight Inc. [1] suggests that the molecule OC=CN would generate the following patterns:

0-bond paths:CON1-bond paths:OCC=CCN2-bond
 paths:OC=CC=CN3-bond paths:OC=CN

Despite the fact that many patterns are produced for each molecule, fingerprints only indicate a probability that a given pattern is present. However, they do enable an investigator to definitely determine that a pattern is not present; thus fingerprints are not as definite as structural keys.

Fingerprints have three main advantages over structural keys. The first is that one fingerprint may search all databases and queries from all domains (such as the pharmaceutical and petrochemical, given as examples earlier). Secondly, a fingerprint can be much smaller than a structural key with the same discriminating power. Finally, the more complex a compound, the more accurately it may be characterised by a fingerprint. However, information may be sparsely distributed within the fingerprint; attempts to solve this problem have led to the folding of a fingerprint to increase information density and variable-size fingerprints [5].

11.2.4 Variable-sized fingerprints

Fingerprint folding allows the information density to be optimised which leads to an optimisation of the screening speed. The complexity of the molecule and the desired success rate of the screening process determine the size of each molecule's fingerprint. Optimisation of the distribution of information density in the fingerprints leads to a reduction in data storage requirements and an increase in screening speed [6,7].

However, evolutions in screening techniques for organic compounds have led to problems for those implementing the screening task. Two of these problems are that, using existing techniques, the variable sizes of fingerprints need to be determined before screening takes place and that the common structure being sought in the compounds needs to be represented in varying sizes of fingerprints. Furthermore, it is possible that an unknown functional structure will be the cause of common functionality in the compounds being screened, and we may not determine the structure because it is not being sought.

These variable size, vast binary compounds need to be compared for commonality in a manner which is accurate and which will enable the user to determine the real common compound from its binary representation irrespective of prior knowledge of the compound functionality.

Potential solutions to this problem appear to be offered by a knowledge-based-systems approach which relies on unsupervised data mining (implemented in the functional programming language Gofer) as the underpinning technology.

11.3 Functional programming language Gofer

The functional programming language Gofer possesses five key attributes which appear to make it suitable for the task of prototyping a data-mining tool for this feasibility trial [8,9]. These attributes are power of expression, pattern matching, parametric polymorphism, higher-order functions and lazy evaluation, as well as the ability to rapidly prototype. The last two attributes are particularly useful. The lazy evaluation possessed by Gofer enables common key characteristics of compounds to be compared, irrespective of compound size. The ability to rapidly prototype enables us to readily determine whether or not data mining does possess the potential to provide the technical underpinning for knowledge-based compound comparitor tools. A further advantage of the use of Gofer is that it may be readily specified using Z and hence any system lockups may be determined and alleviated.

The following paragraphs expand the advantages of the key attributes of Gofer as well as providing an introduction to functional programming to the uninitiated.

11.3.1 Functional programming

Bird and Wadler [8] state that programming in a functional language consists of building definitions and using the computer to evaluate expressions. The primary role of the programmer is to construct a function to solve a given problem. Each function definition gives a name to an expression which is built from function applications. The output of a functional program is a pure mathematical function of its inputs. Functional programs use variables to denote values in the mathematical sense as opposed to the conventional procedural programming sense where variables denote storage locations containing values at different times. The focus is on describing data values by expressions. Functional programming languages, e.g. Gofer, like logic languages, e.g. Prolog, are labelled as declarative – their design is not so much influenced by particular machine details but by a clear mathematical understanding of descriptions. The following paragraphs discuss some recognised merits of functional languages which play a crucial role in our application.

11.3.1.1 Power of expression

As Reade [9] observes, in a conventional procedural language the programmer must:

(i) describe what is to be computed;
(ii) organise the computation sequencing into small steps;
(iii) organise memory management during the computation.

However, a functional language allows the programmer to concentrate on the first task without being distracted by the other two more administrative tasks. Economy of expression is provided by allowing the programmer to express computation in terms of functions without having to explicitly allocate memory for data structures.

11.3.1.2 Pattern matching

In a functional language all data structures are created using constructors. The main data structure used is the list which provides a mechanism for grouping together a sequence of values of the same type.

A list is either empty or has a head (the first item in the list) and a tail (a list containing the second item onwards). Thus a list has two constructors – one to create the empty list ([]) and one to create a nonempty list (:) and the list of numbers [1,2,3] is an abbreviation for the construction:

1 : 2 : 3 : []

New data types, called algebraic types, can be introduced with new constructors. For example, the following algebraic type defines the days of the working week:

data workday = Monday | Tuesday | Wednesday | Thursday | Friday

Functions may be defined using pattern matching on the argument(s), with a separate case being defined for each form of construction for the argument. For example, function isempty determines whether a given list is empty, and function head returns the head (first item) of a given list or signals an error if the list is empty:

isempty [] = true
isempty (h : t) = false

head (h : t) = h
head [] = error 'head of empty list'

11.3.1.3 Parametric polymorphism

In a functional language it is possible to define functions which exhibit parametric polymorphism. A polymorphic function is one that is equally applicable to a range of types. For example, consider the length function which calculates the number of items in a given list:

length [] = 0
length (h : t) = 1 + length t

This function will return the length of any list no matter what the type of the constituent elements.

11.3.1.4 Higher-order functions

A higher-order function is one that either accepts another function as one of its arguments or returns a function as a result. For example, consider the definition of map:

map f [] = []
map f (x : xs) = f x : map f xs

This function returns as a result a list created by applying the given function (first argument, f) to each item of the given list (second argument).

Higher-order functions are extremely valuable as they provide reusable components. By passing different functions as argument, a higher-order function may be specialised in quite different ways. This greatly aids software reuse. For example, consider the two uses of map below; the first adds 1 to every element in a list of numbers, the second places the letter f at the beginning of each of a list of strings (n.b. in functional programming a string is a list of characters, e.g. 'hello' is a syntactic abbreviation for [h, e, l, l, o]):

map (+ 1) [2, 3, 4, 5]
map (f :) [ine, unctional, uture]

11.3.1.5 Lazy evaluation

In modern functional languages, e.g. LML, Haskell, Gofer, expressions are evaluated using lazy evaluation. Here expressions and components of expressions are evaluated in a demand driven manner and are not evaluated more than is necessary to provide a result at the top level. The main benefit of lazy evaluation for our application is the ability to use infinite data structures in computations. For example, consider the definition of higher-order function filter:

filter p [] = []
filter p (x : xs) =
| p x = x : filter p xs
| otherwise = filter p xs

This function returns as a result a list which contains those items of a given list (second argument) that satisfy some predicate (Boolean-valued function passed as first argument). This function can be used even if the argument list is of infinite length as the construction of the result list is overlapped with evaluation of the argument list.

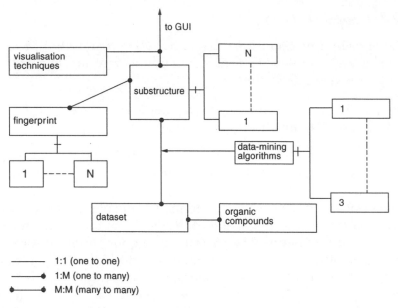

Figure 11.1   Rumbaugh OO information model depicting the prototype tool

It can be seen that lazy evaluation will readily enable Gofer to screen compounds irrespective of, and without prior knowledge of, the size of the fingerprint.

11.4 Design of prototype tool and main functions

11.4.1 Design of tool

Prior to design the tool was specified using Z [10]. However, this is beyond the scope of this chapter and the Z specification for this tool is described elsewhere [11].

Figure 11.1 shows a Rumbaugh object-oriented information model depicting the prototype tool. It can be seen from the Figure that a dataset contains many compounds which are composed of many substructures. The substructures may be represented by various sizes of fingerprint depending upon the required density of information. The fingerprints may be mined by various data-mining techniques which are all functional programming algorithms (being developed at Plymouth). The functional programming algorithms make particular use of the key attributes of the functional programming language Gofer in order to mine the structural data on the organic compounds of interest.

11.4.2 Main functions

The tool comprised three main classes of function. Two of these classes were concerned with file-accessing functions inputting the fingerprint data to the tool from files and outputting the data on binary representation of common compounds to a file. These file-accessing functions will not be discussed because they are variations on standard functions in Gofer which are described in detail by Jones [12]. The third function class was concerned with data mining.

11.4.2.1 Data-mining functions

Each of the three subclasses of this class represented data-mining algorithms, which are being developed at Plymouth. Further discussion of the specific algorithm functionality will not be given, but all of these algorithms inherited the functionality of the comparitor function common which is discussed here.

11.4.2.2 Common

A simplified version of the function common is shown below:

```
common ::([int],[int]) -> a -> [Int]
common (compound1,compound2) =map eogla (zip
                              (compound1,compound2))
```

This shows that common takes two lists of integers as input, combining them into a list of paired integers. It then produces a list of integers based on the contents of the list. For example, if the fingerprint describing compound1 was

[1,0,1,1]

and that describing compound2 was:

[0,1,0,1]

the paired list produced would be

[(1,0),(0,1),(1,0),(1,1)]

This paired list would then be transformed into:

[0,0,0,1]

The list [0,0,0,1] would be a binary representation of the common pharmacophores in compound1 and compound2. However, the combination operation is order dependent and the effect which this has on the result needs to be eliminated (this will be discussed later).

In essence, no matter how long the input strings, common will apply (map) the function eogla to a zipped version of the input strings and then output the results to a file.

The function eogla is a simple function outputing 1 or 0 depending on certain coincident values of the input strings and is defined as follows:

```
eogla :: (int,int) -> Int
eogla (f,s) =1, f==s && s==1
            =0, f==0 && s==0
            =0, f==1 && s==0
            =0, f==0 && s==1
```

This function demonstrates how the inherent lazy evaluation afforded by the use of Gofer is so suitable to fulfilling this task.

11.5 Methodology

The tool was used to determine the common key characteristics of 64 test compounds, and hence classify the compounds according to common pharmacophores, i.e. unsupervised data mining was implemented. 16 compounds of length 256, 512, 1024 and 2048 bytes (sets A–D), each representing a different degree of information density for the 16 compounds shown in Figure 11.2, were tested.

Each set of 16 compounds was compared, by each algorithm, in order to determine the key common characteristics of all 16 members of the set or the key common characteristics of members of a subset of the initial set (in other words, the compounds were classified according to their key common characteristics). The common key characteristics were displayed on screen to the user and written to a file, for later investigation.

It is known that the 16 compounds contain at least four main classes, each with two subclasses. However, the precise nature of the compounds was not disclosed until after these investigations had been completed.

11.6 Results

Table 11.1 presents the classification results described in Sections 11.6.1 and 11.6.2, with results produced by all three algorithms. The strong commonality shown in these results is due to the fact that little additional functionality, over and above that inherited, has been added to each subclass of algorithm.

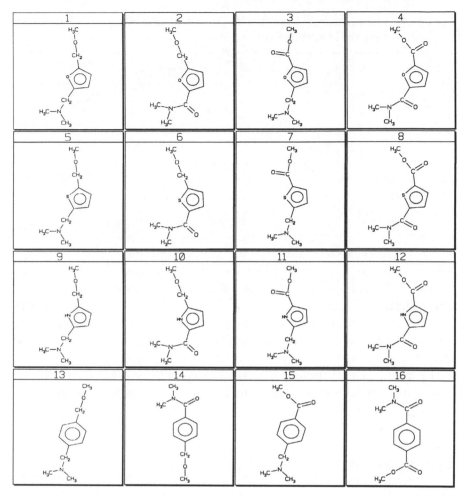

Figure 11.2   Graphical representation of the organic compounds being investigated

11.6.1 Sets A, B and C (256, 512 and 1024 bytes)

Table 11.1 shows that the tool was able to accurately determine the four main classes of compound which existed in the samples and the two subclasses in each sample.

11.6.2 Set D (2048 bytes)

Table 11.1 shows that the tool was not able to determine the four main classes of compound, with only three classes (with many subclasses) being determined.

Table 11.1   *Classification of data sets A–D (for all three algorithms) i.e. all algorithms produce the same results*

Data set	Class 1	Class 2	Class 3	Class 4
A	2,2	2,2	2,2	2,2
B	2,2	2,2	2,2	2,2
C	2,2	2,2	2,2	2,2
D	2,1	1,1,1,1,1	1,1,1,1	1,1,2

Note: 2,2 represents a four-member class with two subclasses each containing two members

The results show that up to, and including, 1024 bytes of information the functional programming technique which we used is capable of classifying the organic compounds according to common strings in their binary representation (representing common pharmacophores). The technique was unable to determine key compounds at strings greater than 1024 bytes, i.e. ones in which there was a sparse information density.

It is thought that the order dependency of the operations will have a bearing on the results and methods, and this will need to be investigated.

11.7 Conclusions

The data-mining tool was able to determine accurately the key common characteristics (or classify the compounds using unsupervised data mining) as long as the compound was less than (or equal to) 1024 bytes long. The apparent failure of this technique is due to the low information density in the binary representation of the compounds used in this investigation.

These initial results suggest that data mining may hold the key to decision support in the pharmaceutical industry. It would appear that the ability of Gofer to provide lazy evaluation makes it a particularly suitable language for prototyping such a tool owing to its ability to determine common pharmacophores in fingerprints of unknown, and variable, length.

Gofer has yet to make a transition from its use for prototyping into market products (perhaps this could be the occasion).

11.8 Future work

Future work will include testing the tool on a larger test set and larger compound size so that we may determine both the accuracy of the tool and the size of compound with which the tool is readily able to perform classification.

Additionally we will investigate methods for eliminating the effect of order-dependent operations on the results.

Further work will involve the addition of knowledge-based support so that unskilled and semiskilled users may readily determine the key common characteristics which are being identified by the tool.

11.9 References

1 http://www.daylight.com (the web site for Daylight Inc.)
2 MARTIN, Y.C., DANAHER, E.B., MAY, C.S. and WEININGER, D.: 'MENTHOR, a database system for three-dimensional structures and associated data searchable by substructure alone or combined with geometric properties', *J. Computer-Aided Molecular Design*, 1988, **2**, pp. 15–29
3 MARTIN, Y.C., BURES, M.G., DANAHER, E.B, DANAHER, E.A., DELAZZER, J., LICO, I. and PAVLIK, P.A.: 'DISCO: A fast new approach to pharmacophore mapping and its application to dopaminergic and benzodiazepine agonists', *J. Computer-Aided Molecular Design*, 1993, **7**, pp. 83–102
4 DOWNS, G.M. and BARNARD, J.M.: 'Techniques for generating descriptive fingerprints in combinatorial libraries', *J. Information and Computer Sciences*, 1997, **37**, pp. 59–61
5 BRADSHAW, J.: memo to K. Burn-Thornton, April 1998
6 PICKETT, S.D., MASON, J.S. and McLAY, I.M.: 'Diversity profiling and design using 3D pharmacophores: pharmacophore-derived queries (PDQ)', *J. Chem. Inf. Comput. Sci.*, 1996, **36**, pp. 1214–1223
7 GILLET, V.J., WILLETT, P. and BRADSHAW, J.: 'Identification of biological activity profiles using substructural analysis and genetic algorithms', *J. Chem. Inf. Comput. Sci.*, 1998, **38**, pp. 1165–179
8 BIRD, R. and WADLER, P.: 'Introduction to functional programming' (Prentice-Hall, 1988)
9 READE, C.: 'Elements of functional programming' (Prentice Hall, 1980)
10 SPIVEY, J.M.: 'The Z notation: a reference manual' (Prentice Hall, 1992)
11 BURN-THORNTON, K.E.: 'Using Z to specify a tool for determination of pharmacophores', submitted to *J. Funct. Program.*
12 JONES, M.P.: 'A system of constructor classes: overloading and implicit higher-order polymorphism', *J. Funct. Program.*, 1995, **5**, (1)

Chapter 12
Data mining with neural networks — an applied example in understanding electricity consumption patterns

Philip Brierley and Bill Batty
Cranfield University, UK

Data mining is the process of analysing data in order to extract useful information. Many techniques exist that can be used in the analysis of data, one of which is artificial neural networks.

In this chapter we explain what a neural network is and how one was used in analysing electricity consumption data from a utility in the UK. Total daily loads over an eight-year period were examined and the influencing factors identified. Rules were subsequently extracted from the neural network by pruning weights in order to ease comprehension of how the data was being processed. A half-hourly model for a single year was created and more subtle factors which influence the load in this timescale were identified.

The ethos in this work is to utilise the modelling capabilities of neural networks in order to identify anomalies to the model. The network results merely provide clues as to why such anomalies might exist, but it is the human ability to interpret the results which is the actual knowledge-discovery process. The neural network is simply employed as a data-mining tool that can model large amounts of data but it has no intelligence for knowledge discovery whatsoever. It is hoped that the approach taken will demonstrate that neural networks can be very powerful tools for analysing large amounts of data, if they are understood and taken for what they are.

The appendixes contain a proof of the backpropagation weight update rule and code that should enable keen readers to program a neural network for themselves. The code is included to show that

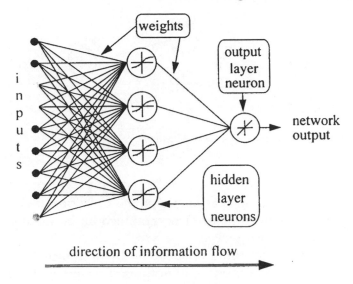

Figure 12.1   A fully connected feedforward multilayer perceptron

implementing a neural network can be a very simple process which does not require sophisticated simulators or supercomputers.

12.1 Neural networks

12.1.1 What are neural networks?

Artificial neural networks are simple computer programs which can automatically find nonlinear relationships in data without any pre-defined model. Several types of neural network exist, of which the most popular is the feedforward multilayer perceptron (MLP) which was the type used in this analysis. Figure 12.1 shows the structure of a typical MLP.

MLPs consist of an input layer, one or more hidden layers and an output layer. Data is fed into the input layer and transformed by weights and neurons as it flows through the network. The network output is the resultant transformation that forms the relationship between the inputs (independent variables) and the output (dependent variable). In a feedforward network there are only weight connections in the forward direction. Networks with neurons whose outputs can feed back into themselves or other neurons in the same or previous layers are known as recurrent neural networks. Fully

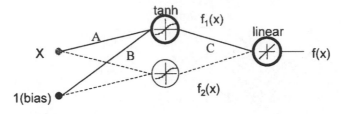

Figure 12.2   Number processing within a network

connected means that all possible weight connections are present, so strictly speaking there could be direct connections between the inputs and the output neuron.

MLPs are trained to find a relationship by presenting the network with historical values of inputs and outputs. Training is the search for a set of weights which best matches the inputs onto the output for the examples (training patterns) in the historical database. Training the network is thus an optimisation problem where the optimal solution lies somewhere in weight space.

There are numerous methods by which this optimisation can be performed, such as random walks [1] or genetic searches [2,3], but the most popular are based on gradient-descent techniques of which there are numerous variations which have evolved from the original backpropagation algorithm or generalised delta rule (see appendixes, Section 12.9.1).

12.1.2 Why use neural networks?

The most common application is to train a neural network on historical data and then use this model to predict the outcome for new combinations of inputs. The hope is that the network has extracted a general relationship which holds for all combinations of inputs. In classification problems the output will have one of two values, representing 'belongs to the set' and 'does not belong to the set', whereas in regression problems the output is a continuous variable.

12.1.3 How do neural networks process information?

Figure 12.2 shows a neural network with one input (x), one hidden layer containing two neurons and one neuron in the output layer. An extra input known as a bias is created and has a constant value, which is 1 in this case. The bias has weight connections to all hidden neurons

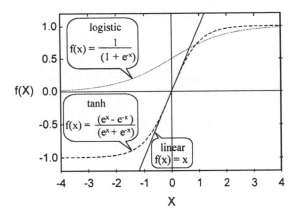

Figure 12.3 Common activation functions

and there can also be a bias weight connection to the output neuron. Each input is connected to each hidden neuron by an associated weight. Each hidden neuron sums all the weighted inputs (the input multiplied by the connecting weight value, i.e. $xA + 1B$) that feed into the neuron and passes this value through an activation or squashing function. The result is then multiplied by another associated weight (C) and the network output is again the summation of all weighted inputs passed through the output neuron activation function.

Any function can act as the activation function but for gradient descent learning it must be continuously differentiable. Two popular sigmoidal-shaped activation functions are the logistic and the hyperbolic tangent (tanh) (Figure 12.3).

The nonlinearity of these sigmoidal activation functions is what enables neural networks to model nonlinear functions. Figure 12.3 shows how they squash the output between limits (0,1 logistic and $-1,1$ tanh). This is commonly used as an output activation function for classification problems as it acts as a decision boundary where a continuous-valued input is classified as 0 or 1 (in the case of the logistic) with a region of doubt for any value in between. Because of this the required output of the network must be appropriately scaled to lie within the limits of the associated output activation function.

For regression problems the output activation is often the identity or linear function (Figure 12.3) as there is no real gain in the output nonlinearity as any further transformation could be achieved in previous layers. It can be seen from Figure 12.3 how the sigmoidal functions have near-linear regions, which enables them to be used to

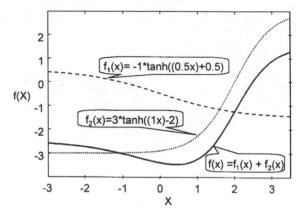

Figure 12.4   How two neurons can transform a linear input into a complex nonlinear output

approximate linear problems. A network with no hidden layer and a linear output activation function becomes a linear regression model.

The output of the network in Figure 12.2, which has tanh and linear activation functions in the hidden and output layers, respectively, is:

$$\text{network output} = f_1(x) + f_2(x)$$

where:

$$f_1(x) = C \tanh(xA + B)$$

and weights A, B and C which provide a good solution must be found for each neuron.

Figure 12.4 shows how a linear input can easily be transformed into a nonlinear output by mapping it onto sections of the tanh activation function. The importance of the bias input acting as a shift operator becomes evident.

12.1.4 Things to be aware of . . .

12.1.4.1 Overfitting and generalisation

Given enough hidden neurons a neural network can map any number of points, but there is the danger that the network has just learned to memorise the data. Figure 12.5 shows five points which can be perfectly mapped by a neural network which it could be assumed has learned the relationship. This is not the case, however, as is demonstrated when more data is shown and a linear relationship with

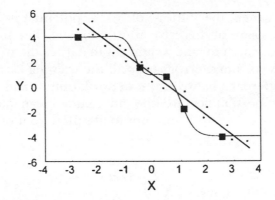

Figure 12.5   An apparently perfect model with poor generalisation properties

noisy data becomes evident. This is what is known as overfitting the training data and the generalisation properties of the network become unreliable.

To create a model with good generalisation properties the training data needs to be plentiful and the number of hidden neurons should be restricted. Training with sparse data and adding hidden neurons until there is no error can give a mistaken sense of achievement.

12.1.4.2 Extrapolation

Neural networks do not give an exact physical model but learn to represent the relationship in terms of the activation functions of the neurons. The nature of the sigmoidal functions is such that neural networks cannot extrapolate with any usefulness outside the domain of the training data. In reality no model can extrapolate with confidence into the unknown. Figure 12.6 demonstrates this for the function $y = 2x^2 - 1$.

Within the training range two hidden neurons can accurately mimic this polynomial, but outside this range the neural representation does not hold. The manner with which sigmoidal neurons become saturated outside their training range has potential for stable neurocontrol applications. Figure 12.6 also demonstrates the power of neural networks for mapping polynomial functions.

12.1.4.3 The function being minimised

Training a network involves the search for a set of weights which provides a good solution to the problem, but what is a good solution?

In order to gauge the fitness of each potential solution some quantitative measure of the error must be made. The most common procedure is to search for the weight set that gives the minimum total squared errors (or r.m.s. error) over all the training cases, where the error is the difference between the network output and the required output. Other possibilities are the minimum mean absolute error (m.a.e. or L_1 norm) or the minimum total square root of the absolute error. Specifically:

$$\text{r.m.s.e.} = \sqrt{\frac{\sum_{i=1}^{i=n} (act_i - pred_i)^2}{n}}$$

$$\text{m.a.e.} = \frac{\sum_{i=1}^{i=n} |act_i - pred_i|}{n}$$

where n is the number of training cases, *act* is the actual value and *pred* is the model value.

The choice made depends on the purpose of the model. Figure 12.7 demonstrates this for a neural network with one hidden-layer neuron. Minimising the r.m.s. error drives the solution towards what may be three outliers and the final solution is neither here nor there. By minimising the absolute error there is less importance given to these three cases and they become easily identifiable.

A third option would be to define an acceptable error tolerance and the fittest solution would be that which models the most training cases within this tolerance. The line in Figure 12.7 passing close to all but

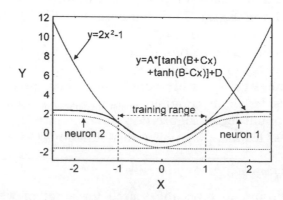

Figure 12.6   Neural networks cannot extrapolate

three of the points would be the optimal solution in this case, given a small error tolerance.

For data-mining problems the purpose should be to identify those cases which stand out from the rest with the objective of trying to understand why this is so and hence learning about the data. It can thus be seen how the choice of fitness function can affect the nature of this task.

12.1.4.4 Local minima

A common analogy to training a neural network (searching for the best weight set) is a kangaroo jumping around a mountain range. The kangaroo is searching for the lowest point in the range and does so by jumping around to see if the place where he lands is lower than the place from which he started. If he cannot jump very far then he might get stuck in the bottom of a local valley when a lower point actually exists in the next valley. This is what is known as a local minimum solution but in order to find the global minimum he needs the power to jump over the ridge between the two valleys and land at a lower point.

Training a neural network is a similar search procedure and most training algorithms do not guarantee the global solution. Figure 12.8*a* shows a neural network trapped in a local minimum. The required *x–y* mapping is possible with four hidden neurons but the weights are such that small weight changes result in the overall fitness function error increasing. Figure 12.8*b* shows the global solution that is possible but unlikely to develop from the situation in Figure 12.8*a*.

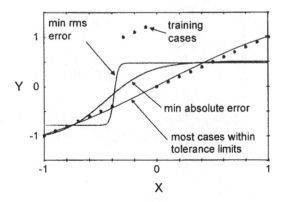

Figure 12.7   Defining the network fitness function for mapping x onto y

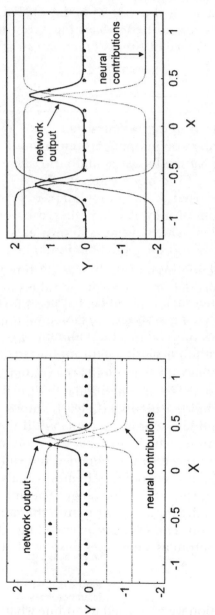

Figure 12.8   Training algorithms can become trapped in suboptimal solutions

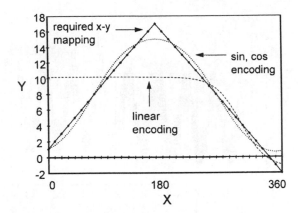

Figure 12.9   Input encoding schemes giving different results for a single hidden neuron

12.1.4.5 Data encoding

The ability of a neural network to extract relationships in data depends on how the data is encoded to represent the values or features of the inputs. The neural network is only as good as the information which it is given and failure to perform satisfactorily is often not the fault of the neural network but rather of the modeller in understanding how networks process the input data. Consider Figure 12.9 where a network with one hidden neuron is used to model the triangular *x–y* mapping over the range *x*=0 to *x*=360. Trying to map *x* directly onto *y* (linear encoding) with one hidden neuron is clearly impossible and would require at least two hidden neurons to get close. If the single input is encoded into two inputs which are the sine and cosine of *x* (in degrees), then a better result can be obtained but still only using one hidden neuron. These two encoding schemes will also give different extrapolation results outside the 0–360 range. The linear encoding will give constant values as the input will map onto the saturated flat parts of the activation function. The sine, cosine encoding scheme will result in repetitions of the output as *x* increases in steps of 360.

12.1.5 Summary

In this brief introduction we have tried to outline what an MLP is, what it can do, how it does it and what to be aware of. Successful use of neural networks is as much an art as a science, and there is no substitute for experience. The hardest step in neural networks is the

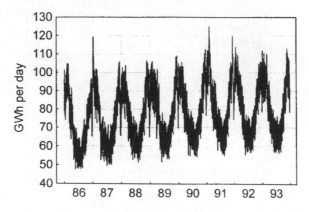

Figure 12.10   Total daily load over an eight year period

first, actually knowing how to use them after reading all the great reports of their success. It is a common misconception that because they are often referred to as artificial intelligence that some sort of supercomputer is required. A neural network is simply a small piece of computer code which iterates away in its search for a solution. In the Appendixes is included some sample code which forms the heart of the neural network.

12.2 Electric load modelling

12.2.1 The data being mined

The purpose of the investigation in this chapter is to understand what factors influence the electricity consumption of a region of the UK. Figures 12.10 to 12.12 show the data in question for the total daily load (throughout this chapter load refers to the total amount of energy consumed in a given period). Figure 12.13 shows typical half-hourly profiles for a week in summer and winter.

Figure 12.10 shows that there is an annual cycle which peaks in the colder winters with the load in the warmer summers being almost half of this peak value. Figure 12.11 shows that there is also a weekly cycle with abnormal activity at Christmas. Figure 12.12 highlights this weekly cycle, clearly showing that there is a reduced load demand at weekends. The difference between summer and winter half-hourly profiles is seen in Figure 12.13. In winter there is a large peak after midnight caused by an off-peak tariff which exists for electric storage

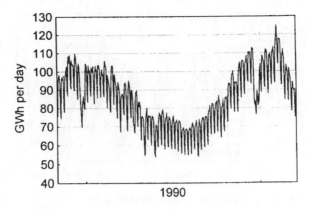

Figure 12.11   Total daily load over a one-year period

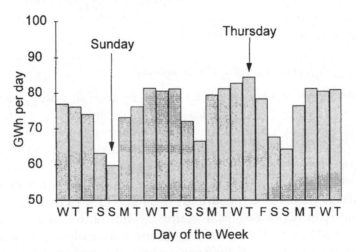

Figure 12.12   Total daily load over a three week period

heating, this peak being absent in summer. There is also a large evening peak in the winter whereas in the summer there are two smaller distinct evening peaks. The two summer peaks coincide with people returning from work (cooking) and dusk (when lights will be switched on). In the winter, as the number of daylight hours reduces these two periods coincide to create one peak which is probably amplified through heating requirements.

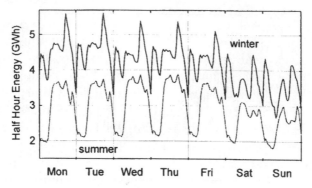

Figure 12.13   Half-hourly profiles for summer and winter

Electricity consumption is a dynamic process depending on numerous independent and interrelated factors and is a challenge for any modelling technique. Consumption patterns vary depending on the location as is shown in Czernichow *et al.* [4] where summer and winter weekly profiles are given for several countries.

12.2.2 Why forecast electricity demand?

In the long term, future trends in electricity consumption need to be forecast so that an energy policy can be formulated to ensure that there will be enough generation plant available to meet the projected requirements. In the medium term, demand needs to be known so that required resources such as coal can be stockpiled. Short-term load forecasting involves predicting electricity consumption hours to days ahead and is required to ensure an adequate electricity supply which is generated in an economical manner. The nature of load profiles (Figure 12.13) means that certain plant may only be required to generate electricity periodically throughout the day, so the prediction is required to formulate an operating schedule. The total cost of generation, and hence price, includes start-up and shut-down costs, which vary depending on the nature of the plant. For example, it is expensive to shut down nuclear reactors so their most economic operation is continuous generation. Coal-powered steam turbines require several hours for preheating the boilers, so once fired they will want to operate for extended periods. Hydroelectric generators, on the other hand, can be fully operational in about three seconds, a feature which allows them to command a high price under certain conditions.

In England and Wales the electricity pool (see Doyle and Maclaine [5] for a detailed description of the UK electricity-supply industry) administrates the wholesale trading of electricity. On a daily basis generators bid in prices at which they are willing to supply electricity for each half hour of the next day. In order to minimise costs, an optimised unit-commitment schedule [6] is calculated based on forecast demand and the bid prices. The bids are stacked starting with the cheapest until the forecast demand is met, and the actual traded price for all generators to distributors is based on this marginal bid price. Thus, in theory, nuclear operators are likely to bid a minimal amount to ensure that they are selected to supply for all hours, but the actual amount which they receive will be based on the system marginal price. The forecast is generally required at least 24 hours in advance so that the generators can be informed of their required schedule.

In the shorter term, forecasts seconds to minutes ahead are required to keep the frequency stable. This is particularly important during television commercial breaks when the switching on of kettles causes surges which have to be balanced by plant with fast reaction times.

With deregulation of the electricity industry, forecasting consumption is becoming more important at the utility level owing to the complex nature of electricity trading.

Reports on the potential energy savings that could be made by increasing the accuracy of the forecasts are limited [7,8].

12.2.3 Previous work

It was noted [9] that the volume of published papers in electric load forecasting is cyclical, with initial great interest gradually declining. Checking the dates from a recent review paper [4] would indicate that the current cycle peaked around 1993. There is no doubt that this current wave of interest is due to load forecasting being developed as another application area for the pattern-matching abilities of neural networks. The work appears to have been initiated in 1990 [10,11] and commercial load-forecasting software is now available and operational [12].

Early papers laid the groundwork and more recent papers tend to report on the results of various modifications. The models usually group input data by individual day types or weekdays and weekends [13–17] and divide data into seasons [15,18] or shorter periods. Holidays are often assumed to resemble weekends [14,19] or the data is adjusted [20,21] or removed [13]. In the literature, growth is seldom mentioned [21–26] as the time period being investigated is often deemed too short for it to make any difference to the model. The common approach is to adjust the data to eliminate its effect, often by some assumed linear growth rate. The reasons stated for such decisions are frequently based on prior knowledge about the load profiles and are probably due to experience of linear modelling techniques.

Such assumptions based on human judgement underestimate the capabilities of neural networks to indicate themselves how data should be modelled. Dividing up the dataset reduces the amount of training information and inhibits a general analysis of long-term trends. By including as inputs the relevant information on why the datasets are different it is possible to create one model for all the data, this single model being easier to analyse and improve. There has been little reported work on improving and hence learning about systems by visualisation of trends in the model performance [27].

Many published papers show excellent results from systems tailored to individual requirements and generally satisfy the needs of the users in the sense that they are at least as good as previous nonlinear models. It is hard to see how future improvements will emerge if the technique is viewed as a black box which cannot explain how it did or did not arrive at a good solution.

In this chapter the approach is to use the neural network as a data-mining tool to try and discover exactly what influences the load profile. This is achieved by examining network errors and finding reasons why they are such.

12.2.4 Network used

A feedforward multilayer perceptron trained by standard back-propagation was used for the analysis. Details are given in the appendixes. The fitness measure being evaluated was the minimum r.m.s. error over all the training examples, but it would have been a simple task to use any other error measure. Network performance is reported as the mean absolute percentage error (MAPE) as it is frequently used in similar work, although this was not the fitness function being minimised by the network training algorithm. The MAPE is only used as a yardstick to gauge model improvement and should never be used as a means of comparing various techniques on different datasets. For example, if a constant load was added to all the data (for instance if a factory with a constant demand was commissioned) then this would give the same model apart from the required constant term but the MAPE would be reduced. Different methods of

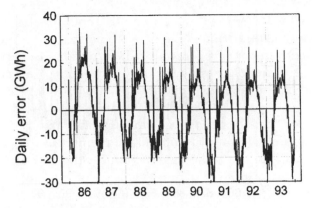

Figure 12.14   Day of week (MAPE = 15.00)

reporting errors and comments are given in Czernichow *et al.* [4], Rahman and Drezga [9], Agosta *et al.* [28] and Zebulum *et al.* [29].

12.3 Total daily load model

Figure 12.10 shows the data being investigated, the total daily load over eight years (1986–1993) for a region with approximately ten per cent of the total UK demand. The load for each day will be the output of the MLP (the dependent variable) and the inputs are what are required to be found. Thus, the data-mining problem is to establish what the factors are which determine the electric load.

Figure 12.12 shows that there appears to be a weekly pattern so this is the initial clue used. There are two commonly used methods of encoding the day of the week. Seven inputs could be created with the day in question having a value of 1 and the remaining six days having a value of 0, a system known as flagging. Alternatively, the day could be transformed into an angle (in steps of $2\pi/7$) and the sine and cosine of this angle used as the inputs. This second scheme was chosen, the consequences of which will become apparent later.

All 2922 examples of the day/load relationship were used to train the neural network, the errors for which are shown in Figure 12.14. In Figures 12.14 to 12.23 the *y*-axis is the daily error in GWh and the caption identifies the added input and MAPE achieved.

An annual cycle in the errors is clearly evident from Figure 12.14, with overestimates in the summer and underestimates in the winter. Weather patterns follow an annual cycle, so the average daily

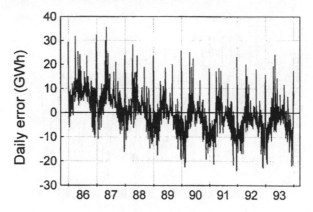

Figure 12.15   Average temperature (MAPE = 7.31)

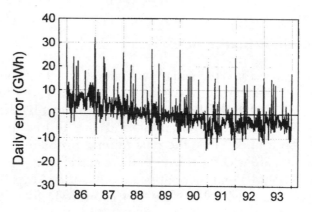

Figure 12.16   Seasonal term (MAPE = 5.28)

temperature was included as the second input; the errors for this network are shown in Figure 12.15.

Including the average temperature significantly reduced the error, but an annual cycle is still evident. The length of daylight is another factor that varies seasonally which would affect electricity demand owing to lighting requirements. In the UK during the summer month of June sunset is around 8.30 p.m., whereas in December it is at 4 p.m. As light levels were not available a continuous term was required as an input which had an annual cycle. A simple number (1–365) is not

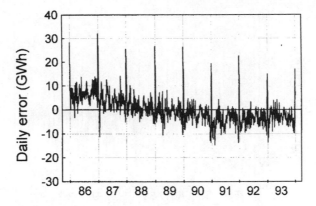

Figure 12.17   Bank holidays (MAPE = 5.00)

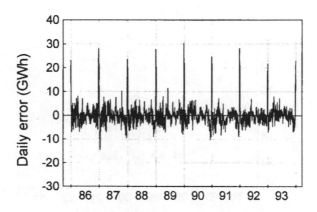

Figure 12.18   Growth term (five hidden neurons; MAPE = 3.10)

sufficient for this as it places adjacent days (31 December, 1 January) at opposite extremes. Taking the sine and cosine of the day-of-the-year angle produces the required cyclical seasonal term. Figure 12.16 shows how this has extracted the seasonal variation.

What is evident now are bank holiday Mondays and Good Friday. There are generally six bank holidays each year which are public holidays, as is Good Friday. A flag was created for these days, excluding those in the Christmas period which is evidently a more complex time and is dealt with separately.

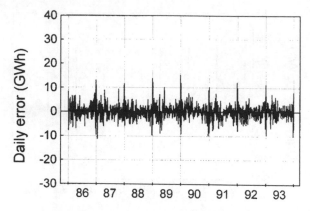

Figure 12.19　Growth term (ten hidden neurons; MAPE = 2.35)

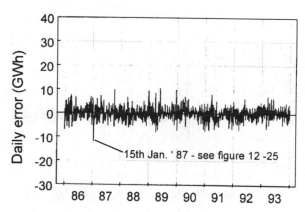

Figure 12.20　Christmas (MAPE = 2.18)

Figure 12.17 shows the errors when a flag to indicate the bank holiday is included as an input and a slow trend over the eight-year period becomes clearer. This can be explained by growth for which a linearly increasing term (1–2922) was included to represent this feature.

Figures 12.18 and 12.19 highlight the effect of the number of hidden neurons. In all previous cases and that of Figure 12.18 only five hidden neurons were used. Figure 12.19 has the same inputs as Figure 12.18 but with ten hidden neurons. The overall error is significantly

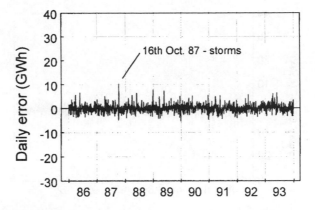

Figure 12.21   Past weather (MAPE = 1.46)

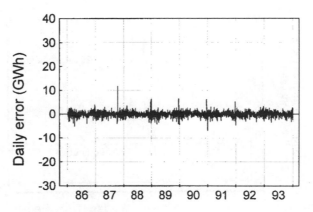

Figure 12.22   Other holiday effects (MAPE = 1.25)

reduced but it is clear that this reduction is due to efforts by the extra neurons to improve the Christmas errors. This is a consequence of minimising the r.m.s. error where outliers are given more significance. From a data-mining approach the network with only five hidden neurons is more informative.

In order to further examine the Christmas effect the errors were averaged over the eight years on a date basis, shown in Figure 12.24. With five hidden neurons it can be seen how the Christmas error is reduced by lowering the whole period from mid November to early

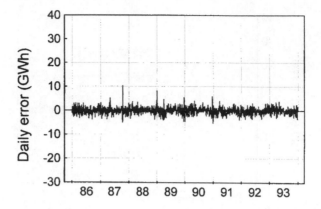

Figure 12.23   Yesterday's and last week's load (MAPE = 1.06)

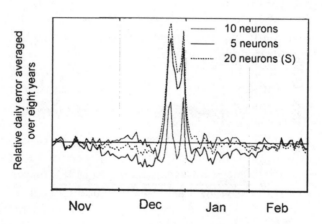

Figure 12.24   Averaged Christmas errors

February by manipulating the seasonal inputs to show a reduced load over this period. With ten hidden neurons there is more resolution available and the Christmas error can be significantly lowered with less interference in the adjoining days. The Christmas period is obviously special, but training with this data without any inputs to represent the feature causes distortion of the network. The third case shown in Figure 12.24 (S) used 20 hidden neurons but only trained on patterns where the initial error was below the overall r.m.s. error. Even with

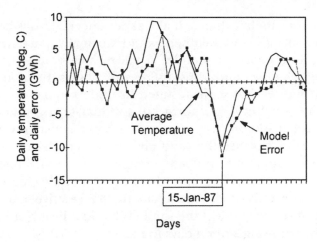

Figure 12.25   The effect of a sudden drop in temperature on the error

more hidden neurons there is little distortion and the residuals are clearly identified because they are never allowed to affect the training of the network. With this technique all patterns should first of all be presented for training before selective training begins to give them the opportunity to 'stake their claim'.

The errors over the Christmas period were significant from 22 December to 4 February with peaks on 26 December and 1 January. These errors indicate that this period is anomalous but their magnitude also gives some indication of the degree of variation from the norm, which is valuable information that can be used by the model. Inputs were created for these dates where the magnitude of the input was related to the magnitude of the average error. These inputs can be considered to be the degree of membership of Christmas, with 26 December having a membership value of 1. The errors of the trained network are shown in Figure 12.20.

Figure 12.20 shows there is residual on the 15 January, highlighted in Figure 12.25. Investigation showed that this error corresponded to a sudden cold front where the average temperature dropped to − 10 degrees Celsius on that day. The model error indicates that more electricity is being consumed than would normally be expected. This could be expected, as off-peak heating systems will not anticipate the sudden drop and ancillary heating devices will be used to make up the required balance. Further examination revealed that other periods experiencing sudden changes in temperature resulted in large model errors. A sharp drop in temperature in the middle of summer gave load predictions higher than actually experienced. This is because the uncharacteristically cold weather would normally warrant a higher daily load, but people generally react to weather as opposed to anticipating change, and thus there will always be a time delay. Conversely, sudden hot spells resulted in underestimations and there was a distinction between short-term gradual changes and sudden changes. The loads on very windy days were constantly underestimated, probably because the wind chill factor can have the effect of reducing the apparent ambient temperature and buildings can become draughty, requiring more heating. Days following windy days were also underestimated, due again to the reactive nature of the system response. People feel the wind chill and adjust heating systems accordingly, requiring several days to restore normality.

To account for these findings maximum, minimum and average temperature and wind-speed values were included for the day in question and the three previous days. The error was significantly reduced by these additional inputs as shown in Figure 12.21. For the obvious residual date now evident (16 October 1987) it was found that:

> On the 16th a violent storm with heavy rain brought chaos to southern England. The winds were probably the strongest for 250 years. Millions of trees were uprooted or broken, many crashed into power lines . . . Some large areas were without electricity for up to a fortnight . . . a mean hourly wind of 72 knots was recorded just before a power failure stopped the recorder. (Whittaker's Almanac 1989)

Examining the dates giving the largest errors in Figure 12.21 revealed certain clusters. These are shown in Figure 12.26 where the errors are averaged over the eight years. Although the exact dates are not the same every year, four clusters of consistent overestimates are evident. Three of these were identified as Easter bank-holiday weekend, August bank-holiday weekend and the week of the bank holiday in late May (Whitsuntide, traditionally a school half-term holiday). The remaining anomaly was late July to early August, which is when most schools have extended summer breaks.

Flags were created for the bank-holiday weekends and Whitsuntide, and a rising and falling linear term for the summer period, mimicking the nature of the error in Figure 12.26. Figure 12.22 shows the result of this trained network.

A causal model has been created which describes the load as a function of known events, but there is obviously a limit to the

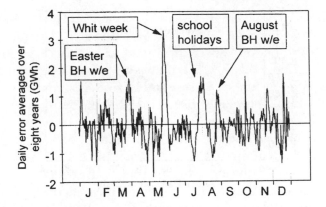

Figure 12.26   Averaged annual errors

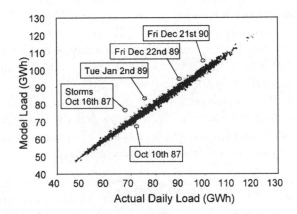

Figure 12.27   Actual against modelled loads

information available for a complete model of this type. Recent loads will contain information about local events which is captured in the load value and cannot be extracted otherwise. The final model shows this by also including yesterday's load and the load on the same day the previous week as inputs giving a final MAPE of 1.06 over all the eight years. Caution should be used here as generally the errors are reduced but days or weeks after certain special days can give increased errors.

Figure 12.27 was created from the model of Figure 12.22 and shows several residuals which can easily be explained. The underestimate on

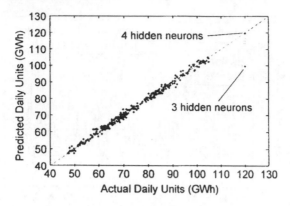

Figure 12.28   Overlearning by the addition of an extra neuron

10 October could be a result of the network trying to reduce the error for the storms on 17 October, one week later. 2 January 1989 was a Tuesday but also a bank holiday. Generally, New Year's day is the bank holiday or the Monday if 1 January falls at the weekend. Because 1 January was a Monday an extra day's holiday was given. Friday 22 December 1989 and 21 December 1990 are special because they are the last full weekdays before Christmas Eve. 21 December was not included in the Christmas period but in 1990 it was obviously taken as a holiday owing to the fact that Christmas fell the following Tuesday (when else would the office party be held?). This was the only example of Christmas falling on a Tuesday in the eight cases.

12.3.1 Overfitting and generalisation

To be of any use it is important that a trained neural network has the ability to generalise and not learn specific information in a photographic memory type of manner. It must extract general relationships between data rather than specific relationships relating only to explicit data. The ability to learn specific information is known as overfitting and can become a problem if too many hidden neurons are used, as illustrated by Figure 12.5.

Figure 12.28 shows the results of a network that can learn to fit an erroneous datum into a model. The data is the total daily load values for a particular year of the model already created with one value being significantly changed to represent a residual or erroneous reading. The network minimises the r.m.s. error. For a perfect model all the points will lie on a straight line, the situation where the network

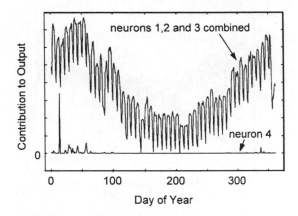

Figure 12.29   How the extra neuron enables overlearning

correctly repeats all the loads. With three hidden neurons the erroneous point is easily identified as standing away from this line. When an extra neuron is added the network can fit the spurious point on this line without much distortion to the remaining points.

Figure 12.29 shows how the neural network has done this. A set of weights has been found that activates the extra neuron for the inputs of the erroneous day. For most other days the combination of weights and inputs are below the operational threshold of the activation function of this extra neuron (in other words it is saturated). This neuron is used to provide the additional load required to account for the error. For days around the erroneous day (day 14) this neuron is also active, inducing errors and thus poor generalisation to days which have similar input patterns.

This is an extreme example as the induced error was rather large, but it demonstrates that there is more gain in dedicating a neuron to correcting a single day than reducing the errors for the remaining 364 days. Without careful examination extreme erroneous readings could quite easily go unnoticed and liberally adding more hidden neurons does not necessarily lead to a better model.

Three networks with three, eight and 15 hidden neurons were trained on the same year's data giving MAPEs of 1.09%, 0.46% and 0.59%, respectively. On this evidence the network with eight neurons appears superior. All weather inputs in this data were then replaced with the average day's weather (the weather for each day of the year being the same) and passed through the trained networks. Figure 12.30 shows that for certain days the two larger networks do not give

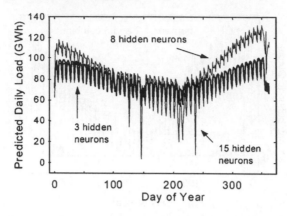

Figure 12.30   Poor generalisation of networks with large hidden layers

realistic predictions. The apparently most reliable network for generalisation is the one with three hidden neurons, although it gave the largest MAPE.

What has happened is that specific groups of neurons are only active for local features in the data. This can clearly be seen for the network with 15 hidden neurons which during learning has associated the bank holidays with the actual weather patterns in order to give a good model fit. When the actual weather is replaced by the average weather the neurons cannot give a general solution. With only three hidden neurons all data is learned by the same core neurons which experience the full range of values and have the ability to generalise. This is an example of how the quest for a minimum error can have its pitfalls.

12.4 Rule extraction

The model created in Section 12.3 was arrived at by deducing reasons for the model errors. As these reasons were identified and encoded as network inputs, improvements were seen. The question now becomes 'how is the neural network processing the data?'. We know that the inputs make sense and that a neural network is a very simple number-processing machine, so an explanation should be simple to find. Without explanations there will be continued distrust of neural networks.

Consider the neural network in Figure 12.1. The network output is simply the summation of a number of terms originating from each hidden neuron, which in turn have formed connections of varying

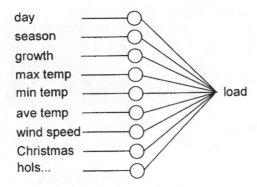

Figure 12.31   Schematic of the pruned network

strength to the inputs. This basic idea makes neural networks a powerful tool for analysing relationships in data. In its simplest form a neural network with two hidden neurons and a linear output neuron is decomposing the output into two components, the natures of which were investigated for the causal inputs identified (i.e. not including past loads).

It was found that one of the neurons was acting as a filter in that it only appeared to be processing day of the week information. This was obvious when the two components were viewed and confirmed by inspecting the weights feeding into these two neurons, with those weights connecting the day inputs with one of the hidden neurons being much larger than the remaining weights.

A new network was created with three hidden neurons, one neuron with weights removed or pruned so that it only processed day inputs and the remaining two being fully connected. In a similar manner to before the seasonal component was filtered. This process was continued and eventually all the inputs had been isolated and a network similar to that in Figure 12.31 was created.

12.4.1 Day of the week

The inclusion of a single neuron dealing only with day of the week inputs gave disproportionately large errors for Mondays. Examination of the output of this neuron revealed that it was operating close to one extreme ($+1$) of the tanh activation function for weekdays and close to the other extreme (-1) for Sundays. The addition of a second, third and fourth dedicated neuron improved the overall errors and reduced the errors for Mondays to the same level as those for all other days.

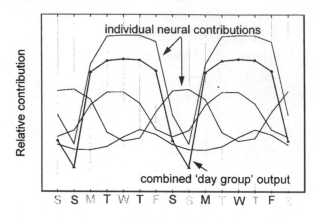

Figure 12.32   Four hidden neurons and combined contribution to output

Figure 12.32 shows how the final contribution for each day is the summation of the outputs of the four hidden day neurons. One neuron gets close to the solution but the extra neurons are required to increase the resolution. The manner in which the day of the week input was encoded is directly related to the number of hidden neurons required. Fortunately, the daily load requirement follows a cyclical pattern over the week, which is suited to the sine, cosine input encoding. If, for example, Wednesday afternoon was a public holiday the load would drop on Wednesday and more neurons would be required to model this effect as the continuity of the cycle would be broken. It would appear that a better encoding scheme for general cases if a continuous weekly cycle is not evident would be seven inputs as described previously which would only require one hidden neuron.

Figure 12.33 shows the first rule, the contribution to the load based only on day of the week.

12.4.2 Time of year

The seasonal component of the load with the summer correction included is shown in Figure 12.34. Figure 12.35 shows how this was formed by the summation of four hidden neuron outputs. The sine, cosine encoding is the only practical method of representing this cyclical term as a network input.

The variation between summer and winter is similar in magnitude to the difference between Sunday and Thursday. The significance of the school-holiday effect is also clearly evident. The overall nature of the curve closely resembles the patterns of sunset and sunrise times, with

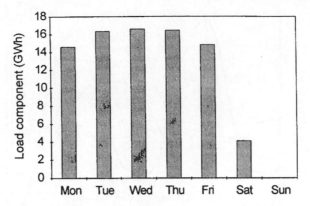

Figure 12.33 Rule 1—what day of the week is it?

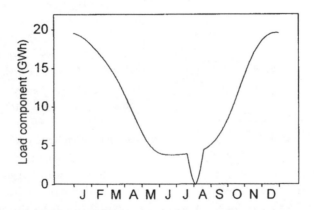

Figure 12.34 Rule 2—what day of the year is it?

the nights drawing in quickly from September to December characterised by the steepness of the slope. From January to May the nights gradually get lighter as the sun reenters the northern hemisphere. Figure 12.34 is the second rule.

12.4.3 Growth

The linear input included to represent growth is transformed by four hidden neurons as shown in Figure 12.36. The nature of the curve

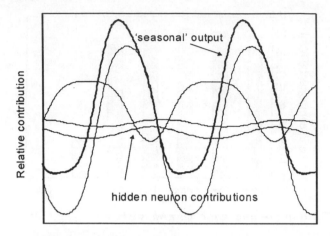

Figure 12.35   How the seasonal term is formed

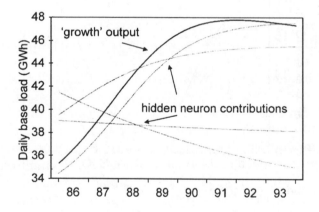

Figure 12.36   Rule 3—what is the base load?

follows the economic climate of the time with the UK recession starting in 1991 clearly reflected by a reduction in the demand for electricity.

A second method of calculating the growth was performed using weather correction. A network was trained for each individual year and then the weather inputs were replaced with the averaged eight-year weather for each day. If the neural network generalises well, this gives

Table 12.1   The relative importance of past weather conditions

	T (today)	T − 1 (yesterday)	T − 2	T − 3
Max temp	1.00	0.59	0.43	0.29
Min temp	1.00	0.19	-	-
Ave temp	1.00	1.08	-	0.63
Wind speed	1.00	0.37	0.13	0.12

a weather corrected load or the load which would have occurred if the weather had been average. The weather-corrected average annual daily load was then calculated for each year and assumed to occur at the median day of each year. Eight points resulted which were then curve fitted with a linear input neural network which was used to give a value for each day over the eight years. This weather-corrected load resembled that of Figure 12.36.

12.4.4 Weather factors

By introducing a single dedicated neuron to process specific weather inputs as opposed to grouping all weather-related inputs together, it was found that the increase in error was negligible. Furthermore, weight examination over several tests revealed consistencies in weight ratios for the time-lagged (previous day's) weather inputs (Table 12.1). Generally, the lag coefficients are as expected, the importance declining with time. Average temperature is different with yesterday's average temperature being slightly more important than today's, which is not unexpected, as today's average is not finalised until the end of the day when most electricity has already been consumed. What is surprising is that the average temperature two days ago is insignificant while that of three days ago is relatively important.

Because of the consistencies in weight values the data can be preprocessed to create a single-valued input for each weather variable. Figure 12.37 shows these factors and the contribution to the load, where the temperature factors are in degrees Celsius and the wind speed in knots and they are calculated from the coefficients in Table 12.1. The nonlinearity of these curves illustrates the effect of the nonlinear regression capabilities of neural networks. The gradients of the maximum and average temperature curves imply that, as the weather gets warmer, electricity consumption decreases. The minimum temperature curve gradient is opposite indicating that there is a

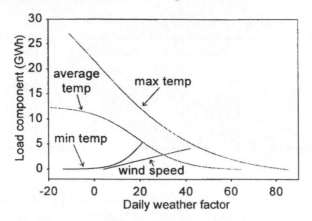

Figure 12.37   Rule 4 — what is the weather like?

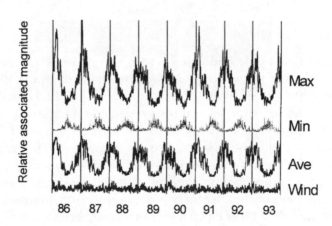

Figure 12.38   The weather components of the load

load component which increases with increasing temperatures. This could be the effect of the limited air conditioning or refrigeration. The wind-speed load component increases as it gets windier. Figure 12.38 shows the weather components of the load over the eight years.

12.4.5 Holidays

Six holiday neurons were created for summer, Christmas, bank holidays and the special days around the bank holidays. No day could

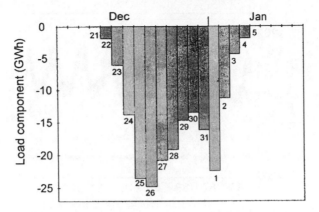

Figure 12.39 Christmas corrections

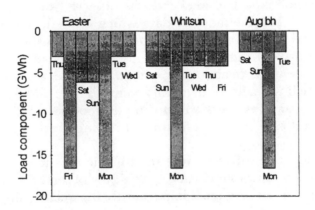

Figure 12.40 Holiday corrections

be a member of more than one holiday type. Figures 12.39 and 12.40 show the corrections deduced by the neural network.

The Christmas corrections were based on observed errors from Figure 12.24 but improvements could be made after the anomalous days around Christmas (Figure 12.27) had been identified, as these will distort the average errors. This exemplifies how adding certain information reveals more detailed information which allows refinement of the initial information—a circular process.

For the Easter weekend, shoulder days were identified from the data which indicate an extended holiday period. This fits with observed

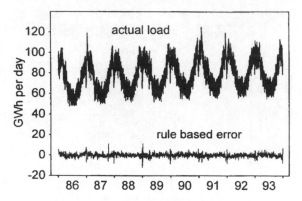

Figure 12.41   Rule-based model

behaviour as people take extra days of holiday to make the most of the two public holidays. The weekend was observed to have more of a holiday effect than the shoulder days, which was reflected in the input encoding. Whitsun week and weekend were all classified as the same holiday group and thus will all have identical corrections. In a fully connected network relationships with day of the week will also be formed which will add to the accuracy and is an example of why this drastically pruned network will not be as good as a fully connected network, as it cannot extract features involving more than one input type.

Only independent factors were used in the creation of this model, mainly to keep things simple and graphically observable. Interrelated factors were tested, the most important being relationships between day of the week and day of the year, and day of the year and growth. Figure 12.41 shows the actual load and the errors with the rule-based predictions. Figure 12.42 shows the change in the cumulative error distribution caused by pruning the network.

12.5 Model comparisons

The fully connected model was used to give next day predictions using the previous 800 days as a training set, with the weather for the prediction day being used retrospectively. A training set of 800 days was used to capture at least two years of examples for periods such as Christmas. An initial network was trained and used to predict the load for the next day's previously unseen data. This data with the actual

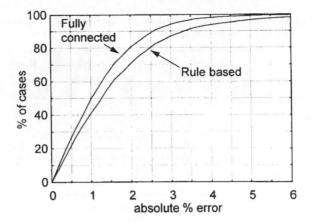

Figure 12.42 Cumulative percentage error distributions

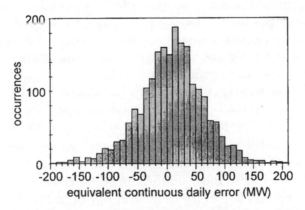

Figure 12.43 Error distribution for one-day-ahead predictions

observed load was then added to the training set with the distant-most day being removed. For each prediction the weights from the previous day's network were used as a starting point and ten epochs of training were allowed (an epoch is where all the patterns are presented once).

A network with ten hidden neurons and inputs including yesterday's and last week's load gave an MAPE of 1.3% over the 5.8 years of predictions. Figure 12.43 shows the errors translated into an equivalent continuous error throughout the day. In context 60 MW represents approximately 20 watts per customer (not person) for the

Table 12.2   Model errors by day type — mean absolute error (MAE) is an equivalent continuous daily error (MW)

	Fully connected MAE	Rule-based MAE	Prediction model MAE	Prediction model MAPE
Christmas	60	144	85	2.38
Bank holidays	51	86	54	2.06
Summer	28	47	31	1.13
Nonspecial weekends	41	51	39	1.26
Nonspecial weekdays	42	48	45	1.22

region (a light bulb is typically 60–100 W). Table 12.2 shows the errors analysed by day type for this prediction model, the fully connected model and the rule-based model.

Christmas is the worst period to model but this would be expected as there is a limited number of examples available for training. The rule-based and prediction model performances are relatively poor which is not unexpected as there is no information relating the date to the day of the week for the rule-based model and there are only two years of examples for the prediction model.

Bank holidays were generally underestimated in the prediction model but the overall error MAE was comparable to the fully connected model. The period classified as summer holidays gave the best prediction results which were again close to the fully connected errors.

The errors for all nonspecial days would indicate that weekdays gave better results than weekends if the MAPE was used as the indicator, as reported in Peng *et al.* [30]. This is not the case, however, when the mean absolute error (MAE) is examined, a result that is due to the reduced weekend load. This highlights the fact that reporting percentages, although common practice, is really meaningless in electric load forecasting.

This error analysis would indicate that, for prediction purposes, improvements would result for the nonspecial days if those days identified as holidays were omitted from the dataset.

12.6 Half-hourly model

For the half-hourly model the data used ranged from 10 January to 6 December 1994, giving 15 888 load values. This range was restricted only by the size of the spreadsheet used for data preprocessing but conveniently missed the Christmas period. Hourly-valued weather data was available for temperatures and wind speeds. The missing half hours were created by simply repeating the previous value. For descriptive purposes the hours range from 0.5 to 24. The energy consumed between midnight and 00:30 is described as happening in hour 0.5. Similarly, hour 13 is 12:30 to 13:00.

12.6.1 Initial input data

Based on the previous experience the initial time inputs for this model were created to represent:

- hour of the day;
- day of the week;
- time of year;
- growth.

For temperatures and wind speeds the current value and moving averages [31] of the previous five, 24 and 48 hours were used as inputs, the time length based on intuition rather than any scientific findings. By filtering in this way, as opposed to using time delays, fewer inputs are required and noise is suppressed. From a common sense point of view the load in any half hour will not depend on an exact temperature 48 hours previously, more a general underlying temperature.

Another term that was included in the initial model indicated whether the data were taken during Greenwich Mean Time (GMT) or British Summer Time (BST), an hour change which makes summer evenings lighter. A flag was used to indicate to which set each data point belonged.

12.6.2 Results

The errors of the initial network are shown in Figure 12.44. The four bank-holiday Mondays along with Good Friday (1 April) have clearly been overestimated, meaning that the load is lower than usual on these days. A flag was created as an input to indicate bank holidays.

Overestimates occur in the period October–March, Figure 12.47 showing the hours at which the largest daily overestimates occur. It can be seen quite clearly that the model has problems with hour 24 from November to March and hour 1 in April and May. The change occurs distinctly on 27 March, which corresponds to the start of BST.

Figure 12.48 shows a typical winter day for this model and it can be seen that hour 24 is a cardinal point [32] and thus important in load

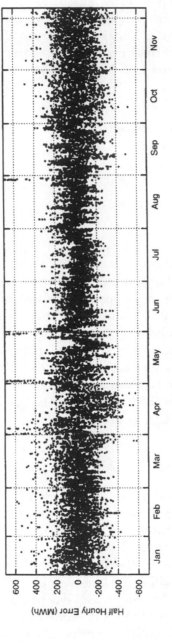

Figure 12.44   Errors with only weather and time as inputs (MAPE = 2.9%)

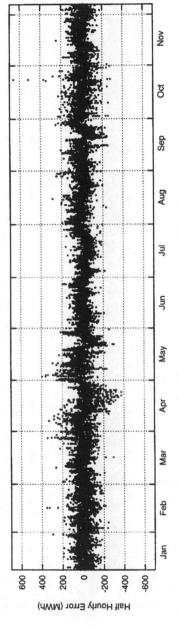

Figure 12.45   Errors with weather, time, holidays, tariffs and daylight as inputs (MAPE=1.8%)

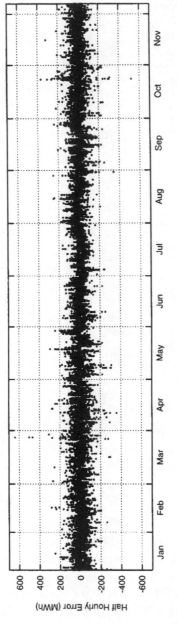

Figure 12.46   Errors with weather, time, holidays, tariffs, daylight and previous loads as inputs (MAPE=1.4%)

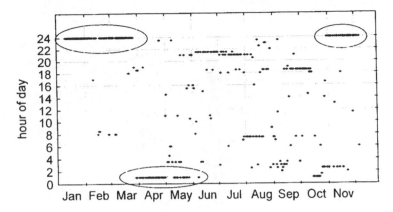

Figure 12.47   *The hours at which the largest daily overestimates occur for the initial model*

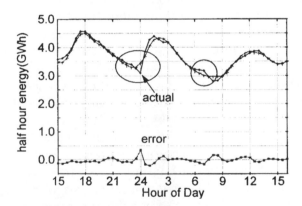

Figure 12.48   *The off-peak tariff is the reason why the errors occur*

forecasts. What is happening is that there is a sudden surge in consumption in hour 0.5 caused by a special tariff for which water heating and storage radiator circuits are automatically switched on for seven hours during the night. There are over one million customers on this tariff of which 80 per cent are on a fixed clock time-switching mechanism explaining why there is a difference between GMT and BST. The remaining 20 per cent are radio teleswitch controlled.

From Figure 12.48 it can be seen why the neural model has problems. The model inputs are generally smooth and continuous and

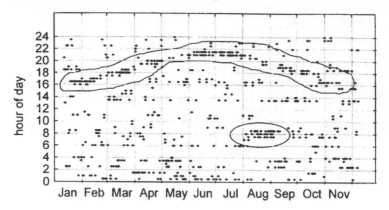

Figure 12.49   The two largest daily overestimates on the improved model now highlight lighting-up time

so are fitting a smooth continuous curve through the data. There is a discontinuity in the load at midnight with the surge from the off-peak tariff. The neural model has compensated for this effect by rounding off the discontinuity so that a smooth curve can be fitted, resulting in the overestimates for hour 24. A similar effect is seen in Figure 12.9. The opposite effect can be seen at hour 7 when the heating and water-charging circuits are automatically switched off. A discontinuity is also seen at hour 3 which corresponds to a similar tariff switching on at 2:30 a.m. In order to model the effects on the load due to the tariffs it is necessary to create an input which indicates the hours for which the tariffs are in operation. Flags were created for each tariff.

Figure 12.49 shows the two largest daily overestimates on the improved model, illustrating that the problems with hour 24 have been eliminated (exactly how this was achieved is demonstrated later). What are now evident are problems that correspond to lighting-up times in the dusk period [33].

With experience gained from how the neural model reacted to the surges due to tariffs, it is assumed that lighting surges cause the new overestimates. Data on effective illumination [34] were unavailable so a day/night indicator was used, the transitions being sunrise and sunset times. An input to represent the dusk period used the half hours before and after sunset as the cut-off points.

Figure 12.49 also reveals a cluster around hour 8 in August, which corresponds to school summer holidays and is explained if fewer people are getting up at this time, resulting in reduced demand. This cluster supports the findings in the daily load model which identified

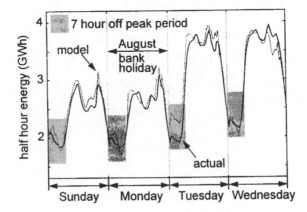

Figure 12.50 August bank-holiday period modelled only with one indicator that Monday was a holiday; reduced load requirement on Sunday and the early hours of Tuesday is very evident

a summer anomaly, but in the half-hourly case the anomalies extend further into August and early September.

Further inputs were created for the Easter weekend and Whitsun week. It was evident that the effect of bank holidays extended to around 6 a.m. the following morning, which makes sense if people on night shifts take this period as their holiday. This is clearly shown in Figure 12.50 with the model overestimating the early-morning load. Errors the day after holidays were also identified in Bakirtzis *et al.* [20] and Hsu and Yang [35].

Figure 12.45 shows the errors of the model modified thus far. Further investigation revealed reasons for some remaining anomalies.

The overestimates in early May occur the morning after the bank holiday in the two half hours following the new cut-off of the bank-holiday indicator (6 a.m. on Tuesday), suggesting that the influence of the bank holiday extends an extra hour in this case. There is also consistent reduced load in the working hours of this day, confirming that many people will take it as a day's holiday to make the most of the long weekend. The overestimates at the end of August occur the evening before and the late morning following the bank holiday. The big dip towards the end of May is actually the week before the bank holiday, indicating that in the run up to the holiday period more electricity than usual could be being consumed, possibly owing to increased industrial output. Another likely reason is that the model is compensating so that the errors during Whitsun are reduced.

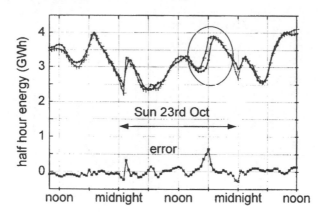

Figure 12.51   An anomaly the day the clocks change

At lighting-up time the day the clocks changed on Sunday 23 October the model seems to be an hour early in its predictions (Figure 12.51). This would be the result if the clocks for street lighting which came on with time switches were not adjusted until the Monday. A second suggestion might be a kind of jet-lag effect where people have not adjusted to the extra hour change. Another possibility that cannot be discounted is that the data has somehow been adjusted to account for the extra hour so that the data base will still have 24 hours in this day (how the data was dealt with was unknown). The overestimates that occur when BST starts on Sunday 27 March are in the early hours of the following Monday morning, especially around dawn (Figure 12.52).

The overestimates in February occur in the late morning of the 15. On the previous evening blizzards swept across Britain bringing many areas to a standstill, so presumably people were turning up late to work the following day, reducing the load (Figure 12.53).

There is a period at the end of September when there are hardly any load overestimates. Examination of the weather conditions revealed that this was peculiar in that the temperature stayed almost constant at 11 degrees Celsius for three days, both day and night.

The greatest anomaly is in the second half of April when there are large underestimates. These all occur in the off-peak tariff hours which gives a clue to their cause. What is thought to be happening is that people are gradually switching their night storage radiators off throughout April, as the weather gets warmer. The model can deal with them being all on or all off but struggles unless it knows exactly how many are on or off.

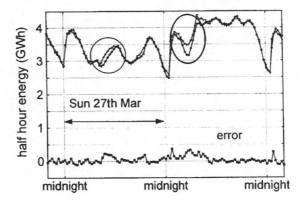

Figure 12.52   More anomalies the day they change back

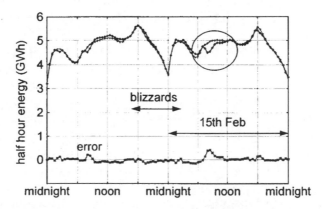

Figure 12.53   Reduced load because of severe weather conditions

It would be expected that there should be similar problems in October as heaters are switched on again, which is slightly evident but not as extreme as in April. This can be explained by people's tolerance of overheating but not under heating. In October all heating will probably be switched on at the first cold spell, and then left on knowing that it could always be cold again tomorrow. In April as it gets warmer heaters will be turned off gradually over a period of a few weeks as people get around to it. The problem of modelling April was also encountered in Hyde and Hodnett [26,33] where the data were for Ireland, a country with similar climate, tariffs and probably a greater proportion of storage radiators. A possible explanation given by the authors was that the errors were due to the hour change occurring in this bimonthly model (March–April).

12.6.3 Past loads

Thus far no previous load values were included in the model and the MAPE was around 1.8%. Past loads were deliberately overlooked because we wanted to identify and explain what causes the load to be what it is, not how the model responds to good initial guesses of what the load might be. A causal model as opposed to a time-series model was required.

The situation in April is an example of how including past loads might help if causal information is unavailable. The load is determined by variables such as weather, not past loads, i.e. the load depends on the underlying conditions. But since previous loads are a consequence of previous underlying conditions, they will contain information about near past conditions which may not be available in raw data form.

In Kiernan *et al.* [36] a feature-selection algorithm showed that the previous half-hour load and the load at the same time a week before were the most important input variables, with the load at the same time yesterday also being important, a finding which is not unsurprising. Loads for the same half hour the day before and the week before were included as inputs to the model, the resulting errors shown in Figure 12.46. The previous half-hour load was not included as this would have to be based on predictions in a 24-hour ahead forecaster (even though forecast temperatures would have to be used). Figure 12.46 shows how the problems with April disappear and the MAPE is now around 1.4%. Comparing Figures 12.45 and 12.46, the main improvements gained by including past loads are clearly in the transition periods of April and October, with no significant visible improvement in other months. What can also be seen is that, although the overall error is reduced, some periods are markedly worse. These stand out clearly and there will be reasons for the errors, such as the period 24 hours or one week previous being a special event.

12.6.4 How the model is working

By including previous loads as inputs improvements were seen in the off-peak load in the transition period of March to April. By resetting all the binary flags so that no events occur and passing these new patterns through the initial weights, it is possible to visualise what is happening.

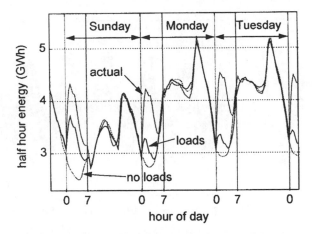

Figure 12.54   How the network models the off-peak period in February

Figure 12.54 shows this for a winter day for the two cases with and without previous loads included in the input data. It can be seen that the model with no previous loads fits a smooth underlying load whereas when previous loads are included there is an influence from past values in the early hours. The 'no loads' curve can be thought of as the model's estimation of what the load would have been if the off-peak tariff did not exist (although the whole profile would change if these tariffs did not exist). Comparing Figure 12.54 with Figure 12.48 it is evident how the improved models use the flag to deal with the discontinuity and improve the predictions for the cardinal point.

12.6.5 Extracting the growth

The linear growth term was pruned from all hidden neurons and connected to its own dedicated neurons in an attempt to extract the growth. Figure 12.55 shows the resultant base load for 1994 following the same trend as the base load extracted for the previous eight years in the daily model.

12.6.6 Populations of models

When creating the models it was noted that identical models with an identical number of hidden neurons always converged close to a certain value, the only difference being the random starting values given to the weights. It could be assumed that the models were almost identical, but this was not the case if viewed on a half-hourly scale. As noise will exist in the loads owing to unpredictable random effects and

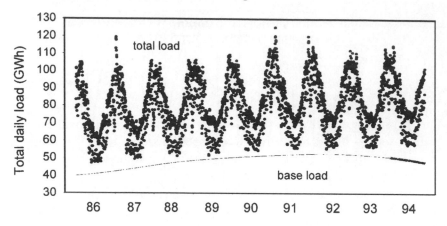

Figure 12.55   The extracted growth for the daily (86–93) and half-hourly (94) models

Table 12.3   Improved performance is seen by averaging several seemingly identical networks

	1	2	3	4	5	Average
RMSE	63.75	65.80	63.91	64.26	64.36	59.50
MAPE	1.42	1.46	1.43	1.44	1.43	1.30

an incomplete set of variables for the inputs (the model will always be to some degree ill posed), the neural fit has relaxed constraints and the model will describe a path through the noisy data. There are many paths that can be made through noisy data that give similar errors and always limits on the accuracy which can be achieved, assuming that the number of hidden neurons is limited.

The question then is which model to choose? For any given point the average of two predictions will always be better than the worst, unless both are the same. Carrying this idea forward as more models are created, the better and more robust should be the averaged performance. Five identically created models were trained, the results shown in Table 12.3.

The overall errors of the averaged model outputs are a significant improvement on any particular individual model. Creating populations of models was a technique used in Feuston and Thurtell [37], but in this case each model (inputs and topology) was different. This was done to overcome the uncertainty of which inputs and connections were relevant.

12.7 Summary

The primary objective of this work was achieved, a neural network being used to bring meaning to a vast amount of data. By doing so, experience and knowledge was gained that would be very beneficial in the load forecasting problem.

It is not proposed that the inputs selected for this model are generally applicable to all regions, as electricity consumption will vary depending on both tariffs and, primarily, the weather. In many regions the air-conditioning load is significant so humidity will have an influence on the load. What is proposed is that each system be analysed carefully and a neural network is a quick and easy way of doing this.

Training times for the neural networks were not excessive (minutes rather than hours on a Pentium 133) with speed improvement best being achieved by adding the extra information required.

The power of neural networks as data-mining, modelling and analysis tools has been shown and in comparison with other techniques the results/effort ratio is very high. Once one application has been performed the transition to other datasets is very simple; it is the same principle but with different numbers.

Familiarity with the tool is as important as the familiarity with the data being modelled. Neural networks are only tools and only as good as the data which goes into them; they are not magic boxes that produce an answer for no apparent reason. The benefits that neural networks can deliver depend on the time and effort which is put into the problem. It is common practice to ignore what is actually happening within the network and to dismiss neural networks when they give wrong answers. This results from the ignorance of the modeller as opposed to the neural networks not working. At the end of the day, neural networks are only nonlinear regression models which are as useful and informative as any other modelling technique.

12.8 References

1 SOLIS F. and WETS, J.: 'Minimisation by random search techniques', *Math. Oper. Res.*, 1981, **6**

2 KRISHNAKUMAR, K.: 'Genetic algorithms—a robust optimization tool'. AIAA report 93-0315

3 YOON, B., HOLMES, D.J., LANGHOLZ, G. and KANDEL, A.: 'Efficient genetic algorithms for training layered feedforward neural networks', *Inf. Sci.*, 1994, **76**, pp. 67–85

4 CZERNICHOW, T., PIRAS, A., IMHOF, K., CAIRE, P., JACCARD, Y., DORIZZI, B. and GERMOND, A.: 'Short-term electrical load forecasting with artificial neural networks', *Eng. Intell. Syst. Electr. Eng. Commun.*, 1996, **4**, (2), pp. 85–99 (review)

5 DOYLE, G. and MACLAINE, D.: 'Power as a commodity' (Financial Times Energy Publishing, 1996)

6 MA, X., EL-KEIB, A.A., SMITH, R.E. and MA, H.: 'A genetic algorithm based approach to thermal unit commitment of electric power systems', *Electr. Power Syst. Res.*, 1995, **34**, (1), pp. 29–36

7 RANAWEERA, D.K., KARADY, G.G. and FARMER, R.G.: 'Economic impact analysis of load forecasting', *IEEE Trans. Power Syst.*, 1997, **12**, (3), pp. 1388–1392

8 BUNN, D.W. and FARMER, E.D.: 'Comparative models for electrical load forecasting' (John Wiley & Sons Ltd, 1985) pp 3–9

9 RAHMAN, S. and DREZGA, I.: 'Identification of a standard for comparing short-term load forecasting techniques', *Electr. Power Syst. Res.*, 1992, **25**, (3), pp. 149–158

10 PARK, D., EL-SHARKAWI, M., MARKS, R., ATLAS, A. and DAMBORG, M.: 'Electric load forecasting using an artificial neural network'. Presented at the IEEE Power Engineering Society winter meeting, 1990

11 PENG, T.M., HUBELE, N.F. and KARADY, G.G.: 'Conceptual approach to the application of neural network for short-term load forecasting'. Proceedings of the IEEE international symposium on *Circuits and systems*, 1990, pp. 2942–2945

12 KHOTANZAD, A., AFKHAMI-ROHANI, R., LU, T.L., ABAYE, A., DAVIES, M. and MARATUKULAM, D.J.: 'ANNSTLF—a neural-network-based electric load forecasting system', *IEEE Trans. Neural Netw.*, 1997, **8**, (4), pp. 835–845

13 RANAWEERA, D.K., HUBELE, N.F. and PAPALEXOPOULOS, A.D.: 'Application of radial basis function neural-network model for short-term load forecasting', *IEE Proc., Gener. Transm. Distrib.*, 1995, **142**, (1), pp. 45–50

14 XIAO, B. and MCLAREN, P.G.: 'An artificial neural network for short term load forecasting', Proceedings of the *Communications power and computing* conference, *WESCANEX '95*, 95CH3581-6/0-7803-2741-1/95, pp. 129-132

15 DASH, P.K., SATPATHY, H.P., LIEW, A.C. and RAHMAN, S.: 'A real-time short-term load forecasting system using functional link network', *IEEE Trans. Power Syst.*, 1997, **12**, (2), pp. 675–680

16 MANDAL, J.K., SINHA, A.K. and PARTHASARATHY, G.: 'Application of recurrent neural network for short term load forecasting in electric power system'. Proceedings of the IEEE international conference on *Neural Networks*, 1995, 0-7803-2768-3/95, pp. 2694–2698

17 EL-SHARKAWI, M.A., MARKS, R.J., OH, S. and BRACE, C.M.: 'Data partitioning for training a layered perceptron to forecast electric load'. Proceedings of the IEEE 2nd international forum on *Applications of neural networks to power systems*, April 1993, Yokohama, Japan, 0-7803-1217-1/93, pp. 66–68

18 AL-RASHID, Y. and PAARMANN, L.D.: 'Short-term electric load forecasting using neural network models'. Proceedings of the 39th Midwest symposium on *Circuits and systems*, 1997, 0-7803-3636-4/97, pp. 1436–1439

19 SINGH, S.P. and MAILK, O.P.: 'Single ANN architecture for short-term load forecasting for all seasons', *Eng. Intell. Syst. Electr. Eng. Commun.*, 1995, **3**, (4), pp. 249–254

20 BAKIRTZIS, A.G., PETRIDIS, V., KLARTZIS, S.J., ALEXIADIS, M.C. and MAISSIS, A.H.: 'A neural-network short-term load forecasting model for the Greek power-system', *IEEE Trans. Power Syst.*, 1996, **11**, (2), pp. 858–863

21 PAPALEXOPOULOS, A.D., HAO, S.Y. and PENG, T.M.: 'An implementation of a neural network based load forecasting model for the EMS', *IEEE Trans. Power Syst.*, 1994, **9**, (4), pp. 1956–1962

22 MOHAMMED, O., PARK, D., MERCHANT, R., DINH, T., TONG, C., AZEEM, A., FARAH, J. and DRAKE, C.: 'Practical experiences with an adaptive neural-network short-term load forecasting system', *IEEE Trans. Power Syst.*, 1995, **10**, (1), pp. 254–265

23 CONNOR, J.T.: 'A robust neural network filter for electricity demand prediction', *J. Forecasting*, 1996, **15**, (6), pp. 437–458

24 SHIMAKURA, Y., FUJISAWA, Y., MAEDA, Y., MAKINO, R., KISHI, Y., ONO, M., FANN, J.Y. and FUKUSIMA, N.: 'Short-term load forecasting using an artificial neural network'. Proceedings of the IEEE 2nd international forum on *Applications of neural networks to power systems*, April 1993, Yokohama, Japan, 0-7803-1217-1/93, pp. 233–238

25 MATSUMOTO, T., KITAMURA, S., UEKI, Y. and MATSUI, T.: 'Short-term load forecasting by artificial neural networks using individual and collective data of preceding years'. Proceedings of the IEEE 2nd international forum on *Applications of neural networks to power systems*, April 1993, Yokohama, Japan, 0-7803-1217-1/93, pp. 245–250

26 HYDE, O. and HODNETT, P.F.: 'Modelling the effect of weather in short-term electricity load forecasting', *Mathematical Engineering in Industry*, 1997, **6**, (2), pp. 155–169

27 RASANEN, M., HAMALAINEN, R.P. and RUUSUNEN, J.: 'Visual interactive modeling in electric load analysis'. Proceedings of the 13th IASTED international conference on *Modelling, identification and control*, February 1994, 0-88986-138-8, pp. 339–342

28 AGOSTA, J.M., NIELSEN, N.R. and ANDEEN, G.: 'Fast training of neural networks for load forecasting'. Proceedings of the American *Power* conference, 1996, **58**, (1), pp. 219–224

29 ZEBULUM, R.S., VELLASCO, M., PACHECO, M.A. and GUEDES, K.: 'A multi-step hourly load forecasting system using neural nets'. Proceedings of the 38th Midwest symposium on *Circuits and systems*, 1996, 0-7803-2972-4/96, pp. 461–464

30 PENG, T.M., HUBELE, N.F. and KARADAY, G.G.: 'Advancement in the application of neural networks for short-term load forecasting', *IEEE Trans. Power Syst.*, 1992, **7**, (1), pp. 250–257

31 MACKAY, D.J.C.: 'Bayesian nonlinear modeling for the prediction competition', *ASHRAE Trans.*, 1994, **100**, (2), pp. 1053–1062

32 HANNAN, J.M., MAJITHIA, S., ROGERS, C. and MITCHELL, R.J.: 'Implementation of neural networks for forecasting cardinal points on the electricity demand curve'. 4th international conference on *Power system control and management*, April 1996, pp. 160–164

33 HYDE, O. and HODNETT, P.F.: 'An adaptable automated procedure for short-term electricity load forecasting', *IEEE Trans. Power Syst.*, 1997, **12**, (1), pp. 84–93

34 KIERNAN, L.A., HANNAN, J.M., BISHOP, M., MITCHELL, R.J. and KAMBHAMPATI, C.: 'Neural networks for load profile reshaping'. Proceedings of the 29th universities *Power engineering* conference, 1994, pp. 358–361

35 HSU, Y.Y. and YANG, C.C.: 'Design of artificial neural networks for short-term load forecasting 1. Self-organizing feature maps for day type identification', *IEE Proc., Gener. Trans. Distrib.*, 1991, **138**, (5), pp. 407–413

36 KIERNAN, L., KAMBHAMPATI, C., MITCHELL, R.J. and WARWICK, K.: 'Automatic integrated system load forecasting using mutual information and neural networks', *Control of power plants and power systems, SIPOWER '95*, Cacun, Mexico, 1995, pp. 503–508

37 FEUSTON, B.P. and THURTELL, J.H.: 'Generalized nonlinear regression with ensemble of neural nets: the great energy predictor shootout', *ASHRAE Trans.*, 1994, **100**, (2), pp. 1075–1080

38 WERBOS, P.J.: 'Beyond regression: new tools for prediction and analysis in the behavioural sciences'. PhD thesis, 1974, Harvard University, MA, USA

39 RUMELHART, D.E., HINTON, G.E. and WILLIAMS, R.J.: 'Learning internal representation by error propagation' *in* RUMELHART, D.E. and McCLELLAND, J.L. (Eds.): 'Parallel distributed processing: exploration in the microstructure of cognition' (MIT Press, 1986)

40 'Back propagation family album'. Technical report C/TR96-05, Department of Computing, Macquarie University, NSW, Australia (available online via www.comp.mq.edu.au/research.html as 9600005.gibb March 1999)

12.9 Appendixes

12.9.1 *Backpropagation weight update rule*

This idea was first described by Werbos [38] and popularised by Rumelhart *et al.* [39].

Consider the network of Figure 12.56, with one layer of hidden neurons and one output neuron. When an input vector is propagated through the network, for the current set of weights there is an output

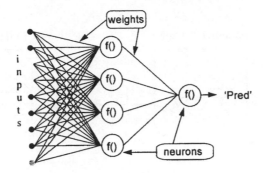

Figure 12.56   A multilayer perceptron

pred. The objective of supervised training is to adjust the weights so that the difference between the network output *pred* and the required output *req* is reduced. This requires an algorithm that reduces the absolute error, which is the same as reducing the squared error, where:

$$\text{network error} = pred - req$$

$$= E \tag{12.1}$$

The algorithm should adjust the weights such that E^2 is minimised. Backpropagation is such an algorithm that performs a gradient descent minimisation of E^2.

In order to minimise E^2, its sensitivity to each of the weights must be calculated. In other words, we need to know what effect changing each of the weights will have on E^2. If this is known then the weights can be adjusted in the direction that reduces the absolute error.

The notation for the following description of the backpropagation rule is based on Figure 12.57. The dashed line represents a neuron *B*, which can be either a hidden or the output neuron. The outputs of *n* neurons $(O_1 \dots O_n)$ in the preceding layer provide the inputs to neuron *B*. If neuron *B* is in the hidden layer then this is simply the input vector.

These outputs are multiplied by the respective weights $(W_{1B} \dots W_{nB})$, where W_{nB} is the weight connecting neuron *n* to neuron *B*. The summation function adds together all these products to provide the input, I_B, which is processed by the activation function $f(\bullet)$ of neuron *B*. $f(I_B)$ is the output, O_B, of neuron *B*.

For the purpose of this illustration, let neuron 1 be called neuron *A* and then consider the weight W_{AB} connecting the two neurons.

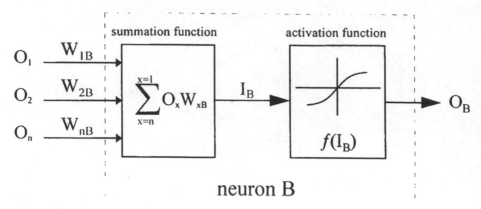

Figure 12.57

The approximation used for the weight change is given by the delta rule:

$$W_{AB(new)} = W_{AB(old)} - \eta \frac{\partial E^2}{\partial W_{AB}}$$ (12.2)

where η is the learning rate parameter, which determines the rate of learning, and

$$\frac{\partial E^2}{\partial W_{AB}}$$

is the sensitivity of the error, E^2, to the weight W_{AB} and determines the direction of search in weight space for the new weight W_{AB} as illustrated in Figure 12.58.

From the chain rule:

$$\frac{\partial E^2}{\partial W_{AB}} = \frac{\partial E^2}{\partial I_B} \frac{\partial I_B}{\partial W_{AB}}$$ (12.3)

and

$$\frac{\partial I_B}{\partial W_{AB}} = \frac{\partial \sum\limits_{x=n}^{x=1} O_x W_{xB}}{\partial W_{AB}}$$

$$= \frac{\partial (O_A W_{AB})}{\partial W_{AB}} + \frac{\partial \sum\limits_{x=n}^{x=2} O_x W_{xB}}{\partial W_{AB}}$$

$$= O_A$$ (12.4)

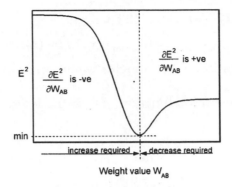

Figure 12.58 *In order to minimise E^2 the delta rule gives the direction of weight change required*

since the rest of the inputs to neuron B have no dependency on the weight W_{AB}.

Thus from eqns. 12.3 and 12.4, eqn. 12.2 becomes:

$$W_{AB(new)} = W_{AB(old)} - \eta \frac{\partial E^2}{\partial I_B} O_A \qquad (12.5)$$

and the weight change of W_{AB} depends on the sensitivity of the squared error, E^2, to the input, I_B, of unit B and on the input signal O_A.

There are two possible situations:

1 B is the output neuron;
2 B is a hidden neuron.

Considering the first case:

Since B is the output neuron, the change in the squared error owing to an adjustment of W_{AB} is simply the change in the squared error of the output of B:

$$\partial E^2 = \partial (pred - req)^2$$

$$\frac{\partial E^2}{\partial I_B} = 2(pred - req) \frac{\partial pred}{\partial I_B}$$

$$= 2E \frac{\partial f(I_B)}{\partial I_B}$$

$$= 2Ef'(I_B) \qquad (12.6)$$

combining eqn. 12.5 with eqn. 12.6 we get:

$$W_{AB(new)} = W_{AB(old)} - \eta O_A 2Ef'(I_B) \tag{12.7}$$

the rule for modifying the weights when neuron B is an output neuron.

If the output activation function, $f(\bullet)$, is the logistic function then:

$$f(\mathbf{x}) = \frac{1}{1 + e^{-x}} = (1 + e^{-x})^{-1} \tag{12.8}$$

differentiating eqn. 12.8 by its argument X:

$$f'(x) = -1(1 + e^{-x})^{-2} \cdot -1(e^{-x}) = \frac{e^{-x}}{(1 + e^{-x})^2} \tag{12.9}$$

But:

$$f(x) = \frac{1}{1 + e^{-x}} \tag{12.10}$$

$$\Rightarrow e^{-x} = \frac{(1 - f(x))}{f(x)} \tag{12.11}$$

inserting eqn. 12.11 into eqn. 12.9 gives:

$$f'(x) = \frac{(1 - f(x))}{f(x)} \bigg/ \frac{1}{(f(x))^2}$$

$$= f(x)(1 - f(x)) \tag{12.12}$$

similarly for the tanh function:

$$f'(x) = (1 - f(x)^2)$$

or for the linear (identity) function:

$$f'(x) = 1$$

which gives:

$$W_{AB(new)} = W_{AB(old)} - \eta O_A 2EO_B(1 - O_B) \qquad \text{(logistic)}$$
$$W_{AB(new)} = W_{AB(old)} - \eta O_A 2E(1 - O_B^2) \qquad \text{(tanh)}$$
$$W_{AB(new)} = W_{AB(old)} - \eta O_A 2E \qquad \text{(linear)}$$

Considering the second case:

B is a hidden unit:

$$\frac{\partial E^2}{\partial I_B} = \frac{\partial E^2}{\partial I_O}\frac{\partial I_O}{\partial O_B}\frac{\partial O_B}{\partial I_B} \tag{12.13}$$

where the subscript, O, represents the output neuron:

$$\frac{\partial O_B}{\partial I_B} = \frac{\partial f(I_B)}{\partial I_B} = f'(I_B) \tag{12.14}$$

$$\frac{\partial I_O}{\partial O_B} = \frac{\partial \sum\limits_{p} O_p W_{pO}}{\partial O_B} \tag{12.15}$$

where p is an index that ranges over all the neurons including neuron B that provide input signals to the output neuron. Expanding the right hand side of eqn. 12.15:

$$\frac{\partial \sum\limits_{p} O_p W_{pO}}{\partial O_B} = \frac{\partial O_B W_{BO}}{\partial O_B} + \frac{\partial \overset{p \ne B}{\sum\limits_{p}} O_p W_{pO}}{\partial O_B} = W_{BO} \tag{12.16}$$

since the weights of the other neurons, W_{pO} ($p \ne B$), have no dependency on O_B.

Inserting eqns. 12.14 and 12.16 into eqn. 12.13:

$$\frac{\partial E^2}{\partial I_B} = \frac{\partial E^2}{\partial I_O} W_{BO} f'(I_B) \tag{12.17}$$

Thus $\partial E^2 / \partial I_B$ is now expressed as a function of $\partial E^2 / \partial I_O$, calculated as in eqn. 12.6.

The complete rule for modifying the weight W_{AB} between a neuron A sending a signal to a neuron B is:

$$W_{AB(new)} = W_{AB(old)} - \eta \frac{\partial E^2}{\partial I_B} O_A \tag{12.18}$$

where:

$$\frac{\partial E^2}{\partial I_B} = 2E f_o'(I_B) \qquad \text{—} I_B \text{ is the output neuron} \tag{12.19}$$

$$\frac{\partial E^2}{\partial I_B} = \frac{\partial E^2}{\partial I_O} W_{BO} f_h'(I_B) \qquad \text{—} I_B \text{ is a hidden neuron} \tag{12.20}$$

where $f_o(\bullet)$ and $f_h(\bullet)$ are the output and hidden activation functions, respectively.

Example:

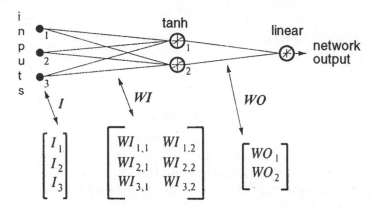

$$\text{network output} = [\tanh(I^T \cdot WI)] \cdot WO$$

let:

$$HID = [\tanh(I^T \cdot WI)]^T$$

the outputs of the hidden neurons.

$$\text{error} = (\text{network output} - \text{required output})$$

$$LR = \text{learning rate}$$

The weight updates become:

linear output neuron

$$WO = WO - (LR \times \text{error} \times HID) \qquad (12.21)$$

$$\underset{\text{local gradient}}{\diagup} \qquad \underset{\text{input signal}}{\diagdown}$$

tanh hidden neuron

$$WI = WI - \{LR \times [\text{error} \times WO \times (1 - HID^2)] \cdot I^T\}^T \qquad (12.22)$$

$$\underset{\text{local gradient}}{\diagup} \qquad\qquad\qquad \underset{\text{input signal}}{\diagdown}$$

Eqns. 12.21 and 12.22 show that the weight change is an input signal multiplied by a local gradient. This gives a direction which also has magnitude depending on the magnitude of the error. If the direction is taken with no magnitude then all changes will be of equal size, which will depend on the learning rate.

The algorithm above is a simplified version in that there is only one output neuron. In the original algorithm more than one output is allowed and the gradient descent minimises the total squared error of all the outputs. With only one output this reduces to minimising the error. It is prudent to use only one output if possible as noise from unrelated outputs can affect the network and more hidden neurons will be required anyway.

There are many algorithms [40] that have evolved from the original algorithm with the aim to increase the learning speed.

12.9.2 Fortran 90 code for a multilayer perceptron

The following source code is for a multilayer perceptron trained with the original backpropagation algorithm. The weights are updated after the presentation of each pattern. The hidden neurons have tanh activation functions and there is one output neuron which has a linear activation function. Hidden and output layer bias inputs of 1 are created; there are two individual learning rates for each layer of weights. The patterns are presented in a random order and an epoch said to have occurred when as many patterns have been presented as there are in the training set. On completion of each epoch it is decided whether or not to accept the new weights depending if the cost function has been lowered. This procedure could be performed after each pattern presentation rather than after each epoch.

The code is written in Fortran 90 as it has convenient matrix multiplication routines. All undeclared variables are real unless the variable name begins with the letters I–N, in which case they are integers. The routine for setting the random seed is specific to the ftn90 compiler for PCs by NAG/Salford software, otherwise it should work on any Fortran 90 compiler. In the code anything following a '!' is a comment.

```
PROGRAM Neural_Simulator
!!coded in Fortran 90 by Philip Brierley

!! declare arrays !!
REAL,ALLOCATABLE :: DATA(:,:),TRAININP(:,:),TRAINOUT(:)
REAL,ALLOCATABLE :: WIH(:,:),WHO(:),HVAL(:)
REAL,ALLOCATABLE :: WIHBEST(:,:),WHOBEST(:)
REAL,ALLOCATABLE :: INPUTS_THIS_PAT(:),DUMMY1(:,:),DUMMY2(:,:)

!! define some constants which can be varied!!
```

```
NO_OF_EPOCHS=10000        !number of epochs
NHIDDEN=5                 !number of hidden neurons
ALR=0.1                   !learning rate for input-hidden weights
BLR=0.01                  !learning rate for hidden-output weights
```

!! *open pattern file* !!
```
OPEN(UNIT=10,FILE='AVE.PAT',STATUS='OLD')
READ(10,*)NPATS,INPUTS    !read no.  of patterns, no. of inputs
NOUTPUTS=1                ! number of outputs (fixed)
```

!! *number the neurons* !!
```
NHIDDEN=NHIDDEN+1         !accounts for bias to output
NDU=INPUTS+NOUTPUTS      !Number Data Units
INPPB=INPUTS+1           !INPut Plus Bias
NHS=INPPB+1              !Number Hidden Start
NHF=INPPB+NHIDDEN       !Number Hidden Finish
NOS=NHF+1               !Number Output Start
```

!! *set the array dimensions* !!
```
ALLOCATE(DATA(NPATS,NDU))              !raw data read from file
ALLOCATE(TRAININP(NPATS,INPPB))        !input patterns
ALLOCATE(TRAINOUT(NPATS))              !output
ALLOCATE(WIH(INPPB,NHS:NHF))           !input-hidden weights
ALLOCATE(WIHBEST(INPPB,NHS:NHF))       !best weights
ALLOCATE(WHO(NHS:NHF))                 !hidden-output weights
ALLOCATE(WHOBEST(NHS:NHF))             !best weights
ALLOCATE(HVAL(NHS:NHF))                !hidden neuron outputs
ALLOCATE(INPUTS_THIS_PAT(INPPB))       !pattern being presented
ALLOCATE(DUMMY1(1,NHS:NHF))            !dummy matrix
ALLOCATE(DUMMY2(INPPB,1))              !dummy matrix
```

!! *read patterns from file* !!
```
DO I=1,NPATS
READ(10,*)(DATA(I,K),K=1,NDU)
ENDDO
CLOSE(10)
```

!! *create training inputs and outputs* !!
```
TRAININP(:,1:INPUTS)=DATA(:,1:INPUTS)
TRAININP(:,INPPB)=1              !create input bias
TRAINOUT(:)=DATA(:,NDU)
```

```
DEALLOCATE(DATA)                    !the array 'data' is no longer required

!! generate initial random weights !!
CALL DATE_TIME_SEED@                !set seed for random number generator
DO K=NHS,NHF
WHO(K)=((RANDOM()-0.5)*2)/10        !generate initial weights
DO J=1,INPPB
WIH(J,K)=((RANDOM()-0.5)*2)/10      !generate initial weights
ENDDO
ENDDO


WIHBEST=WIH                         !record of best weights so far
WHOBEST=WHO                         !record of best weights so far
RMSEBEST=100000000                  !the best rms error, initially set high


!!!!!!!!!!!!!!!!!!!!!!!!!!!!!!!
!!! LETS START !!!!!!!
!!!!!!!!!!!!!!!!!!!!!!!!!!!!!!!

PRINT *,'epochs   rms_error'       !print to screen

DO M=1,NO_OF_EPOCHS

 DO I=1,NPATS

  !! select a pattern at random !!
  IPAT_NUM=NINT(RANDOM()*(NPATS-1))+1
  INPUTS_THIS_PAT(:)=TRAININP(ipat_num,:)
  OUTPUT_THIS_PAT=TRAINOUT(ipat_num)

  !! calculate the network output !!
  HVAL=MATMUL(TRANSPOSE(WIH),INPUTS_THIS_PAT)
                                     ! inputs × weights
  HVAL=TANH(HVAL)                    ! tanh activation function
  HVAL(NHF)=1                        ! acts as output bias
  OUTPRED=SUM(WHO*HVAL)              ! model output
  ER_THIS_PAT=(OUTPRED-OUTPUT_THIS_PAT)  ! model error

  !! change weight hidden - output !!
  WHO=WHO-(ALR*HVAL*ER_THIS_PAT)
```

```
!! change weight input - hidden  !!
DUMMY2(:,1) = TRAININP(IPAT_NUM,:)
DUMMY1(1,:) = ER_THIS_PAT*WHO*(1-(HVAL**2.00))
WIH = WIH-(MATMUL(DUMMY2,DUMMY1)*BLR)

ENDDO      !! (I) one more epoch done


!!!!!!!!!!!!!!!!!!!!!!!!!!!!!!!!!!!!!!!!!!!!!!!!!!!!!!!!!!!!!!!!!!!!!!!!!
!! evaluate 'fitness' of the network  after each epoch      !!
!!!!!!!!!!!!!!!!!!!!!!!!!!!!!!!!!!!!!!!!!!!!!!!!!!!!!!!!!!!!!!!!!!!!!!!!!

SQERROR=0       !! in this case the fitness function is the squared errors

DO J=1,NPATS
  INPUTS_THIS_PAT(:) = TRAININP(J,:)
  OUTPUT_THIS_PAT = TRAINOUT(J)
  HVAL = TANH(MATMUL(TRANSPOSE(WIH),INPUTS_THIS_PAT))
  HVAL(NHF) = 1
  OUTPRED = SUM(WHO*HVAL)
  ER_THIS_PAT = (OUTPRED-OUTPUT_THIS_PAT)
  SQERROR = SQERROR+(ER_THIS_PAT**2)
ENDDO !(J)

RMSE = SQRT(SQERROR/NPATS)          !! root of the mean squared error

IF (RMSE<RMSEBEST) THEN             ! if the rms error has improved then
  WIHBEST = WIH                     ! keep the new weights
  WHOBEST = WHO
  RMSEBEST = RMSE
ELSE                                ! else if it has increased then
  WIH = WIHBEST                     ! go back to the old weights
  WHO = WHOBEST
ENDIF

!! print errors to screen !!
PRINT *,M,RMSEBEST

ENDDO      !! (M) after all the epochs have been done !!

END PROGRAM Neural_Simulator
```

The following is the contents of the demonstration pattern file called 'ave.pat'. The output is the average of the three inputs. The first line is the number of patterns and the number of inputs.

patterns, inputs

5,3

0.1,0.3,0,0.133 ←————————— *pattern 1*

0.2,0.01,0.2,0.137

0.6,0.3,0.3,0.400

0.2,0.05,0.2,0.150

0.3,0.2,0.1,0.200 ←————————— *pattern 5*

input 1   *output*

input 3

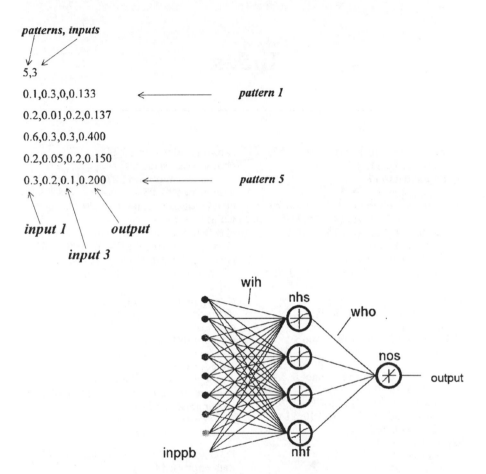

Figure 12.59   The neuron numbering convention in the code

Index

activation function 162, 163, 164, 167, 168, 243, 244, 245
aggregate data 117
aggregate operator 68
aggregated probability distribution 70
aggregation 67–70, 79, 84, 114, 119, 120, 121, 122, 123, 130, 131–2, 133, 134, 135
association pattern 134
association rule 100, 104–5, 107–9, 122, 123, 134
attribute 4
auto insurance dataset 19, 27, 28, 29
autoclass-c 184
AVD (attribute value distribution) 47–63

babies at risk of asphyxia database 149, 153–5, 158
back pain 160, 161–3, 168–78
back propagation 161, 162, 210, 218, 219, 240, 242, 254, 292–9
Bayes' theorem 48
beam search 5
beam width 27
bias 4, 5, 9, 28
bitmap indexing 119
bitmap representation 228, 229
blurring 3, 11-5, 16, 17, 19, 20, 26
BNF grammar 100
bottom-up approach to data mining 140, 150
breast cancer dataset 19, 20, 27
business 88, 115, 116

C4.5 19, 27, 39–40
C5.0 197, 198, 199, 218, 219
case-based reasoning 208, 210-1
causal model 263, 285

causal relationship 96, 97
characteristic rule 95
chemical compound 227–30, 234–8
chemistry 228, 234–8
chess endgame dataset 19, 20, 27
ChiMerge 19
classification 186, 208, 218
classification rule 46, 95, 97, 100, 120–1
cleaning (of data) 142–4, 157–8
Clementine 197, 198, 199
cluster analysis 148
cluster detection 214
clustering 186
concept 3
concept difficulty 3–29
concept dispersion 7, 8, 25
concept hierarchy 71, 72, 75, 83
connectionist paradigm 210
contact lens dataset 47, 48, 49, 55–60
contingency table 79
cross-entropy 13
customer credit ratings 95

DAG (directed acyclic graph) 96
data capture 141
data cleansing 214–5, 216
data conversion 196
data cube 115, 121, 128
data encoding 249
data extraction 212, 216
data loading 216
data mining 33, 46, 47, 48, 64, 65, 67, 71, 82, 83, 87, 95, 97, 98, 101, 114–35, 139, 140–1, 147, 180, 188–95, 204, 205, 217, 222, 227, 230, 234, 235, 238, 240, 289
data processing 215–6
data prospecting 214
data refreshing 216

data transformation 212, 216
data vector 37, 38, 39, 40, 41
data warehouse 64, 114–35, 180, 205,
    212, 216, 224
data-based detection 9, 10
data-based difficulty measures 10–1
database
    relational 83, 200, 201
    object 201
    temporal 88, 94
database functionality 196
database re-engineering 74–5, 77, 78
database relation 66
database table 83
DBMS (database management system)
    73
decision support 114, 115, 116, 117,
    161, 177, 205, 227
decision threshold 42
decision time 94, 102
decision tree 199, 200
Dempster-Shafer mass function, 83
deviation 95, 96
diabetes dataset 19, 27
dice (range selection) operation 118
dimension (OLAP) 117, 118
discarding data 184
discretisation 186
distributed database 82
domain hierarchy (OLAP) 117
domain knowledge 33, 35, 36, 37, 38,
    39, 41, 44, 161, 167, 176–7, 178,
    181, 197, 199, 221–2
drill-down 118, 124, 133, 134

eager aggregation 132
electricity supply 240, 250–3, 255–89
EM (expectation maximisation)
    algorithm 71
entropy 12–15, 16, 187
error analysis 254, 255, 258–65, 266,
    276, 278, 282, 283, 292–8
error tolerance 246–7
estimation 34, 37, 143, 184
Euclidean distance 152
evaluation function 189
event 94, 95
event relationship 96, 97
exclusive-OR 5, 17
exhaustive rule discovery 50, 51, 53, 59,
    60, 61
expert knowledge 37, 39, 64, 65, 71, 74,
    83, 147, 155, 161, 167, 176–7, 178,
    181, 197, 199, 205, 210, 212, 216,
    221
explanation facility 161, 170, 177
extrapolation 245, 246

fact table 118, 213
false alarm 42, 43
fault detection 42, 43
feature construction 188
feature detector neurons 163–4, 168,
    169
feature interaction 8, 9, 28, 29
feature selection 184–5, 187–8, 189,
    196
feedback sandwich model 114–5,
    123–4, 125–8, 133, 135
feedforward MLP 241, 249, 254, 255,
    299–303
filter selection 189
fingerprint 229–30, 234, 238
Fisher algorithm 186, 196
FLTIS (finding large temporal item
    sets) 107–8
forecasting 181, 205, 208, 210, 217,
    220, 252, 289
Fortran 299–303
fuzzy set 181

generalisation 129, 244–5, 264, 265,
    266
generalised data model 66
generalised delta rule 242
geographical factors 151, 180–1, 187,
    196, 197, 205, 206, 251, 289
glass dataset 19, 20
glaucoma 38, 39, 40–1, 43
Gofer (functional programming
    language) 227, 230, 231–4, 235,
    236, 238
granularity 122, 123, 133, 134, 135, 213,
    216
graphs 182, 196, 206, 208, 209, 214,
    228, 237
greedy search 5, 10
greedy splitting algorithms 6, 26
GRI (rule induction algorithm) 217
group-by operation 132, 133
GTAR (generating temporal
    association rules) 107, 109

health 139, 144–7, 149
hepatitis dataset 19, 27, 28

heuristic 47, 53, 54, 55, 56, 57, 58, 59,
     60, 62, 114, 119, 123
heuristic search algorithm 189
hill climber search engine 196
historical data 115,116, 125, 128–30,
     131, 132
house votes dataset 19, 20, 27
hypercube 212
hypothesis-based detection 9, 10

ID3 (tree induction algorithm) 187
imprecise data 65, 66, 67, 69, 83
incomplete data 64, 65, 66, 143, 155,
     157, 208
incorrect data 214–5
index function 91
induced rule 167, 170, 172–3, 176, 177
induction 65, 196, 199, 200, 217
infertility database 149, 155–7, 158
information density 230, 238
information extraction 213–4
information gain 187, 197, 199
information theory 187
integrated architecture 127–8, 135
integrity constraint 65, 71, 73, 75, 79,
     83–4
intelligent assistant 210
intensional historical data 128, 130,
     131, 132
interestingness 64, 65, 81–2, 100, 110
interpolation 215, 216
intrinsic accuracy 7
iris dataset 19, 20
irrelevant attributes 17–8, 19, 20, 21,
     25, 26, 29
irrelevant data 214–5
irrelevant field 143, 144, 157
iteration 69, 70, 78, 79, 80–1, 82, 83,
     84, 147
ITRULE 51

J measure 13, 14, 20, 26, 46
join operation 118, 119

knowledge discovery ix–x, 64, 83, 88,
     95, 176, 177, 180, 204, 217, 240
knowledge elicitation 221–2
knowledge guided discovery 47, 139,
     140–1
knowledge modelling 217
Kohonen self organising map 148–9,
     150, 154, 157
Kullback-Leibler information
     divergence 70, 71

lazy aggregation 132

lazy evaluation 233–4, 236, 238
learning 7, 37, 147, 148, 161, 162, 210,
     292
linear inverse problem 71
local minima 247
logic programming 72, 83
lymphography dataset 19, 20, 27

machine learning 37, 64
MADAME (meteorology and data
     mining environment) 205, 211
MAPE (mean absolute percentage
     error) 254, 255, 256, 257, 258,
     259, 260, 265, 275, 276, 277, 278,
     279, 280, 285, 286, 288
materialised view 131, 132, 133, 212,
     215, 217, 218
maximum-likelihood estimator 83
maximum-likelihood ratio 36
medicine 35, 38, 82, 88, 96, 144–7, 160,
     177
meteorology 180–3, 187, 188, 196–200,
     204–24
minimum r.m.s. error 254, 264, 265,
     288
missing data 143, 155, 157, 181, 182–5,
     187, 190, 194, 196, 197, 198, 199,
     208, 215, 216
MLP (multilayer perceptron network)
     161–78, 208, 210, 241, 249, 254,
     255, 299–303
multiattribute count operator 76
multidimensional analysis 117, 140
multiple-level data mining 115
multiple materialised view 212
multiple strategy method 210

negated significant inputs 164–6, 167,
     170, 173, 175, 176, 177
network training 242, 247–8, 254, 255,
     261, 264, 274, 289
neural classifier 219, 220, 222, 223
neural network 140, 147, 154, 157, 158,
     160–78, 181, 184, 208, 210, 214,
     218, 219, 220, 222, 240–50, 253,
     255, 264, 266, 277, 282, 287, 288,
     289
neuron activation function 162, 163,
     164, 167, 168
Newton–Raphson procedure 83
noise 20, 23, 33, 34, 38, 41, 43, 44, 64,
     65, 208, 215, 288, 299
nonvariant field 143, 144–5, 152, 154,
     155, 157
nonlinear regression 289

nowcasting 205, 206, 210, 217, 219–21, 222, 223
null value 66–7
numerical models 208, 210

object database 201
offline data mining 128
OLAP (online analysis processing) 114–35
onchocerciasis 38, 42, 43
online data mining 128
outliers 32–44, 143, 145–6, 152, 157, 214–5
overfitting 244–5, 264

parametric polymorphism 232
partial value 66, 67, 69, 70, 71, 72, 73, 82, 84
pattern 96, 98, 99, 101, 103, 140, 141, 147, 157, 180, 217, 228
  association 134
  influence 134
  sequential 96
  temporal 88, 97, 98, 100
pattern matching 232, 253
periodicity of patterns 97, 101, 110
periodicity of time 92–4
petrochemical 229
pharmaceuticals 227, 238
pivot 118
pivot table 79
potential knowledge 95, 98
prediction 181–2, 200, 205, 206, 210, 242, 275, 276
premining 124–5
preprocessing 142–5, 152, 154, 157–8, 180, 181, 182–8, 196, 212, 222
primary tumour dataset 19, 27
principal components analysis 33
PRISM 48, 57
probability 37, 38, 46–63, 70, 82–3, 229
project outcome dataset 60–1
Prolog 72

quasi-independence 79–82
query 114, 115, 117, 120, 132
query language 100, 102
query tool 140
query transformation 132

recurrent sigma-pi neural network 210
reference function 91
relational database 83, 200, 201

relational DBMS 116, 117
relational OLAP 117
RELIEF 22, 24, 25, 26, 29
RELIEFF 23–4, 25, 26
RELIEVED 25, 26
retail 88, 96, 97
ROC (receiver operator characteristic) analysis 42, 43
roll-up 117
rule 46–63, 65, 161, 167, 180, 181, 185, 186, 188, 189, 190–5, 196, 198, 199, 200, 218, 219, 220
  association 119, 122, 123, 134
  characteristic 95
  classification 95, 97, 100
  induced 95, 167, 170, 172–3, 176, 177
  temporal 88, 97
rule-based approaches 218, 219, 220, 274, 275, 276
rule discovery 46–63, 134–5
rule extraction 266–74
rule induction 83, 95, 181, 197, 217
rule interest 46, 47
rule ranking 46
Rumbaugh object-oriented information model 234

sales 95, 104–6, 120, 121, 122, 129–30, 131–2, 133, 134
science 88, 96
search 5, 6, 10, 26, 27, 103, 104, 107–9
search algorithm 189
search engine 196
semantic knowledge 119, 120
semantics of rules 114, 121, 122
sensitivity analysis 122–3
sequential pattern 96, 219
sigmoidal function 162, 163, 243, 245
significant inputs 164–6, 167, 168, 170, 173, 174, 176, 177
similar pattern 96
simple aggregate operator 68
simple count operator 67–8, 76
simulated annealing 181–200
simulation model 210
skewed field 143, 145, 152, 157
slice operation 118
snowflake schema 213
SQL 68, 73, 89, 92, 100, 102, 103, 116
SQL3 94, 110
standard relational database 66, 67, 84
star schema 118, 119, 125, 131, 213

statistics 32, 33, 34, 35, 64, 79, 82, 83,
    84, 147, 150, 151, 152, 154, 210,
    215
stock market 88, 96, 97
structural key 228–9
structural zero 79, 82
supervised learning 147, 162, 214, 292
synthetic data 143–4

t-test 151, 152, 154
table-based constraint 73
table-based predicate 74
target concept 3, 4, 7, 9, 10, 28
target dataset 46, 141, 142, 152, 158
target field 186
target rule 47–63
Templar framework 196
temporal data 87–110
temporal data mining 88–110
temporal query language 94
threshold 101
time 89, 181, 185, 187, 200, 205, 206,
    212, 216, 217, 219, 220, 250–1,
    253, 255
time model 89, 90–3, 104, 110, 285
time semantics 89, 94
time sensitive data 129
time stamp 98, 99, 105
time value 98
TQML (temporal query and mining

language) 100–1, 102, 104, 106,
    110
toolkit for knowledge discovery 189,
    195–6, 197, 200, 201
top-down approach to data mining 140
transaction time 94, 102
tree induction 196
trends 95–6, 100, 140, 141, 147
TSQL2 94–5
type-1 and type-2 problems 3, 20, 21

uncertainty 82, 181
unreliable data 185–6, 190, 193–4, 195,
    200
unsupervised clustering 184
unsupervised data 230, 238
unsupervised learning 147, 148
user-defined time 94, 102

variation 11, 15, 16, 17, 24–5, 29
visualisation 182, 196, 212

wealth factors 151
WHO 'Health for all' database 149–52
Wilks's multivariate outlier test 35, 38
workbench 210
wrapper selection 189

XCAVATOR 46

Z notation 231, 234